THE NIGHT BLITZ
1940–1941

Also by John Ray

The Battle of Britain
The Second World War

THE
NIGHT BLITZ

1940–1941

JOHN RAY

CASSELL&CO

To Nicholas

Cassell Military Paperbacks

Cassell & Co
Wellington House, 125 Strand
London WC2R OBB

Copyright © John Ray 1996

First published by Arms and Armour 1996
This Cassell Military Paperbacks edition 2000

British Library Cataloguing-in-Publication Data
A catalogue record for this book is available from the
British Library

ISBN 0-304-35676-X

Edited and designed by Roger Chesneau/DAG Publications Ltd

Printed and bound in Great Britain by
Cox & Wyman, Reading, Berks

CONTENTS

ACKNOWLEDGEMENTS

I should like to thank the many people whose advice, wisdom and practical assistance have aided me in the preparation and production of this book. They include, in particular, Mrs Beryl Houson, Captain Alan Ellender, Mr Roy Ripley, Professor R. V. Jones, Mrs Jenny Last, Mrs June Appleton and Mrs Marjorie Stewart. A special debt is due to Dr W. H. Penley, formerly of the Telecommunications Research Establishment, Swanage, whose experience in, and knowledge of, the early days of radar are exceptional. There are many others, civilians and Service personnel, who have recounted and shared their memories of the years 1940 and 1941.

I also acknowledge a debt to several people and institutions for their assistance with comments on the text, for photographs or for permission to reproduce short extracts from documents in their possession: Mr Sebastian Cox, of the Air Historical Branch, Ministry of Defence; the staffs of the Imperial War Museum's Department of Printed Books and Documents and Department of Photographs; the staffs of the City Archives of Portsmouth and Southampton; the North-East Aircraft Museum, Sunderland; the Museum, St Helier, Jersey; Lady Douglas of Kirtleside; and the House of Lords Record Office. Crown Copyright material in the Public Record Office is reproduced by permission of the Controller of Her Majesty's Stationery Office.

I have also benefited from the guiding hand of Mr Rod Dymott, Director of Arms and Armour Press, and of Mr Roger Chesneau. My daughters, Jenny and Margaret, have been assiduous in helping me to produce typescripts. Finally, as ever, the unvarying support and encouragement of my wife, who, like me, lived under the Night Blitz, have gone far to make the writing of this book possible.

John Ray

INTRODUCTION

When they declare that they will attack our cities, then we shall wipe out their cities—Adolf Hitler, Berlin, 4 September 1940

For one year, from the surrender of France in June 1940 until the invasion of the Soviet Union in June 1941, German armed forces launched three active and intense campaigns to overthrow the British homeland. The first was the daylight Battle of Britain, the second the Night Blitz and the third the Battle of the Atlantic. The first was an attempt by the *Luftwaffe* to overwhelm the Royal Air Force, especially Fighter Command, preparatory to a seaborne invasion of the British mainland; generally, this lasted from mid-July to the end of October. The third, which started in earnest at the end of 1940 and continued for the rest of the war, was aimed at Britain's sea trade. A common factor of these two campaigns was that servicemen trained in war fought against each other.

This book examines the second campaign, the Night Blitz. The battle extended from September 1940 for some eight months until May 1941, with hardly a night's break. The *Luftwaffe* attempted to pound Britain into submission by bombing economic and civilian targets, hoping to cause material destruction and to break morale. Unlike the other two campaigns, this was a contest mainly between *Luftwaffe* aircrews and British civilians, the one group skilled and the other untrained in killing. The Night Blitz, though described as an assault on economic targets, was primarily an attempt to erode the morale of civilians through the destruction of areas where they lived and worked. In this it failed. Further aerial attacks were launched against Britain throughout the remainder of the war, from 'Baedeker Raids' to Operation 'Steinbock', and from V1 flying bombs to V2 rockets. None, however, reached the intensity of the Night Blitz either in numbers of casualties caused or in physical destruction.

In choosing industrial cities and seaports as their main striking points, where thousands of civilians lived close by legitimate targets, the *Luftwaffe* were implementing theories of aerial warfare proposed since the 1920s. These held that wars could be won, either exclusively or principally, through the exercise of strategic air power. The ideas, emanating from Douhet and Mitchell and strongly supported by Wever in Germany and Trenchard in Britain, called for the exercise of concentrated bombing over the enemy's homeland.

In that respect, in 1940 the *Luftwaffe* suffered a particular disadvantage. The Night Blitz over Britain was conducted without the use of a true heavy bomber. The *Luftwaffe*, prepared since the Spanish Civil War to act as a tactical force in close support of ground attack, had not been allowed to develop the Heinkel 177 which would have made a cardinal difference over Britain. The widespread devastation and thousands of deaths and injuries inflicted across the country resulted from the actions of medium bombers, the largest of which was the Heinkel 111.

Today, most of the visible scars of the Night Blitz have disappeared, and they are seldom reflected on by generations unused to war as they walk or ride daily across sites once demolished and burnt. This is particularly true in a number of city centres, where swathes of destruction were cut through areas of historic buildings and shops, offices and homes. Post-war reconstruction has covered acres of smashed and burnt houses, workplaces, schools and churches, as is particularly evident in, for example, Plymouth and Coventry. Inevitably, the extent of the damage has been removed from sight, and consequently from people's minds. Scars, however, have not always been removed from the memories of an older generation, which includes the author. Memories of crouching in shelters, or under the stairs, while an aerial pounding descended, the like of which had never previously been experienced by any nation, will remain: for that generation, when walking over the sites of bombing, going through supermarkets or shopping malls, or driving along crowded streets, recollections of the dead and injured, of fire and falling buildings, will never be far distant.

The story of the Night Blitz was also one of remarkable technical achievement, and this is particularly true with regard to the application of science to warfare. The Germans pioneered the guidance of aircraft by radio beams. To counter them, British scientists worked with considerable skill and energy to introduce methods of locating aircraft in darkness and to cooperate closely with servicemen in halting *Luftwaffe* raids. In this respect praise must be given to the scientists of the Telecommunications Research Establishment, whose contribution is often overlooked or ignored. Some of the pioneers later carried their skills into the fields of space exploration and telecommunications, bringing benefits to the post-war world.

Since 1945 the effects of aerial bombing and the morality of its employment have been closely examined, often by those who never experienced it. The first point to be acknowledged is that the Germans, from the First World War, were pioneers of air attacks on civilians. Zeppelin and Gotha raids then, although comparatively small, set a standard which they followed with greater intensity in 1940. Some people compare the damage and casualties caused by the Germans in the Night Blitz with the far greater devastation and killing which resulted from the Allied attacks on the *Reich* later in the war. Such critics often imply that Bomber Command and the United States Army Air Forces overdid the response to German raids. This is not true. The only limiting factor on *Luftwaffe* strategy in 1940 and 1941 was the lack of a bomber to compare with the Allied 'heavies', for example, the Lancaster and the Flying Fortress, which operated later. Had the *Luftwaffe* developed the Heinkel 177 and built enough of them, German leaders would have had no reservations over killing more people and causing wider damage in Britain than they did. Destruction of the economy and the smashing of civilian morale was their stated aim. With bigger bombers, more cities in the United Kingdom would have been 'Coventrated' and Dresdens and Hamburgs would have been seen in Britain. It is noticeable that, at the time, no German voices were raised in protest at the destruction of homes and historic buildings by the *Luftwaffe*, nor at the death and injury meted out to the British people.

Bomber Command learned lessons from the *Luftwaffe*'s methods of night attack and employed them until, by 1945, Germany was 'a fortress without a roof'. Those who denigrate the Command's activities, which began in embryonic form as *Luftflotten II* and *III* were attempting to annihilate British cities, ignore the general welcome given to the campaign by those who had suffered so much at the hands of the German Air Force. It is easy for critics to advance destructive comments. They do not propose any constructive and practical suggestions of an alternative strategy which Britain could have followed at the time in the fight against one of history's most evil regimes.

The Night Blitz against Britain failed in one important respect: civilian morale did not snap, and the British Government consequently was not forced to sue for peace. The stress exerted on ordinary citizens in the areas raided was intense and at times the burdens of loss of relations and friends, homes and property were difficult to bear. Inevitably, morale was affected by fire and explosion, especially when there were repeated raids within a short time. In this, however, the *Luftwaffe*'s tactics helped the defenders, because in a few places only, notably London, Merseyside and Plymouth, were concentrated assaults launched against single targets within the space of a week. In general, public determination to cling on, then to hit back, was strengthened, its full effect being seen from 1942.

Over recent years some historians have suggested that there was public fragility in what Churchill termed the 'finest hour'. They claim that reports were suppressed by the Government. Others have blamed the Prime Minister for urging the British people to fight on rather than trying to make peace with Hitler, a policy which, they assert, left Britain bankrupt in resources and power. Such arguments overlook the general feeling of the nation at the time, basing their case on the thoughts and writings of a small minority. For a whole year the United Kingdom stood alone amid disaster and depredation, offering resistance to tyranny—an example admired and respected across the world. Small imagination is required to estimate the effects not only to the population of the British Isles, but also to others, especially Russians and Jews, if Britain had failed. This was indeed an *annus mirabilis* in British history and one which should never be forgotten or dishonoured by succeeding generations. Sometimes these lessons are evaded by denigrators whose pens inscribe with metaphorical glee on the graves of the dead.

This book tries to pay tribute to those who died in the Night Blitz, civilians as close to the battle line as any servicemen. In view of their sacrifice and the spirit of the survivors, it is surprising that, in a nation which accords proper remembrance to the glorious dead of the armed services, no suitable national memorial exists to the 60,000 civilians—men, women and children—whose lives were taken in war. There is still time to honour them properly.

John Ray

CHAPTER ONE

THE SATURDAY RAID:
7 SEPTEMBER 1940

THE AFTERNOON RAID

A turning point in the Second World War was reached In the late afternoon of Saturday 7 September 1940. At about 3.45 p.m., British time, *Reichsmarschall* Hermann Goering, Commander-in-Chief of the *Luftwaffe* and a senior member of the Nazi hierarchy, stood at Cap Gris Nez on the French Channel coast, among a group of his officers. The weather that day had been sunny, and through powerful binoculars he could see the white cliffs of southern England, only twenty-two miles away across the deceptively peaceful waters. Gathering overhead was the most powerful force ever to have been assembled in war for one operation against a single target. Under Goering's orders, seven single-seat fighter *Jagdgeschwader*, together with scores of twin-engine *Zerstörer*, were preparing to escort five *Kampfgeschwader* of bombers into action: from the cream of the *Luftwaffe*, a force of 617 fighters would escort 348 bombers. The whole array was being dispatched on a mission which the *Reichsmarschall* hoped would bring a rapid and successful end to the Battle of Britain and thereby to the war. Goering knew well that his reputation, together with that of his air force, would rest considerably on the results of the ensuing action.

His airmen understood the importance of their task and appreciated that timings and courses had to be met exactly. Heinkel 111s, Dornier 17s and Junkers 88s were to be flown in carefully stacked formations, giving their gunners the best angles of fire for mutual support. Above and around them weaved Bf 109s and Bf 110s in close escort, although many of their pilots were frustrated at having to fly slowly near their lumbering charges.

When the armada had assembled, it moved away north-westwards across the Channel, prepared to follow the explicit instructions given. Pilots and navigators kept a wary eye on their watches, as it was imperative to arrive over the target at the correct time, bringing the fullest effect to the bombing pattern in a single attack. At exactly 5 p.m. one *Kampfgeschwader* of II *Fliegerkorps* would approach from the east and open the assault, while forty minutes later the remainder of *II Fliegerkorps* would make the main raid from the south. With meticulous timing, *I Fliegerkorps* would arrive five minutes afterwards, adding to the devastation below.

Most aircrews had taken part in previous strikes, especially in southern England, where fighting in the Battle of Britain had built in intensity throughout August. From the start they had learned to be wary of the *Kanal*, which had to be crossed twice and whose waters had already swallowed many planes and their crews. In addition, they had come to respect the tenacity of their opponents in the Royal Air Force who had fought unremittingly in defending the last nation left unconquered after Germany's previous triumphs in the Western Campaign. They had discovered that, in an uncanny way, most raids were confronted by Hurricanes and Spitfires. They had seen scores of *Luftwaffe* machines destroyed or damaged by an unyielding enemy. The gentle English countryside was littered with the graves of blazing aircraft, while empty seats in the Mess were a constant reminder of the closeness of death.

Nonetheless, as the great formations crossed the English coast, many pilots believed that victory was not far distant. Numbers brought confidence, and their air fleet extended for mile after mile across the sky. During the previous fortnight they had concentrated on targets well inland, especially the airfields of No 11 Group Fighter Command, whose commander, Air Vice-Marshal Keith Park, was under unrelenting pressure. His all-important sector stations, the hub of RAF defences, had been raided. Hornchurch, Biggin Hill, Kenley and North Weald had been bombed, with Park's squadrons suffering heavily in trying to defend them. In that period Fighter Command had lost about 260 aircraft and 109 aircrew, and some squadrons had had to be withdrawn from the firing line. Unknown to the German airmen in flight, that very afternoon a conference was being held by Air Chief Marshal Sir Hugh Dowding, Commander-in-Chief Fighter Command, to plan 'for Fighter Command to go downhill'.[1] There appeared to be a good chance that another week or two of airfield attacks would break the RAF defences and that the necessary domination would be achieved to pave the way for a seaborne invasion—or a British surrender.

But today's raid was not intended for airfields. The engines of almost one thousand aircraft were beating through the skies of Kent towards a new target, previously spared any large-scale attacks. The destination had been given the code-name *'Löge'*.

The first intimation that British defences had of the raid came through radio direction finding (RDF) stations on the Kent coast. Just before 4 p.m. plotters noted signs of enemy aircraft gathering in increasing numbers over the Pas de Calais, followed by the progress of formations as they crossed the Channel. Although the Germans had been ominously quiet during the previous hours of the day, it appeared that they were about to continue their strikes against airfields. However, the signals staff had never had to deal with so many simultaneous reports and found themselves under pressure because of the size of the attack. 'The number of aircraft appearing on the RDF tubes,' recorded an official narrative, 'was at times too great to be reported by the operator accurately enough to give a clear picture. On occasions the amount of information passed was sufficient to swamp the Filter Room.'[2] RAF fighters were scrambled with the main object of defending their bases and soon about a dozen squadrons were airborne on patrol. Yet as they gained height and came into position to tackle the enemy, British pilots sensed a different element to this raid. Never before had they seen so many German bombers and, more worryingly, never before had they been confronted by so many fighters. 'As we broke through the haze,' one pilot wrote later, 'you could hardly believe it. As far as you could see, there was nothing but German aircraft coming in, wave after wave.'[3] The *Luftwaffe* numbers were daunting. Another pilot, flying with No 609 Squadron, called up hastily from Middle Wallop, remembered that 'the whole German Air Force was just flying along two or three thousand feet below me. The air was just crawling with these planes with black crosses on them . . . I'd never seen so many planes in my life.'[4]

It was some time before the new German intentions became clear. Consequently some British squadrons received aimless or contradictory instructions from controllers and were dispatched from place to place until, finally, HQ No 11 Group recognised that the vast formations were not about to attack airfields or aircraft factories. The realisation dawned that the bombers were heading for another destination, and fighters were diverted, all too late, to defend it. For the packed masses of *Luftwaffe* aircraft were now approaching their target, *'Löge'*. That was the German code-name for London.

On the German side, instructions had been followed explicitly. For example, the aircraft of *I Fliegerkorps* were given exact heights and routes to follow in Operational Orders issued the previous day. The Junkers 88s of *KG 30* had gathered over St Omer, left France south of Cap Gris Nez at about 15,000 feet and crossed the Channel. They had aimed a straight course for the railway fork just north of Sevenoaks station, and then proceeded to the main target. Protecting them were Bf 109s of *JG 26 'Schlageter'*, which had made their mark in battle over previous weeks. The Heinkel 111s and Junkers 88s of *KG I* had rendezvoused at St Pol, crossed the Channel at 18,000 feet and made for the Kentish village of Riverhead before moving on to *'Löge'*; their escort was provided by *JG 54*, the famous 'Greenhearts'. Dornier 17s of *KG 76* had formed up at 16,000 feet above Hesdin, left France at the northern perimeter of Boulogne and set course at the English coast for Westerham, the site of Winston Churchill's country home. Then, guarded by the experienced pilots of *JG 27*, they closed on the target.

Because the German change of plan caught the defences by surprise, only some four squadrons of Fighter Command were moved quickly to confront the intruders. As a result, attacks on *Luftwaffe* formations were not concentrated and, because of overwhelming fighter cover, easily brushed aside. The bombers were given a free run over their targets.

The main objective was the great area of dockland in the East End of the city, including Silvertown, Woolwich, Deptford and Millwall. 'The miles of quays, the colossal warehouses, the vast basins filled with shipping of every description,' noted an old guide book, 'provide a sight calculated to stir the blood of the most phlegmatic of Englishmen, and to excite the envy of "our friend the foreigner".'[5] That late afternoon, 'the foreigner' was no friend and was intent on their destruction.

Included in the area were such prime targets as the Beckton Gas Works, the largest in Europe; the six hundred acres of Woolwich Arsenal; the Surrey Commercial Docks, a site of 336 acres on the river's south bank, used principally for timber and grain; the 230 acres of the West India Docks and the similarly sized Millwall Docks; and the Royal Victoria and Albert Docks. They were 'clearing-houses of every imaginable kind of commodity from all parts of the world. Ivory and marble, rubber and perfume, tea and fruit, chilled meat and tobacco, wool and wheat'. One-third of Britain's overseas trade passed through the London Docks, and 'the quantities are so huge that it is difficult to mention them in one breath'.[6] All of these places had been carefully studied by bomb-aimers using maps and aerial photographs.

Between 5 and 6 p.m. the aircraft moved virtually unimpeded across the area on their bombing runs, dropping a rain of high explosives and incendiaries in a concentrated onslaught. The effect below was catastrophic. An official history remarked baldly that 'an area of about $1^1/_2$ miles between North

Woolwich Road and the Thames was almost destroyed and the population of Silvertown was surrounded by fire and had to be evacuated by water'.[7] At ground level experiences were desperate and terrifying. One observer, looking east from the roof of the Home Office building several miles away, recollected the awe-inspiring spectacle. 'Huge clouds of black smoke were billowing and spiralling up into the clear blue sky, great spurts of flame were shooting up; there was a dull thud of bombs as they exploded and reverberated in the distance and an acrid smell of burning was borne in on the wind. The docks looked as if they had been reduced to one great inferno.'[8]

The *Luftwaffe* certainly achieved its object in hitting commercial targets, but even in daylight, when bomb-aimers had a clear view of the ground, many bombs fell on residential areas. Blast respects no boundaries. Scores of terraced houses built in the mid-nineteenth century as homes for dockers, factory workers and their families were destroyed or damaged. Hundreds of civilians were killed or injured, trapped or shaken by the ferocity of an attack concentrated on a small area of the great city.

Relieved of the burden of their bombs, the *Luftwaffe* formations then turned for their French bases. 'On return flight,' the Operational Orders stipulated, 'some loss of altitude is permissible, in order to cross English coast at approximately 4,000 metres.' The homeward course was laid down as 'Maidstone–Dymchurch–escort fighter bases',[9] so throttles were opened as aircraft came lower, making for the coast. Because the RAF fighter effort was brought tardily to the area of the raid, many bombers escaped unharmed. German losses were later estimated at 33 aircraft, in exchange for 28 British fighters.

The *Luftwaffe* considered that the attack had been a great success, and German wireless services made much of it. Broadcasting directly from his headquarters, Goering told his listeners, 'I personally have assumed the leadership of this attack, and today I have heard above me the roaring of the victorious German squadrons which now, for the first time, are driving towards the heart of the enemy in full daylight, accompanied by countless fighter squadrons.' He went on to claim that 'this is an historic hour, in which for the first time the German *Luftwaffe* has struck at the heart of the enemy'.[10]

The attack also marked the real beginning of a new phase of the air war over Britain and in that sense was a turning point in the conflict. Moreover, it acted as a type of pathfinder operation to mark the target area. By the early evening much of the East End of the capital was burning, and acting as an objective for the next stage of the German plan. The great London raid of 7 September was

17

both the forerunner of, and the first step in, the Night Blitz, which was to affect many cities and towns, villages and hamlets across Britain during the following nine months.

THE NIGHT RAID

When the 'All Clear' sounded, at about 6.10 p.m., in the main centres of destruction the survivors emerged from whatever shelter they had managed to find. On the ground they were surrounded by flames and falling buildings, destroyed or damaged homes and dead or injured people. They prayed that their ordeal was past, but these hopes were soon to be dashed. Two hours later, the sirens wailed again.

A report from a *Luftwaffe* liaison officer at Naval Headquarters showed the next step in the German plan: 'The further conduct of the attack on London', he announced, 'is expected to involve day operations by *Luftflotte II*, with very heavy fighter escort, and night operations by *Luftflotte III*, with the object of destroying the city's harbour installations, supplies and power sources.'[11] Consequently a night raid opened which was continued by 250 bombers, mainly from *Luftflotte III*'s bases in northern France. It lasted eight hours.

According to one account, the first wave of attackers was detected ten to fifteen miles north of Cap d'Antifer between 20.08 and 20.14 hours, 'steering for our coasts at a height of some 15,000 feet'. It arrived just west of Beachy Head between 20.22 and 20.34 hours. 'Proceeding unhindered to London, they dropped bombs in Battersea, Hammersmith and Paddington among other places, turned south-west and returned to their bases by way of Selsey Bill.'[12]

For the aircrews, the task was relatively simple. The daylight bombers had illuminated a target which showed in the darkness from the Channel coast. The fiery glow of London's sky could be seen at ground level from distances of well over thirty miles, while in Shaftesbury Avenue one witness remembered that '5 miles from the blaze it was possible to read the evening newspaper'.[13] The safety of bombers was assured in the night sky as they cruised around with no fear of intercepting fighters and unloaded bombs on the inferno. Altogether, 330 tons of high explosive and 440 incendiary canisters were dropped. These landed widely across the East End, concentrating first on the area bombed a few hours earlier and adding to the desolation. The start of the night raid was noted by Ivan Maisky, the Russian Ambassador, at his embassy. 'Exactly at 9 p.m. there began high in the darkened sky a kind of strange and unaccustomed roar.

It seemed as though a multitude of enormous birds was circling in the sky, each of them giving out a protracted howling or piercing sound. At once it was frightening and revolting. Then dull blows could be heard.'[14]

As a contemporary aviation magazine reported, 'For a time bombing was confined to the area attacked originally. Later other parts of London were bombed, possibly because smoke and cloud hid the chosen targets.'[15] A female air raid warden who was to the west of Liverpool Street, about four miles from the docks, wrote: 'By 3 a.m. the raid was heavier than ever and bombs were much closer . . . planes began to circle steadily and monotonously overhead just as we had seen them circling over the East End in the afternoon. It was alarming to think that it was we who were the target.'[16]

By then, some of Dockland's fires were out of control. A fireman at Rum Wharf in the East India Dock admitted that 'the fire was so large that we could do little more than make a feeble attempt to put it out'. The whole of one warehouse, he wrote, 'was a raging inferno against which were silhouetted groups of pigmy firemen directing their futile jets at the wall of flame'.[17]

In the Quebec Yard of Surrey Docks two hundred acres of timber burned furiously with the biggest fire, which ignited even the wooden blocks in the roads. The heat was so intense that fireboats 300 hundred yards away, against the opposite bank of the river, had their paint blistered. In the docks, pepper fires scalded the breath with stinging particles, while barrels of rum exploded. Paint fires gave off a searing flame and rubber burned with a thick, choking smoke. Liquefied sugar, tea and wheat all added heat and light to the conflagrations as warehouses collapsed under the impact of bombs. At quaysides, moored ships and barges started to burn.

The cover of darkness allowed bomber crews to take their time and many circled over the city after dropping their loads. No longer did they fear assault from Spitfires and Hurricanes as they did in daylight raids. For some, a spirit of revenge burned as fiercely as the fires below. One pilot of a Heinkel 111 claimed that the RAF's Bomber Command had launched 'a war of terror' against German civilians and that that, in his opinion, 'overcame our reservations towards repaying like with like'.[18]

The Germans undoubtedly caused damage to the targets they wished to hit, particularly supplies of food and materials useful to the war effort. Transport was also affected, as three main line terminal railway stations were put out of action. However, the devastation extended widely across the densely packed residential areas, affecting homes, shops, public houses and hospitals. The inhabitants of the East End suffered harshly. As dawn broke next morning and the last bombers headed back to the security of their French bases, 430 Londoners lay dead and 1,600 had been seriously hurt. The fires burned on through Sunday; their equal had not been seen in Britain since the Great Fire of London, 274 years earlier. There were nine spreading conflagrations, 54 large fires each needing at least ten pumps, and about a thousand smaller blazes.

After a signal lack of achievement in previous daylight attacks, the Germans were pleased to advertise their success. A communiqué issued on 8 September claimed that over one million kilograms of bombs had fallen on London's port and industrial districts during the afternoon and night attacks and 'quays, merchant ships, docks, warehouses, power, water and gasworks as well as arsenals, factories and transportation installations have been hit and partly destroyed by the heaviest of explosions'.[19]

For Goering and his bomber crews there was a feeling of satisfaction that so much material damage had been caused to such a prestigious target. The cost in aircraft lost was negligible. The uncertain factor was the effect of intense bombing on the will of the British people to continue resistance. Unknown to the civilians of London, the long, hard night of explosions and emergencies, fire and destruction was only the first of many to be borne over the following nine months. This was an ordeal they were to share with others, mainly in cities across Britain. The intensified Night Blitz had only just begun.

RESURRECTED MEMORIES

For those Londoners aged over thirty who had lived in the city during the First World War, the events of 7 September rang alarm bells of memory. Although on a lesser scale, they had experienced bombing before and remembered not only the damage caused but also the shock waves to public morale. Throughout 1915 and 1916 German Zeppelins had attacked the capital on twelve out of the 51 raids they had launched across Britain. These hydrogen-filled airships, some as long as ten cricket pitches, were used by both the German Army and Navy. Admiral Tirpitz explained their value, suggesting that single bombs were 'odious when they hit and kill an old woman'. If, however, 'one could set fire to London in 30 places', that would be, 'fine and powerful'. Then, 'all that flies and creeps should be concentrated on that city'.[20]

Zeppelins moved slowly and were therefore vulnerable, so most attacks were made in darkness. Sometimes this led to poor navigation and targets were missed by up to 60 miles. However, radio direction signals were later emitted from two land stations to give greater accuracy. One was at Kleve, in the Rhineland, an important beam-transmitting point in the Night Blitz of 1940.

The first bombs had landed in Norfolk on 15 January 1915 and on 31 May London was hit, bombs descending on 'Stoke Newington, Dalston, Hoxton, Shoreditch, Whitechapel, West Ham and Leytonstone',[21] areas which suffered twenty-five years later. Zeppelins at first were treated as a nuisance, but soon demands for protection arrived from a public whose morale was in danger of being affected. After a raid on Hull by a single machine which caused 60 casualties and destroyed 40 buildings, rioters sacked shops owned by Germans before troops arrived to restore order. Zeppelins ranged across Britain from Macclesfield to Skegness, from Birmingham to Norwich and from London to Arbroath. Altogether they dropped 200 tons of bombs, killing 557 people and seriously injuring 1,358. The damage caused was valued at £1.5 million.

Defences were sorely pressed to prevent the raids. There was little artillery. 'It soon became current talk among the ribald that of the three most useless things in the world, one was the anti-aircraft gun,'[22] wrote Sir Frederick Pile, later GOC-in-C AA Command. The small biplane fighters of the time were often too slow, lacked firepower and could not reach the airships' height. Zeppelins soon became greatly feared weapons. For one German aviator their value lay not so much in any destructive power as in their 'onslaught upon England's insularity otherwise undisturbed by war'.[23]

The Germans then turned to raiding with aircraft. Aeroplanes were more manoeuvrable than Zeppelins, easier and quicker to build and less easily detected, and they carried smaller crews. Their first bombs fell on the capital on 28 November 1916, landing on 'a baker's shop, a dairy, a private residence, some mews and on the Victoria Palace music hall'.[24] From mid-1917 the Germans began day and night raids, aiming to break British morale.

Four flights of bombers, the *Englandgeschwader*, flew from Belgian bases. Their aircraft, the Gotha, was a three-seat biplane with a top speed of 85mph, a wing-span of 72 feet and a bomb load of 450kg. Their ceiling of 20,000 feet was reached only with difficulty by defending fighters. Their first daylight raid over London came on 13 June. 'Not far off, high in the sky over the Tower of London and coming westward, were a dozen German aircraft,' wrote a young man. 'They looked like summer gnats in the clear sky.'[25] A lady wondered how to escape them, expressing the civilian's feeling of impotence and vulnerability that would be felt equally in the same area by Londoners 25 years later: 'I felt sure they were all looking at me and would drop a bomb just for fun, on the chance of hitting me.'[26] The raiders unloaded 126 bombs, seventeen in the City of London, killing 162 people and injuring 432. The event 'aroused the population to a passion of protest'.[27] The enemy had struck with impunity at the heart of the Empire.

The Government had already reacted to the new aerial threat by establishing the Smuts Committee to investigate it. Their two reports, in July and August 1917, led to the creation of the London Air Defence Area (LADA), under the command of Major-General E. B. Ashmore, with fighters, guns and search-lights. 'London occupies a peculiar position in the Empire of which it is the nerve centre,' suggested one report. By the following year the metropolis might became 'part of the battle front' and required special defences. More-over, as 'an air force can conduct extensive operations far from and independ-ent of both armies and navies', there was no limit to its use. The day would come when 'aerial operations, with their devastation of enemy lands, the destruction of industrial and populous centres on a vast scale, may become the principal operations of war'. Three other recommendations marked a turning point in British service strategy. An Air Ministry should be formed, together with a unified Royal Air Force, which would launch its aerial campaign against Germany through independent bomber forces.[28]

As British defences improved, German bombers raided at night for eight months, from September 1917. This was the same period as the Night Blitz twenty-three years later. The eleven-ton Giant was introduced, with a wing-span of 138 feet, carrying 1,800kg of bombs. Night raids were difficult to counter. The worst single incident occurred on 29 January when the Odhams Press building in Long Acre received a direct hit, killing 37 civilians and injuring 89 others. 'The moonlight aeroplane attacks,' wrote a contemporary historian, 'marked a new era of rhythmic ruthlessness hitherto unknown.'[29] In October Smuts accused the enemy of 'striking at us through our non-combatants, our women and children'. By December Lord Rothermere called for reprisals, to avenge 'the murder' of the innocent.[30] An officer escorting captured German airmen passed through angry crowds: 'He had to keep them off at the point of a revolver, otherwise we should all have been lynched.'[31]

The defences, using searchlights, anti-aircraft guns and night fighters, had some success, but in the main German bombers flew regularly across southern England. By the end of the campaign, 52 aeroplane raids had been made on Britain, nineteen of them on the capital. Altogether 76 tons of bombs fell, killing 857 people and injuring 2,050. These figures were carefully studied by those who, between the wars, estimated the effects of bombing. They also were impressed by the fact that tied down in Britain for Home Defence were 353 searchlights, 266 anti-aircraft guns and 282 day and night fighters.

At ground level, civilian defences were few to counter this novel warfare. There were lighting restrictions, and air raid warnings 'were distributed partly by maroons (or sound bombs) fired into the air'. Also employed were 'policemen on foot, on bicycles or in cars carrying "Take Cover" placards and blowing whistles or sounding horns'.[32] Many families went to their cellars, or to shelters below public buildings or police stations. Thousands used Underground railway stations, while some from the capital's East End 'trekked' to what they considered to be the safer West End. Outside London, caves or mine workings were used. Nevertheless, the majority of people stayed in their own homes, judging that their chances of being hit were slender, a manifestation that recurred in 1940.

An important result of German raids was the expansion of the British bomber force to retaliate. They struck at a few industrial and transport targets in western Germany, in such places as Trier and Mannheim. A little damage was done and there were civilian casualties, though fewer than those suffered in the United Kingdom. Raids started even before the Royal Air Force was formed on 1 April 1918 with the amalgamation of the Royal Flying Corps and the Royal Naval Air Service. By June Major-General H. Trenchard was in command of the Independent Air Force, using his bombers to strike at railways, factories and airfields behind the battlefield. His largest aircraft was the Handley Page O/400, powered by two 250hp Eagle engines and having a wing-span of 100 feet, a top speed of 97mph and a bomb load of 2,000lb.[33]

Trenchard's unwavering belief in the efficacy of air power was shown at this time. He reasoned that the enemy would be forced to employ resources to oppose him, while industry and transport would suffer from bombing. Furthermore, he would affect civilian morale and meet the desire for retaliation felt by many British people at the time. 'If I were you I would not be too exacting as regards accuracy in bombing railway stations in the middle of towns,' Sir William Weir wrote to Trenchard in September 1918. 'The German is susceptible to bloodiness and I would not mind a few accidents due to inaccuracy.'[34]

By the end of the war the Independent Air Force had Berlin in its sights. The four-engine Handley-Page V/1500 was secretly built and tested to carr half a ton of bombs to the German capital then return to the French base at Nancy.

The psychological effect of such a raid would have been remarkable for both sides. However, as the war came rapidly to an end in November, the venture never occurred. Over twenty years were to elapse before Berlin was raided.

Thus, for thousands of Londoners on 7 September 1940, attack from the air was no novelty. Memories of air-raid warnings and searchlights, anti-aircraft fire and falling bombs were stirred. A quarter of a century earlier damage had not been extensive, but the seeds of fear of the aerial threat had been sown. The people were about to re-live those experiences, with attendant demands for retribution, although on a scale unknown in 1918. They were soon to learn that, with the coming of the aeroplane, there were no longer any non-combatants in war.

NOTES

1. Public Record Office, Kew (PRO), AIR 16/330, Reinforcement of No 11 Group, meeting, 7 September 1940.
2. AIR 41/12, Signals IV, 'Radar in Raid Reporting', 122.
3. S. Johnstone, *Enemy in the Sky* (1976), 131.
4. B. Wickes, *Waiting for the All Clear* (1990), 53.
5. Ward Lock, *London, 1910* (1910), 246.
6. E. Fodor (ed.), 1936, *On the Continent* (1985), 1057–58.
7. T. O'Brien, *Civil Defence* (HMSO, 1955), 38.
8. A. Price, *Blitz on Britain 1939–1945* (1977), 78–9.
9. W. Ramsey (ed.), *The Blitz: Then and Now*, vol. ii (1988), 49.
10. Goering broadcast, German radio, 7 September 1940.
11. SKL KTB, Ops Div., Part A, 8 September 1940.
12. AIR 41/17, 'Air Defence of Great Britain' (ADGB), ii, 55.
13. B. Nixon, *Raiders Overhead* (1980), 13–16.
14. I. Maisky, *Memoirs of a Soviet Ambassador* (1967), 107.
15. *The Aeroplane*, 13 September 1940.
16. Nixon, 17.
17. Ministry of Information, *Front Line* (HMSO, 1942), 26–30.
18. H. Hermann, *Eagle's Wings* (1991), 66.
19. OKW Order, 8 September 1940.
20. *Tirpitz Memoirs*, quoted in R. Cross, *The Bombers* (1987), 49.
21. J. Morris, *The German Air Raids on Great Britain 1914–1918* (1927), 31.
22. F. Pile, *Ack-Ack* (1949), 45.
23. Cross, 30.
24. Morris, 206.
25. V. Pritchett, *A Cab at the Door* (1968).

26. Mrs C. Peel, *How We Lived Then* (1929).
27. Morris, 223.
28. Report by General J. C. Smuts to the War Cabinet on 'Defence Arrangements for Home Defence against Air Raids', 17 August 1917.
29. Morris, 233.
30. Lord Rothermere, Chairman of the Air Board, 14 December 1917.
31. C. Lewis, *Sagittarius Rising* (1936), 189.
32. O'Brien, 10.
33. B. Cooper, *The Story of the Bomber 1914-1945* (1974), 26–7.
34. See Morris, 62.

CHAPTER TWO

THE BRITISH BACKGROUND
1918–1939

THE PRESUMED THREAT

In his extensive study of the background of bombing, Bialer wrote that 'the fear of aerial bombardment in inter-war Britain was unprecedented and unique'.[1] Certainly it was unique in British history, although, at the time, other nations shared an awareness of the possible results of massive air strikes. One major concern in the United Kingdom stemmed from the nation's geographical position. Britain's coastline was her frontier. Several thousand miles of boundary offered entry points for intruding bombers. In addition, as no part of Britain is more than one hundred miles from the sea, targets could be easily reached. A number of these were vulnerable ports, such as Liverpool, Hull and Glasgow; others were industrial cities, like Birmingham, Manchester and Sheffield.

The target most threatened was the world's greatest city and Britain's largest port, area of production and commercial centre, as well as the seat of government—London. The capital's proximity to the mainland Continent, with easy access from the south across the Channel or from the east over the North Sea, made it particularly vulnerable to air attack. This had been proved for London's inhabitants through the ease with which Zeppelins and Gothas had arrived during the First World War.

When the Air Staff investigated the capital's vulnerability in 1935 they commented that its proximity to the coast added to the difficulties of defence. In addition, technical developments—for example, improved bomb sights—offered the probability that specific areas such as Whitehall would be heavily bombed. But there was a second and in some ways more decisive factor causing trepidation in the 1920s and 1930s: the defences of the time were unable to locate and shoot down enemy bombers. Fighters succeeded later when technology provided them with a means of intercepting the enemy, together with a superiority in design, performance and armament over bombers, but these did not exist before the later 1930s.

Consequent fears were not held in Britain alone. One of the greatest exponents of the power of aerial bombing was an Italian, General Giulio Douhet. His book, *Command of the Air*, was first published in 1921. Nine years later he wrote a fictional account of a future war between Germany and France, painting a sombre picture of destruction by means of aerial bombardment. The latter book had an unwelcome taste of reality for many readers. They were offered a descriptive story of hundreds of German bombers devastating French cities, causing so much damage that the government sought peace in less than two days. The crux of such a contest, Douhet reasoned, was for the aggressor to move with speed, ferocity and an unyielding purpose. He predicted that, by the second day of a war, thousands of civilians would flee into open countryside to escape the aerial terror. The Douhet Theory accepted the inability of fighters to prevent these raids, because of their inferior performance—a factor which, in reality, had changed by the time of the German attacks on Britain in 1940.[2]

In the United States, the prime apostle of air power was Brigadier-General William ('Billy') Mitchell, who became Director of Military Aeronautics in 1919. Mitchell demonstrated the power of aircraft by using bombers to sink obsolete warships, moored for target practice. In 1921 one of these vessels sank immediately when hit squarely by a 2,000lb bomb. Mitchell shared the beliefs of Douhet and Trenchard concerning the effect of bombing civilians in cities. 'To gain a lasting victory in war,' he wrote in 1930, 'the hostile nation's power to make war must be destroyed.' Potential targets were then listed—'The factories, the means of communication, the food producers, even the farms, the fuel and oil supplies, and the places where people live and carry on their daily lives.' However, Mitchell was no easy colleague and offended fellow officers by the forceful advocacy of his beliefs.[3]

For the British, an island race, treating civilians as a kind of fourth force in war, standing beside soldiers, sailors and airmen, was an unwelcome novelty. Strategists who accepted the reality of a new warfare were quick to explain the situation. Major-General J. F. ('Boney') Fuller wrote in 1923 that 'today entire nations go to war, not only as soldiers, but as moral and material suppliers of soldiers'.[4] In that case, he explained, 'to attack the civilian workers of a nation will then be as justifiable as to attack its soldiers'. Fuller's imagination later ran riot, suggesting that in a future war, London could be raided and 'a fleet of 500 aeroplanes, each carrying 500 ten-pound bombs of let us suppose mustard gas, might cause 200,000 casualties, and throw the whole city into panic within half an hour of their arrival'. In this fashion, he believed, a war could be won inside two days with the victor suffering no losses.[5]

Lord Balfour, presiding over the Committee of Imperial Defence in the previous year, had made similar predictions. As an enemy could drop 75 tons of high explosives daily on London 'for an indefinite period', he believed that at all hours, 'the capital of the Empire would be subjected to unremitting bombing of a kind which no city effectively acting as the military, naval and administrative centre of a country engaged in a life or death struggle has ever had to endure'.[6]

In the view of many strategists, the greatest potential weakness in a nation's defensive chain was civilian morale: if that link could be snapped, a government would be compelled by its citizens to make peace. 'The ultimate objective of air attack is largely achieved by influencing the morale of the enemy population,' Trenchard wrote in an Air Staff memo in 1922. He added that the greatest effect would come from 'aerial bombardment of legitimate objectives in his great centres of production'. In the following year Trenchard told the War Office that 'the moral effect is to the material effect to the ratio of 10:1', although on that point Smith described the Chief of the Air Staff as 'fond of the totally unfounded statistic'.[7] Yet Trenchard was a pragmatist who appreciated that advances in technology had not only turned aircraft into fighting machines but also changed the nature of warfare.

Leaders of the two older services, however, were uneasy and less ready to accept the new circumstances, especially when the brusque Trenchard fought tooth and nail for an independent air force which would conduct its own campaigns. In 1928 the Chief of the Naval Staff claimed that RAF policy went beyond the bounds of international law. The Chief of the Imperial General Staff commented that the Bomber Doctrine, 'put in plain English, amounts to one which advocates unrestricted warfare against the civil population of one's enemy'.[8] Knowing that bomber raids would be reciprocated, the majority of British people suspected their vulnerability in any future war and came, albeit unwillingly, to accept the situation. They relied on their government to act wisely so that these terrors would never occur. Others supported schemes for disarmament, pinning their hopes on the League of Nations. A small number became pacifists, later following such organisations as the Peace Pledge Union. Vivid memories of the travails of 1914–18 lived on. 'Society in the twenties and thirties exhibited all the signs of having suffered a deep mental wound,' Marwick has written. Ordinary people clearly remembered 'the agony and the bloodshed as well as the more generalised revulsion at the destruction of an older civilization'.[9]

As the Germans turned increasingly to throw off what they considered to be the grossly punitive terms laid on them by the Treaty of Versailles, they started to re-establish their fighting forces, especially the *Luftwaffe*. Consequently, for the remaining years until the outbreak of war in 1939, the presumed threat to Britain was seen to come from Germany. This anticipation coloured the perceptions and actions of most British politicians and strategists, who believed that an aerial devastation would arrive inevitably from the east if war broke out. Fear of the bomber became the prime driving force in Britain's relations with other European countries, leading to the expansion of her own forces—but also to the policy of appeasement.

The stark reality behind politicians' anxieties was expressed during a House of Commons debate in 1932 by Stanley Baldwin, Lord President of the Council. The man in the street should appreciate that 'there is no power on earth that can prevent him from being bombed. Whatever people tell him, the bomber will always get through.' Less often remembered are Baldwin's next words, which showed bluntly the equation of destruction required for survival. 'The only defence is offence, which means that you have to kill more women and children more quickly than the enemy if you want to save yourselves.'[10]

Writing three years later, Air Commodore L. E. G. Charlton, formerly Air Attaché to the United States, envisaged bombers flying in close formation and destroying cities while fighters were unable to prevent the offensive. Bombers could be equipped 'with double guns firing forward, broadside and aft'.[11] The defenders' sole advantage would be speed, but even bombers would be flying at over 200mph: in 1936 only the Hawker Fury and the Gloster Gauntlet of the RAF's fighters could exceed that speed in level flight.[12]

The estimate of possible destruction was predicated on what had happened in the First World War. In 1925 the Air Staff said that, in London, air raids would kill 1,700 people and injure 3,300 in the first twenty-four hours, the figures decreasing to 1,275 and 2,475 respectively on the next day and then levelling off at 880 killed and 1,650 injured in each subsequent twenty-four hours. In later estimates, the figures were revised upwards. As a result, even Churchill was tempted to extremity in forecast. At least three or four million inhabitants of London would be driven out into the countryside, he believed, 'without shelter and without food, without sanitation and without special provision for the maintenance of order'. Controlling them 'would certainly absorb the energies of our small Army and our Territorial Force'.[13]

In the *Encyclopaedia of Pacifism*, Aldous Huxley painted a lurid picture of aerial warfare: 'A bombardment with a mixture of thermite, high explosives and vesicants could kill large numbers outright, would lead to the cutting off of food and water supplies, would smash the system of sanitation and would result in general panic.' He went on to describe a rush from towns, and those not crushed to death by that would die later from starvation and disease. The Army, he suggested, would not fight the enemy but would be employed 'to keep order among the panic-stricken population at home'.[14]

Aerial assault on civilians was experienced in practice in three main areas during the 1930s and the events which were captured on film, or described in news reports, fuelled fears. These were in China, under attack from the Japanese, in Abyssinia, invaded by the Italians, and in Spain, during the Civil War. What the bulk of people did not appreciate, however, was that in those countries the air forces of the aggressors were operating against slight, if any, opposition. Any attacks against Britain would meet sterner resistance.

The effect of films was considerable. In 1936, Alexander Korda's version of H. G. Wells' story *Things to Come* portrayed lurid scenes of urban destruction. Visitors to the cinema were able, with a little imagination, to transfer such chaos to their surrounding streets. Again, when in October 1937 newsreel cameras showed the aftermath of death and damage in Guernica, the impression of unstoppable misery was firmly stamped on the public mind.

By the later 1930s a revolution in the design and power of fighters, combined with advances in locating bombers through radio direction-finding (RDF), had altered the balance between the two types of machine. However, this was either unknown to or unappreciated by many people. Writing in 1938 for the Left Book Club, J. B. Haldane predicted that 270 bombers could drop 400 tons of bombs in thirty seconds. 'This would probably kill about 8,000 people, and wound some 15,000. And that could be repeated several times a day.'[15]

Fear of bombing lasted until the opening of the Second World War. Less than a year earlier, at the time of the Munich Crisis, that factor played on Chamberlain's mind as he returned from meeting Hitler. 'He had flown up the river over London. He had imagined a German bomber flying the same course,' the Cabinet were told. His old worries surfaced: 'He had asked himself what degree of protection we could afford to thousands of homes which he had seen stretched out below him.' The effect on his mind was decisive. 'We were in no position to justify waging a war today in order to prevent a war hereafter.'[16]

It is apparent that between 1918 and 1939 the anticipated threat from the air was high. All hoped, though without total conviction, that the RAF would be able to thwart the enemy either through defensive measures or by the threat of counter-attack.

THE SERVICES' RESPONSE

In November 1918 the RAF possessed the world's largest air force, with over 22,000 aircraft and almost 300,000 personnel, of whom 25,000 were women. In addition, large sections of British industry had been turned over to the production and maintenance of aeroplanes. Altogether 188 squadrons world-wide could operate from 475 airfields. Of these massive forces, approximately 200 fighters, mainly Sopwith Camels and Bristols, were employed in the defence of the United Kingdom. The RAF, in spite of some opposition from the two older services, had won a right to stand in its own place.

Within sixteen months, however, British air power had suffered a dramatic reduction. By early 1920 thousands of aircraft had been scrapped and the RAF's strength was down to about 30 squadrons. The main cause of the contraction was the apparent lack of danger to Britain. Germany had been defeated. France, an ally, guarded the Rhineland. Consequently the British Government sheltered behind the 'Ten Year Rule', which based all defence planning on the assumption that no large war would occur within ten years. Accordingly, a small force would be retained, to be rapidly expanded in the event of an emergency. A government anxious to return to peacetime conditions and to curtail service spending paid little heed to the prophetic words of Major-General Sir Frederick Sykes, Chief of the Air Staff in December 1918. 'In the next war, however near or distant,' he wrote, 'the existence of the nation will depend largely upon air power. In peace and in war the nation which thinks in three dimensions will lead those thinking in two.'[17]

When the weaknesses of British defences became apparent in 1922–23, plans had to be laid hastily to resurrect a system of air cover. Ironically, the putative foe was France, Britain's traditional rival, yet more recently a friend and ally in arms. Of the major powers involved in the First World War, the French alone had retained powerful armed forces after 1918, bearing in mind the suffering resulting from two German invasions during the previous half-

31

century. When minor international crises arose—in 1922 over Chanak, then in the following year over the Ruhr—the strength of the RAF either to intervene abroad or to defend at home was questioned. This was done particularly through the Salisbury Committee, which recommended that Britain should have a Home Defence Force of 52 squadrons. That number was estimated to equal the strength of the French Air Force, which was foreseen as the only possible aggressor. Total French air strength included 200 day and 96 night bombers, together with 340 fighters, numbers which the RAF in the United Kingdom could not match.

Meetings were held by senior RAF officers and from these the future pattern became clear: 'The discussions were dominated by the personality of the Chief of the Air Staff (CAS), the main creator of the Air Force, who had an experience and authority which no one else could rival.'[18] Trenchard, with his strong belief in attack by a bomber force, wanted to restrict the numbers of fighters allocated for Home Defence. The agenda for the first meeting, issued on 29 June 1923, asked how many fighter squadrons would be required, and how many of those would be night fighters. The answer was 'Probably 20. 17 of these will be in sectors of the Air Fighting Zone and 3 at interception stations. About 6 night fighting squadrons will be required.'[19]

Subsequent discussions, lasting until 8 August, covered some topics relevant to the later Blitz of 1940. For example, one Air Commodore believed that day bombing would cause more casualties because 'the inhabitants would be at work by day in crowded places, etc.',[20] a view supported by Squadron Leader Portal (CAS from October 1940). He believed that daylight bombing would affect factory workers, 'bearing in mind crowd psychology'.[21] Yet Trenchard wanted night bombing, to destroy factories, 'throwing quantities of people out of work' and 'dislocating their normal life' as well as having a 'moral effect'.[22]

In many respects Trenchard had summarised both his and the Air Staff's view of the RAF's future role at a meeting six days earlier: 'Would it be best to have less [sic] fighters and more bombers to bomb the enemy and trust to their people cracking before ours, or have more fighters to bring down more of the enemy bombers?' he asked rhetorically. Then came the argument employed generally against those, like Dowding fifteen years later, who put faith in fighter defence: 'It would be rather like putting 2 teams to play each other at football, and telling one team that they must only defend their own goal, and keep all their men on that one point.' The defending team would not be beaten, but neither would they win. Although there would be an outcry, 'the French in a bombing duel would probably squeal before we did . . . the nation that could stand being bombed longest would win in the end'.[23] This reflection was supported two years later in the Report of the Air Raid Precautions Committee, established to examine Home Defence. The Committee accepted that in the next war 'it may well be that the nation whose people can endure aerial bombardment the longer, and with greater stoicism, will ultimately prove victorious'.[24]

Consequently, until the opening of the Second World War, the Air Staff's overall faith rested in the power of the bomber. Through the employment of large numbers, heavy damage would be inflicted on an enemy's economy, by bombing industrial and transport targets. They also believed that the enemy would be forced to employ, for home protection, resources that were needed elsewhere, throwing him into a defensive frame of mind. Civilian morale would be eroded, adding to the burdens of the opposing government and possibly shortening the war.

The Air Staff's plans in the 1930s bore the hallmark of this Bomber Doctrine, favoured particularly by Trenchard. For them, fighter defence had never proved its case either by denying air space to bombers or by winning a war. Thus the expansion schemes advanced between 1934 and 1938 were weighted in favour of the bomber. For example, Scheme A of July 1934 proposed 41 bomber and 28 fighter squadrons. By the time of Scheme M in November 1938, even after the Government had acknowledged the need for fighter defence of the home base, the respective figures proposed by the Air Staff were 85 and 50 squadrons.[25]

A decisive factor in RAF planning of the period was the inability of fighters at that time to locate and destroy bombers. The Fairey Fox bomber, which appeared in 1926, was, in Cooper's words, 'not only the fastest bomber of its day, with a speed of 156 m.p.h., but faster and more manoeuvrable than most fighters'.[26] The point is proved when comparing its performance with that of the Armstrong Whitworth Siskin Mk III fighter, which entered service in 1924, with a top speed of 134mph. The Gloster Gamecock of 1926 could manage 155mph and was armed with two Vickers machine guns, giving little or no superiority over bombers of the time. In the early 1930s the differences in performance continued. The Hawker Hart, the RAF's standard light bomber from 1930 to 1937, was better than the single-seater fighters of the period. In fact, Hawker produced the Demon as a two-seat version of the Hart; the bomber's top speed was 184mph while the fighter was 3mph slower.

The superiority of the bomber was demonstrated during the Air Defence Exercises held by the RAF in July 1932. On the first day thirteen 'attacking' bombers were adjudged 'shot down' for the loss of seven 'defending' fighters, although most bombers reached their targets. During the second day, only two out of seven raids were intercepted. The third day saw 20 per cent of the raiders 'shot down', but at the cost of 17 per cent of the defenders. On the last day nine fighters were 'lost' in 'bringing down' twelve bombers. These results offered some comfort to those who hoped that the bomber threat could be met by interceptors, yet they showed that aircraft of an enemy power could still reach and bomb cities in Britain.[27]

Under Trenchard, a system of protection known as the Air Defence of Great Britain (ADGB), was set up. Because of the proven weaknesses of fighters, wide use was made of ground defences to intercept raids by both day and night. These consisted of anti-aircraft guns, searchlights, balloons, sound detectors and the Observer Corps. By the late 1920s the whole organisation came under the control of the Air Ministry.

The defences were arranged in three 'layers' to engage incoming aircraft. At the coast, and extending for 35 miles inland, was an Outer Artillery Zone, whose guns had the task of disrupting enemy squadrons. Behind this came the Fighter Zone, where RAF squadrons would engage bombers in aerial combat. Finally, near London the Inner Artillery Zone was established, a last-ditch protection system for the capital. Telephone communication between guns and searchlights and the Fighter Area headquarters was intended to bring a coordinated defence. It was the best that could be produced at the time, but the scheme had several weaknesses, both by night and by day.

The first was the distance of fighter squadrons from the coast, because, before RDF, there was no effective warning of the enemy's approach. Biplane fighters needed at least a quarter of an hour to climb to 15,000 feet, so required to be positioned well inland to give any chance of interception.

Secondly, there was a dearth of AA guns and searchlights. General Pile has shown how swiftly after 1918 defences were dismantled. All of the guns and searchlights stationed to protect London in November 1918 had been removed by 1920, and with them went the defensive system. By 1926, when the ADGB organisation was being built up, great weaknesses transpired during training exercises. 'The only thing that emerged with an awful clarity,' Pile wrote, 'was that a drive for better technical apparatus, such as sound-locators, was a matter of urgency, that the height-calculating apparatus was far from accurate, and that the control system needed overhauling.' A report on th exercises commented that the only benefit brought by AA fire was to morale, because 'from permanent emplacements, out of 2,935 rounds fired at a target flying on a known course at a known speed and at the best height for shooting only two actual hits were obtained'. In 1931 ground defences were still undermanned and the CAS had to admit that, although the number of Air Force squadrons was increasing, 'if there was an immediate declaration of war we could only man 27 per cent of the guns and 22 per cent of the searchlights out of the total authorized for ADGB'. [28]

The third weakness related to the identification and positioning of incoming enemy raids. Until the advent of RDF, sound detectors were employed, a method tried during the First World War. By later standards the scheme was primitive, but as no better apparatus existed it was incorporated into the defences as an early warning system stretching from the Humber to Kent. Some of the derelict equipment can still be seen near Hythe, on the south-east coast. Large concrete 'sound mirrors' were built at listening stations to cover London, the Thames Estuary and the Kent coast. The concrete bowls, with diameters of twenty or thirty feet, collected sounds acoustically, where they were traced by an operator wearing a stethoscope. By using handwheels and foot pedals he could scan different parts of the sky, searching for aircraft. The largest bowl was a strip concrete mirror 200 feet in length and 30 feet in height, equipped with microphones to detect sounds and relay them to a plotting room. Through taking cross-bearings from several mirrors it was hoped to locate the exact position of the aircraft. This system could detect the general direction of enemy formations, but not their height or size. It was, moreover, susceptible to extraneous noise. For example, a morning test of the mirrors in 1934 was disturbed by a passing milk-float. The milkman was asked not to return in the afternoon, when Dowding would be present. [29]

Results were fed into the Fixed Azimuth System. This was based on messages being relayed to a central Control Room in London and thence to the guns. However, the FAS relied on an enemy approaching the capital on fixed lines, flying a straight course at a steady speed and height, particularly up the Thames Estuary. In the days of slow-moving bombers sound detectors offered some hope to the defences, but with the arrival of faster and more manoeuvrable monoplanes the deficiencies of the system became obvious.

Sound mirrors were tested during the Air Defence Exercises of 1933 and 1934. In the latter year it was reported that the operators' stethoscopes had been replaced by headsets. These left 'both hands free for operating the handwheel controlling the direction of listening, and for dialling messages for transmission to the plotting room'. However, messages from Hythe to the London headquarters had to be sent along ordinary telephone lines shared by the public—hardly the conditions to meet an emergency.[30]

The revolution in detecting aircraft, which was to bring a radical improvement to the RAF's defensive system, came with the use and development of radio beams. In 1934 a committee was appointed 'to investigate the possibility of countering air attacks by utilizing the recent progress of scientific invention'. The members, whose work was to have crucial effects on the war over Britain both by day and night, were led by H. T. Tizard, Rector of Imperial College, London. He was joined by Professors A. V. Hill and P. M. S. Blackett, and by two members of the Air Ministry's Research and Development Department, which was led by Dowding. They were Major H. A. Wimperis, the Director of Scientific Research, and A. P. Rowe. The group was known as the Committee for the Scientific Survey of Air Defence (CSSAD).

At an early stage they were asked to investigate the possibility of employing a 'death ray', which fitted contemporary popular ideas of science fiction, as shown in books and films. The scientists Robert Watson-Watt and A. F. Wilkins investigated the matter, concluding that no such beam could kill people or immobilise engines. Nevertheless, research showed that radio signals might be used to detect aircraft, from which they were reflected, or 'bounced' back to earth. Here was the starting point for a revolution in air defence. 'While I modestly believe myself to be the father of radar,' Watson-Watt wrote later, 'I am convinced that Arnold Frederick Wilkins has a unique claim to the title of mother of radar, for nobody did so much to give the embryonic war-winner its start in life.'[31]

The way was open for experiments with aircraft in flight and, for these, on 26 February 1935 a Heyford bomber flew along a radio beam emitted from the BBC Overseas Station at Daventry. Scientists below followed the bomber on a receiver linked to their cathode ray oscilloscope, with encouraging results. 'We now have in embryo,' Wimperis wrote on 4 March, 'a new and potent means of detecting the approach of hostile aircraft, one which will be independent of mist, cloud, fog or nightfall.'[32] The sum of £10,000 was advanced to promote more experiments, made at Orfordness in Suffolk, where receivers and transmitters were installed below a 75-foot aerial. Work proceeded apace, and soon the nearby Bawdsey Manor was taken over, becoming the centre of investigations. By July an aeroplane was detected and followed at a range of 40 miles; within two months another, flying at 7,000 feet, had its height estimated accurately. Problems with apparatus were gradually solved.

To track aircraft, tall towers were required. Those transmitting signals were 350 feet high, while those receiving were 240 feet. The first five were planned to cover the Thames Estuary and by August 1937 the number proposed had grown to twenty, which would give cover from the Firth of Forth to Portsmouth. As the probable enemy was Germany, cover was essential along Britain's east coast. The tall towers were erected quickly and known as Chain Home (CH) stations.

A further problem to be addressed was the detection of aircraft flying in low, below 3,000 feet. Subsequently, low-level scanners, with smaller apparatus than the tall towers, were evolved and set up as Chain Home Low (CHL) stations. Thus any aircraft approaching the British coast in the area covered could be detected and tracked. The system was destined to be Fighter Command's salvation during the daylight Battle of Britain. By then, there were thirty CH and thirty CHL stations between Scapa Flow and Strumble Head in Pembrokeshire.[33]

Information received by the RDF systems was passed to a Filter Room in Fighter Command's headquarters at Stanmore. From there it was issued to the headquarters of each fighter group, which in turn forwarded the details to their sector stations. The Sector Controller would then 'scramble' squadrons to intercept enemy aircraft, and Dowding's policy was to meet them beyond or over the coast, in a speedy response.

In the words of the Official Narrative, the system aimed 'to ensure that all possible information about enemy movements would simultaneously be displayed in Sector and Group Operations Rooms and on the Command plotting table'.[34] In practice the system worked. It was tested in a series of Air Exercises, culminating in the most extensive test held just before the outbreak of war. This extended from 8 to 11 August 1939, ending with a practice black-out which enveloped south-east England and London. To defend the area, 53,000 men, 700 searchlights, 110 guns and 100 barrage balloons were employed. Nevertheless, the greatest defender was the unseen eye of RDF. 'Weather, as usual, played an important part,' a contemporary report noted, 'and was particularly bad with low cloud, rain, wind and ground fog, hampering attack and defence with incalculable impartiality . . . yet it was the acid test of the success of RDF. Nearly every attack was intercepted.'[35]

This 'Dowding System' of methodical and integrated interception was generally excellent for day defence. Enemy formations could be located and tracked well before reaching the British coastline, their height and bearing detected. On crossing the coast, they would be followed by the sharp eyes of the Observer Corps, civilian 'spotters' whose contribution to the defensive plan has been underestimated. They had 'a Centre, to which posts, situated for the most part at vantage points in the open country, telephoned plots of enemy aircraft'. This information allowed Fighter Command's controllers to know the whereabouts of planes flying inland.[36]

There was another success to help the defences. This was a greatly needed and rapid advance in the design and performance of fighters, so that by the outbreak of war they possessed a speed, manoeuvrability and firepower that had easily overtaken those of bombers. In Britain, the revolution arrived in the form of the Hurricane and the Spitfire. After George Bulman tested the former at Brooklands in November 1935, he told Sidney Camm, the designer, 'Another winner, I think!'[37] This enthusiastic verdict was echoed by others over the following years. Easier to build than Spitfires, Hurricanes were still produced more slowly than Fighter Command wished. By October 1938, just after the Munich Crisis, only Nos 3, 56 and 111 Squadrons were equipped with the new machines; at the outbreak of war there were 347 Hurricanes in the United Kingdom. Their size, speed and firepower were gratifying to those accustomed to smaller and lighter biplanes. There was a world of difference between flying a Fury, with its maximum speed of 223mph and a take-off weight of 3,620lb, and a Hurricane, whose comparable figures were 316mph and 6,040lb.

The first test for the Spitfire was at Eastleigh on 5 March 1936, in front of its designer, R. J. Mitchell. Harald Penrose, who flew one several months later, said, 'Every pilot who flew that Spitfire instantly recognised it as a winner.'[38] Smaller yet faster than the Hurricane (365mph and 5,284lb), the Spitfire was more difficult to produce and therefore entered service slowly. At the time of Munich only fourteen were ready, all non-operational. By the outbreak of war the figure had risen to 187—far from reassuring for Fighter Command.[39]

Changes in the balance between fighters and bombers, however, affected air fighting by day; at night, the balance was virtually unaltered, when defenders were confronted by apparently insuperable difficulties. In general, estimates of forthcoming action made both by the *Luftwaffe* and the RAF anticipated day contests, and aircrews were trained accordingly. The Joint Planning Committee in 1936 believed that 1,000 bomber sorties daily could be launched directly from Germany. 'It is clear that in a war against us,' the Committee alleged, 'the concentration of the whole German air offensive ruthlessly against Great Britain will be possible. It would be the most promising way of trying to knock this country out.' In their belief, most strikes would arrive from the east or north-east during daylight, and Fighter Command's defences should be geared to meet these.[40]

By July 1938 a warning note was sounded when the Assistant Chief of the Air Staff expressed the view that, apart from heavy day raids, attacks would also be made at night. These would be launched by between 300 and 500 aircraft, flying either separately or in small formations.[41] The defences were faced with a seemingly impossible problem, because the Dowding System could not operate in darkness. 'So long as the aircraft was visible, Observer Corps plotting was adequate,' stated the Official Narrative. 'When however they had to rely on plotting by sound, as at night, or under conditions of cloud, the tracks produced were too inaccurate for controlled interception.'[42] RDF was, moreover, an invisible 'eye' looking seawards, but when at night intruding aircraft had crossed the coast there was no reliable method of identifying and tracking them inland.

The obvious counter-measure for the RAF was to have a form of airborne RDF, a small apparatus carried by fighters. The task of producing that was first undertaken by Dr E. G. Bowen and by the end of 1936 a receiver had been built. However, many technical difficulties lay in the path of creating effective ground transmitters and by early 1939 problems had not been overcome. In July of that year the Air Ministry reported that 'while the equipment is still in a relatively early experimental stage, it is considered to have immense possibilities for air fighting at night as in conditions of bad visibility'.[43] Just before the war opened, Mark 1 Airborne Interception (AI) sets were fitted into three Blenheim Mk IVs of No 25 Squadron. The theory was that a ground station could place a fighter within five miles of a bomber, and that airborne radar 'could pick up at 3 miles and guide the interceptor to within two hundred yards'. But practice was far removed from theory, and the failure of trials proved that better apparatus was needed.[44]

By 1939 Tizard told Dowding that he was 'mainly occupied with the night problems now'. Difficulties over day fighting were being solved, 'but the night problem is more serious, and we do want much more [sic] experiments'.[45] Five months later the Deputy Chief of the Air Staff noted that tests were being made with night fighters, 'in view of the present relative weakness of our night defence'.[46] Dowding himself later lamented the inadequacy of the system: 'I had long been apprehensive of the effect of night attacks, when they should begin, and of the efficiency of our defensive measures.'[47]

Apart from the difficulties of locating the enemy at night, the RAF lacked a suitable night fighter. As C-in-C, Dowding considered that the aircraft needed a two-man crew, one to fly the plane while the other operated RDF equipment. At first he suggested that the Defiant would fit these requirements.[48] Later the Beaufighter, planned as a long-range fighter, met the qualifications: the Mk IF was powered by two Hercules engines, giving a maximum speed of 323mph, and carried the formidable armament of four 20mm cannon and six Browning machine guns. Although 300 Beaufighters were ordered after the prototype had flown on 17 July 1939, the first did not reach Fighter Command until September 1940, in too small numbers to make an immediate impact during the Night Blitz. Their effect was not felt until early 1941.

To fill the gap at night, the RAF therefore turned to the Blenheim. From late 1938 about 200 Blenheim Mk Is were modified as fighters at the Southern Railway's Ashford workshops. Their existing two machine guns were augmented by a further four, but with a top speed of 260mph the Blenheim lacked the pace to catch German bombers, especially the Junkers 88. Even by the early months of 1940 Fighter Command included only six squadrons of Blenheims specialising in night fighting.[49]

As the war opened, it appeared that the burden of night defence would be carried by ground forces, as had happened in 1914. By then seven AA divisions had been formed, and the presence of their guns, together with balloons and searchlights, was a great boost to civilian morale. Anti-Aircraft Command, established on 1 April 1939, was under the leadership of General Sir Frederick Pile, who worked closely and harmoniously with Dowding. Pile's greatest difficulty, a shortage of equipment, was not remedied until the Night Blitz was well under way. He recollected that 'on March 1, 1939, only 570 heavy guns and 1,950 searchlights would be capable of going into action. In other words, there was still only half the requirements laid down two years before, and, as far as guns were concerned, only a third of the new scale approved in February.'[50] His task was formidable.

To offer confidence to British citizens who anticipated heavy bombing from the first day of war, Dowding was asked to broadcast just after the last peacetime

Air Exercises. His words summarised the defenders' faith that, although small in numbers, they would offer a strong riposte to attackers: 'It only remains for us to see that our technical equipment keeps ahead of that of our potential enemy.' He then showed his faith in RDF, about which the public knew nothing: 'What we have been doing is to work at increasing interception towards 100 per cent which is our goal.' He finished with the explicit belief that 'serious attack on these Islands would be brought to a standstill within a short space of time'.[51] Dowding here was referring to attacks in daylight. What he obviously did not know was that, a year later, the Germans would be launching a night bombing campaign from just across the Channel.

PREPARING CIVILIANS FOR WAR

The inter-war period saw the growth of a fourth service which, by 1939, was able to stand beside the Army, Navy and RAF in Britain. The difference was that its members were unarmed and part of an organisation whose sole aim was to protect people and property. Their overall tasks came under the general heading of 'air raid precautions' (ARP), and just after the Munich Crisis the force comprised about 1,140,000 men and women. At the time that was more than twice the strength of the fighting services added together.

In 1923, fears of the comparative weakness of the RAF had wide effects. The Air Ministry were concerned not only with the repercussions for Britain's defences, but also with what could be suffered by civilians. They therefore suggested to the Home Office that a scheme of precautions against air attack should be instituted. Consequently, in May 1924 an Air Raid Precautions Committee met under the chairmanship of Sir John Anderson, 'to enquire into the question of Air Raid Precautions other than Naval, Military and Air Defence'.[52] The seven main topics discussed established the limits and purpose of the work of civil defence over the following twenty years.

First, they investigated warning systems, remembering that during the First World War the authorities considered that too many people had been alarmed and had absented themselves from work unnecessarily. Secondly, they explored methods of preventing damage both to people and property, through such means as providing gas masks, and through lighting restrictions. In the third place they foresaw the need to maintain vital services and sustain everyday life. Next they examined the question of damage repair, where the Ministry of Health would have to deal with medical services, and the Home Office with fire brigades. Their fifth question concerned the possible removal of the seat of government from London to another centre, for example Birmingham, or Liverpool, although the general consensus was that this could have an adverse effect on public morale. Sixthly, they investigated anti-gas measures, stressing the need for making buildings gas proof and for setting up decontamination centres. Their last point summarised all the others by pointing out the need for public opinion to be educated in matters of home defence; in this they wanted secrecy maintained so that ordinary people would not panic.

Between 1926 and 1929 the question of air raid precautions did not stand particularly high in Britain. There was a general international desire for peace, with no immediate threat looming for the United Kingdom. However, one domestic conflict did interest the Air Raid Precautions Committee. This was the General Strike of 1926. The reactions to the strike of both the Government and the bulk of the population showed the need in emergencies for a civilian organisation with a general staff to ensure the continuance of everyday life. The use of special constables, motor transport, wireless and the telephone system had enabled this to be achieved—points all noted by the Committee.

By the early 1930s the international situation appeared less settled. Several nations, including France and Germany, produced documents on air raid precautions, and in Britain the potential threat of the bomber was recognised not only by the services but also by politicians. Baldwin's reflection in 1932 was no isolated voice. Therefore, in April 1933, Major-General H. L. Pritchard was appointed Air Raids Commandant, while seven months later the British Government abandoned the 'Ten Year Rule', which had restricted the development of the armed services. Steps were taken towards rearmament.

Pritchard produced a memorandum on the defence of London which laid down an important principle: 'In organising the whole civilian population to defend themselves,' he wrote, 'they must be organised on a civilian basis in their civilian organisation.' The population, he went on, 'must not lean upon some other Service'.[53] After that, although Air Raid Precautions developed into a well-arranged service, with necessarily strict procedures and discipline, its nature as a civilian force was never in doubt. This, however, marked the development of a battle which stretched through the following dozen years, over who was to provide funding for the new service: was it to be central government, or the local authorities?

By 1934, with the Nazis in power, Germany was recognised by the Committee for Imperial Defence as the possible enemy in a future war. The Committee estimated the aerial threat to Britain to be at least equal to the U-boat menace of the First World War. Extra defence therefore should be provided for London and more instructions given to the public. Speaking in a debate on 30 July 1934, one month after 'The Night of the Long Knives' had shown Hitler's ruthlessness in dealing with supporters, let alone enemies, Baldwin asserted that 'since the day of the air [sic] the old frontiers are gone. When you think of the defence of England, you no longer think of the chalk cliffs of Dover; you think of the Rhine. That is where our frontier lies.'[54]

The Government came to acknowledge its responsibility for civil defence and early in 1935 allocated £100,000 for the task. The decision was taken to develop ARP services to match developments in anti-aircraft defence. There was much discussion on whether, in the event of war, the seat of government should remain in or be removed from London, or be dispersed across the capital.

From 1935 the pace of rearmament quickened. A White Paper on defence issued in March admitted that the international situation had deteriorated. Britain's 'desire to lead the world towards disarmament by our example of unilateral disarmament,' it claimed, 'has not succeeded'. At the same time Germany both admitted that the *Luftwaffe* had been re-established and introduced conscription. Against this background the British Government was compelled to respond.[55] Thus on 9 July 1935 the 'First Circular' on air raid precautions was issued, being sent to all local authorities and being available to the public at 2d per copy. By that time Anthony Eden, Minister without Portfolio, had been told by Hitler that Germany had air parity with the RAF, and the Circular admitted that 'it would be impossible to guarantee immunity from attack' by enemy aircraft and that poison gas might be used. Local authorities were asked to prepare emergency services and were given the responsibility of reporting bombs, gas and damage in their areas.[56]

By early 1936 the Government was taking a serious view of the importance of Home Defence, differing from those, like Trenchard, who wished to achieve safety primarily by hitting back at the enemy. In March Sir Thomas Inskip, the Attorney-General, became Minister for the Coordination of Defence, and he favoured the development of defensive systems for the services, for example fighters rather than bombers to protect the home base.

An Air Raid Precautions Department, set up in April, began to examine the practical issues which would follow widespread aerial strikes against Britain. As the majority of British people, after the traumas of 1914–18 and the more recent derelictions of the Great Slump, would not readily accept the idea of an

43

imminent war, the ARP Department was regarded generally with little enthusiasm: 'They were a small, and in some respects amateur, crew making for deep waters in a ship of light tonnage.'[57] Yet they were forced to explore the presumed results of aerial attack on Britain. What shelters were required? How could evacuation from London be effected? Should there be mass burials of the dead? Were water supplies sufficient to combat large fires?

Although some British citizens were strongly opposed to rearmament and others still fostered a hope of 'collective security', by the end of 1936 the prospects of peace appeared less bright. The Italian invasion of Abyssinia, the German reoccupation of the Rhineland and the opening of the Spanish Civil War concentrated minds on Britain's possible involvement in international troubles. A small yet telling example occurred when the Italians employed mustard gas in Abyssinia: 'feeling in England could hardly contain itself'.[58] Civilian indignation at the same time was aware that similar weapons could be employed against cities in the United Kingdom. However, the British people, with a customary reticence and reserve, were still slow to respond to the needs of defence, which Baldwin explained by commenting that 'a democracy is always two years behind the dictator.[59]

Nonetheless, the distant rumbles of thunder during 1936 and 1937 caused the Government to take practical measures for protecting civilians. Gas was considered to be a particular danger, so the production of gas masks was ordered. By the end of 1937 it was hoped that forty million masks, in three sizes, would be available. The facepiece 'included vulcanised sheet rubber, cellulose acetate eyepieces, cotton webbing, slides, buckles, safety pins and other materials'. The complete container, in whose contents civilians were to place their faith, included 'canister bodies and ends, wire diaphragms, cotton pads, muslin diaphragms, filter pads, sprigs and activated charcoal'. However, at that time no suitable masks existed for babies or very small children, a problem not remedied finally until 1938.[60]

Early in 1937 an important development in civil defence came with the establishment of a voluntary Air Raid Wardens' Service. This was open to women as well as men, a total exceeding a quarter of a million people being required for a system based at least partly on the German scheme of *Luftschutze Hauswarte* set up under the Nazis. The qualities required of British wardens, who were later treated with a mixture of admiration, humour, respect and dislike, were laid down. 'The general idea of an air raid warden is that he should be a responsible member of the public,' stated a memorandum, 'chosen to be a leader and adviser of his neighbours in a small area, a street or a small group of streets,' adding, significantly, 'in which he is known and respected.'[61]

The question of air raid warnings exercised the minds of the authorities. It was intended that notice of the approach of enemy aircraft should be given from seven to ten minutes before their arrival to ARP headquarters, fire brigades and the police. There was a fear that general warnings might alarm the public, but by the end of 1937 the necessity of warning all people of impending danger was recognised and siren systems were planned.

Similar questions of public reaction were raised over lighting restrictions, because a total black-out could be counter-productive. In general, RAF commanders wanted very low lighting, while ARP services suggested 'aids to movement', for example, white paint and guide lights. However, the threat of night bombing led, by November 1937, to planning for a strict black-out.

In the spring of 1937 a committee under the chairmanship of Sir Warren Fisher was set up to investigate air raid precautions; it reported to the Cabinet at the end of June. First, the committee suggested that the prime aim of ARP should be to sustain public morale, ensuring that the everyday life of the nation continued and reducing the effects of air raids on people and property as far as possible. Its members examined the figures of likely casualties and showed how, through modern bombs, these had risen alarmingly. The estimate was that an attacker dropping 600 tons of bombs each day could cause 200,000 casualties a week, of which 66,000 would be killed. One of the most important results of the investigation came from examining the relative responsibilities of central and local government for ARP services. Automatically this led to further debate over the proportion of costs to be borne by each side.[62]

During the first half of 1937 tinges of apathy appeared in Britain over civilian defence, compared with what was happening in Germany, the potential adversary. There, a British Chargé d'Affaires referred to the German scheme as 'the third line of air defence', while a later historian of events in Kent noted that 'it was difficult to interest the public and that efforts in that direction were generally criticised as "war-mongering"'.[63] Penrose refers to 'national inertia' and claims that 'the masses remained unmoved by threats of enemy bombs and clouds of poison gas', even into 1938. One reason for the indifference was that 'these were prosperous times'.[64]

At the end of the year the Government introduced an ARP Bill, which came into effect on 1 January 1938. Local authorities were compelled to introduce measures for civilian defence into their areas. War appeared to be closer. In the words of the Act, local authorities should work towards 'the protection of persons and property from injury or damage in the event of hostile attack from the air'.[65] Seventeen duties were laid upon them, varying from the provision of shelters to gas detection and from instructing the public to providing casualty services. Such responsibilities incurred considerable outlay which some local authorities were unable, or unwilling, to meet. Deep discussion followed among the Treasury, the ARP Department and the Local Authorities Association to decide who should pay; generally, that meant who else should pay.

Through the early months of 1938 the Government's stress on bolstering home defence, rather than launching counter-attack, continued. The fear of early massive bombing was shown in Sir Thomas Inskip's Report, which referred to air strikes 'designed to inflict a knock-out blow at the initial stage of the war'. The task of the authorities, he suggested, 'must be to provide adequate defence against this threat'.[66]

The *Anschluss* of March 1938 worried the Government. Toynbee referred to Hitler's 'uncanny manipulation of the Austrian body politic from his wizard's cave at Berchtesgaden',[67] and although a German reply to the British protest suggested that the question was not Britain's business, there was unease. In Churchill's opinion, Europe was faced with 'a programme of aggression, nicely calculated and timed, unfolding stage by stage'.[68] By May, German intentions towards Czechoslovakia caused further apprehension, while the Committee for Imperial Defence learned that air raid precautions were more advanced in France and Germany than in Britain. They were also recommended to appoint a Minister of Home Security in time of war, because of the danger from air raids. There existed 'a real danger, especially at the outset of war,' they were told, 'that the national will to resist might be broken, if the situation in the devastated areas could not be got under control at once'.[69]

On 14 March, in a broadcast, the Home Secretary asked for one million active workers, women as well as men, for ARP services and, at the same time, a pamphlet, 'What You Can Do', was issued to encourage recruitment. Reports were being received of the effects of bombing in the Spanish Civil War and, as the Sudetenland crisis occupied headlines in May, many volunteers came forward; by that time some 400,000 had enrolled. A series of pamphlets and handbooks kept the question of civilian defence in the public gaze. By the end of March 700,000 copies of 'The Protection of Your Home Against Air Raids' had been issued and others, such as 'The Duties of Air Raid Wardens' and 'First Aid and Nursing of Gas Cases' were readily available.[70]

The British propensity for voluntary work emerged in May and June, during the Sudetenland crisis. Under the leadership of the Dowager Lady Reading, the Women's Voluntary Services for Air Raid Precautions was formed. Among the original aims was 'to help bring home to every household in the country what air attack may mean', while another was 'to make known to every household what it can do to protect itself and help the community'.[71] The organisation enabled thousands of women to contribute to civil defence by fostering the spirit of service, which was shown regularly during the Night Blitz two years later.

Decisions over air raid warnings and the black-out were taken in 1938. Over one hundred warning districts were listed, and the responsibility for issuing the necessary signals was vested in Sir Hugh Dowding, Commander-in-Chief Fighter Command, who would have received RDF signals directly from CH stations round the coast. Four grades of message were planned, to be issued by telephone to local civilian headquarters:

1. The Preliminary Caution, Air Raid Message, 'Yellow';
2. The Action Warning, Air Raid Warning, 'Red';
3. Raiders Passed, Air Raid Message, 'Green'; and
4. Cancel Caution, Air Raid Message, 'White'.

For the 'Warning', 'a code of blasts' would be employed as 'a signal of 2 minutes' duration consisting of either a fluctuating or warbling signal of varying pitch, or a succession of intermittent blasts'. For the 'Raiders Passed', there would be 'a continuous signal of 2 minutes' duration at a steady pitch'. The 'Air Raid Warning' and the 'All Clear' were to be heard daily by millions of people, especially during the twelve months from May 1940 to May 1941— and never forgotten by those who heard them.[72] The black-out 'spared no citizen or section of the nation'. By law, the occupant of premises 'would be required to make all lights in his building invisible to an outside observer for the duration of a war'. There was to be neither street lighting nor illuminated signs, and motor vehicles were to be fitted with masked headlamps.[73]

As the Air Staff had raised its figures of the possible scale of attack, estimates were made of the bombing pattern. The Germans, they suggested, could drop either 600 tons of bombs each day for several weeks or, in an attempted knock-out blow, 3,500 tons during the first twenty-four hours. These would comprise 50 per cent high explosives, 25 per cent incendiaries and the remaining 25 per cent gas, which could be replaced by high explosive. The spectre of fire was thereby raised, because the Fire Brigade estimated that a single bomber, carrying a thousand small incendiaries, could cause 150 fires in a built-up area. To prevent widespread conflagration civilians themselves would have to tackle fires: the Incendiary Bomb Committee recommended the use of a pump developed from those employed for spraying foliage or washing cars. Fitted with a foot support, it would be known as a 'stirrup pump' and cost 12s 6d. During the Night Blitz of 1940–41 this small item, seemingly so innocuous in war, was to save hundreds of lives and countless buildings from destruction.[74]

In July 1938 a step was taken which had important consequences later. A Committee suggested that in war Regional Commissioners should be appointed to implement the Government's measures for defending the population in different regions of Britain. Their work would be required particularly if, under the stress of attack, central Government broke down. The Commissioners would be 'figures of wide local, rather than national, eminence', and one described his duties as those of 'the head of a breakdown gang'.[75] Among their tasks were the oversight of evacuation, requisitioning buildings, dealing with casualties and public morale. At first there was slight opposition to their powers, which some criticised as dictatorial and not in the British tradition, but twelve Commissioners were appointed.

The turning point of 1938 for the armed aervices and the nation generally was the Munich Crisis. The unwelcome reality of war was brought home to all citizens, removing doubts over the need for air raid precautions. After the crisis eased, most people realised that war was inevitable, its outbreak being only a matter of time and an appropriate cause. As concern built in September, local authorities were asked on Saturday the 24th to issue gas masks from their storage centres, to have trenches dug and to prepare first aid posts. This work, carried out on the following day, reinforced the imminent threat.[76]

The BBC broadcast the 'wailing, despondent notes of the siren' on the day before Chamberlain flew to Berchtesgaden, and householders were exhorted to set aside a 'refuge room' in the house and dig a slit-trench in the garden. Then, in the evening of 27 September the Prime Minister spoke over the wireless to the nation. 'How horrible, fantastic, incredible it is that we should be digging trenches and trying on gas masks here,' he said, 'because of a quarrel in a faraway country between people of whom we know nothing!'[77]

On 29 September the Government published plans for the voluntary evacuation of two million people from the capital, half a million of them schoolchildren. Already people had left cities on their own initiative in droves reminiscent of Bank Holiday crowds. The relief when Chamberlain returned from his meetings with Hitler, carrying promises of peace, was unfettered and felt across the nation. Yet some recognised the uncomfortable truth of Churchill's comment that 'this is only the first sip, the first foretaste of a bitter cup which will be proffered to us year by year unless by a supreme recovery of moral health and martial vigour, we arise again and take our stand for freedom as in the olden time'.[78]

The Munich Crisis underlined not only the weaknesses of Britain's air defences but also the need for a speedy expansion of the civilian service. A spirit of urgency entered both the Government's and local authorities' planning. Extra duties were allocated to various existing ministries. The Food (Defence Plans) Department of the Board of Trade became responsible for the protection, supply and distribution of food stocks. The Ministry of Labour controlled National Service, while the Ministry of Transport took over air raid precautions on railways and other forms of transport. The Board of Education arranged air raid precautions in schools and the Ministry of Health planned evacuation, casualty services, burials and the provision of water services.

On 21 December Parliament heard that poorer people in vulnerable areas who had an income of less than £250 a year were to be issued with a domestic shelter, soon known as the 'Anderson'. Dr David Anderson, who played a considerable role in its design, had first thought of the shelter as an indoor protection. However, it was usually installed outdoors, after the suggestion that shelterers might be trapped by debris inside a house. The fourteen corrugated steel sheets weighed eight hundredweight and, with measurements of 6 feet by 4 feet 6 inches and with two exits, gave shelter to four people. The unit cost was £5.[79]

Between Munich and the outbreak of war many other shelters were introduced. In some areas caves and disused railway tunnels were adapted, while in Newcastle the Ouseburn Culvert and Victoria Tunnel were opened. Many public shelters were erected, or situated in converted and reinforced buildings. A number of buildings in Whitehall were strengthened, and the use of Underground stations was discussed, although the Government did not want to create a 'shelter mentality'.

The need for such measures increased during 1939. In April the Air Staff, oracles of doom, again raised estimates of the possible scale of attack. They believed that 700 tons of bombs could be dropped daily by 650 aircraft for the first two or three weeks of war. Carrying the warning further, they predicted that by April 1940 the figures would rise to 800 aircraft dropping 950 tons daily, or even 3,500 tons in the first twenty-four hours of conflict. Their reckoning was correct, they claimed, because in bombing attacks on Barcelona in March 1938 each ton of high explosive had caused fifty casualties.[80]

As air raid precautions expanded, in January 1939 every household received a copy of the 'National Service Guide', seeking volunteers for all aspects of work, from wardens to first aid parties and from demolition squads to ambulance drivers. Of the whole ARP force, one-third was to be women, underlining their importance to the nation's defence. They responded well, making up one-fifth of the total of wardens, two-thirds of Report Centre Staff, most members of First Aid Posts and all ambulance drivers. The Women's Voluntary Service (WVS) enrolled widely for nursing services, hospital supply depots and the planning of evacuation. The German occupation of the rest of Czechoslovakia in March 1939 led to more volunteers appearing, noted by *The Times* as 'a steady, and last week almost spectacular, increase in the numbers volunteering for ARP services'.[81]

In the remaining weeks before war began air raid precautions played a widening role in Britain's everyday life. Equipment was produced, gathered and stored by local authorities and training exercises involving black-out and sirens were held. Some took place during the RAF's Air Exercise in July and August, bringing a realistic touch. However, on 11 August in London an observer recalled that 'the darkness came gradually. Leicester Square and Shaftesbury Avenue were already doused and here and there a lamp went off in Piccadilly until only the big triple-headed lamps in the Circus itself remained alight'.[82] The watching crowds treated the event like an inverted firework display. Since the end of June the warning system had been complete, the country being divided into 111 districts. The decision was taken to issue the 'Yellow' Preliminary Warning when raiders were 22 minutes' flying time away, followed by the 'Red' Action signal at twelve minutes. Many kerbstones were painted white and thousands of reflectors were sold.

The ARP Department's work appeared endless, and by early 1939 it had distributed 50 million respirators to adults and older children. For younger children, 1,500,000 smaller masks, each costing 3s 6d and soon to be known as the 'Mickey Mouse', had been issued. For babies an anti-gas helmet had been devised, costing about £1; some 1.4 million were given out. This 'baby bag' was an item of formidable appearance which fitted over the baby's head and upper torso and had a face window, 'and the air was supplied by means of a bellows pump and respirator container'.[83]

Homes were adapted to meet the threat of gas. 'We placed blankets in readiness to be laid at the foot of the living-room door, in case of mustard gas attack,' recollected Peter Ustinov. 'A mustard gas victim, according to the handbook, was to be taken to a zone outside the contaminated area, wrapped in blankets, and administered hot, sweet tea—nice clear thinking to thwart the holocaust.'[84]

Apart from the fear of gas, the greatest threat facing civilians appeared to be incendiary bombs. As early as February 1937 the Government admitted that 'the fire risks from incendiary bombs dropped from aeroplanes present a problem which is beyond the capacity of normal peace-time organisations'.[85] The Germans had used small, 1kg magnesium bombs during the First World War and the fear grew that these would be dropped in thousands on built-up areas. Local authorities were therefore asked to raise and train an Auxiliary Fire Service, and by June 1939 120,000 men and 18,000 watch-room attendants had enrolled. Some districts prepared adequately and a survey in May 1938 showed that these included Birkenhead, Birmingham, Bristol, Cardiff, Newcastle, Portsmouth and Southampton. Among areas less well equipped were Glasgow, Hull, Plymouth, Sheffield and East and West Ham.

When a Fire Brigades Act was passed in July 1938 there were only 6,600 full-time and 13,800 part-time firemen. The need for an Auxiliary Fire Service was crucial, especially in built-up areas where, a report noted, one bomber over a 'fairly closely populated area' might cause 75 fires over three miles, a figure that could rise to 150 fires over 'a congested area'.[86] During the crises of 1938 recruitment for the AFS speeded up, probably because the activity of fighting fires was seen as a more active response in what were basically passive defences. Equipment arrived gradually and in greater supplies, with overalls, rubber boots and oilskin leggings among other items. Early in 1939 the Government announced that any of the AFS who took on full-time fire fighting would, in the event of war, be paid at the rate of £3 per week for men and £2 per week for women.[87]

The trailer pump, the basic equipment for AFS units, soon became a common sight in Britain, although even as late as Munich too few were available. Herbert Morrison, the Leader of the London County Council (LCC), was highly critical of the Government, claiming that whereas 3,000 emergency fire appliances were required in the capital, only 99 had been supplied. The London Fire Brigade, he stated, had 13,500 auxiliaries but only 145 auxiliary appliances.[88] Great acceleration followed, and the total of 2,000 emergency pumps available in September 1938 had risen to 14,000 by the outbreak of war. In addition, by September 1939, 75 fireboats were in operation, 36 of them on the Thames. Yet in some areas equipment was gathered slowly, with hydrants and hoses, water tanks and turntable ladders in short supply, some pieces having to be bought abroad.

The importance of an adequate water supply during air raids was to be driven home, sometimes at tragic cost, in the Night Blitz of 1940–41. The pre-war responsibility of augmenting water supplies was given to local authorities. Some reacted well, their task made easier if there were nearby rivers or lakes, but others were slow. One reason was the heavy costs involved, so in February 1939 the Government gave grants for water schemes to several cities which later were to suffer heavy assaults; these included London, Birmingham, Bristol, Coventry and Liverpool. And yet by September 1939 plans for water provision were insufficiently advanced and some cities suffered cruelly from fire during night raids. One, later hit severely by incendiary attacks, 'refused to install the 5,000 gallon steel tanks provided by the Home Office because the tanks "would disturb the amenities of the city"'. By the summer of 1941, thanks to the *Luftwaffe*, the amenities had vanished.[89]

The Civil Defence Act of 1939 accepted the recommendations of the Anderson Committee that evacuation should be voluntary, but that local authorities in reception areas should be compelled to accept evacuees. The vast scheme of moving thousands of women and children, mainly from the great cities, had been planned by the Ministry of Health and carefully organised, demanding a massive effort from the nation's transport system. 'The first main exodus took place on September 1–3, 1939,' reported a wartime London study, 'about the end of the normal elementary school holiday, when some of the children had been running wild for a month.' In that time 166,300 mothers with 260,300 small children left, together with 735,000 unaccompanied schoolchildren. With them also went 12,000 expectant mothers, together with 76,000 people of other categories, 'making a total of roughly 1¼ million as against some 3½ million considered eligible'. Many of those who left, or their parents, had heeded the dire warnings and came from 'the poorest and most congested areas near river and dockside, railway yards and gasworks, where the threat of bombing was so obvious that their denizens fled, as it seemed, for dear life'.[90]

The greatest number of evacuees, naturally, came from London. 'On the 1st, 2nd and 3rd of September, in the famous three days of evacuation which so many people regretted,' reported an Official History, '607,000 people were got out of London on that planned migration by London Transport alone.' Railways carried even more in a well-scheduled operation. About 1.3 million evacuees were taken in 1,500 special trains, 'not one of them in our crowded Bradshaw, but all of them invented'.[91] Other built-up areas also dispatched those recognised, since the Report of the First ARP Committee in 1925, as 'les bouches inutiles'. They were sent from Manchester, Merseyside, Tyneside, Birmingham, industrial Yorkshire and the southern ports of Southampton and Portsmouth. The chief reception areas were, in descending order of numbers taken, Lancashire, Sussex, Yorkshire, Kent and Cheshire, together with Essex, Northamptonshire, Hertfordshire, Suffolk, Somerset and Surrey. For the children, evacuation brought mixed emotions. 'At last the train came and we all bundled in,' one girl wrote. 'Only the engine driver knew our destination. However, we kept our spirits up, for it was rather an adventure and we were all in it together.' The 'adventure' terminated at Luton.[92]

At the end of August 1939, as war approached with an inevitability which troubled millions of Europeans, the public mood in Britain was calm. The Polish Crisis was the last straw, and there would be no further appeasement. 'The British people, in fact, were fed up with a succession of crises,' wrote the historian of civil defence, 'and in a mood of "as it's got to come, let's get on with it!".'[93] The nation had not completed preparations, but many advances had been made since Munich. With hindsight, it is easy to criticise the weaknesses of a system which had been assembled rapidly to meet a threat of awful yet unknown proportions. However, there should be little surprise that difficulties of provision occurred in a peaceful democracy still emerging from deep economic troubles and which had been drawn inexorably into the vortex of an unsought and unwelcomed conflict. 'Everything I have worked for, everything I have believed in during my public life has crashed into ruins,' Chamberlain confessed in his broadcast to the nation on the bright morning of 3 September.[94] In minutes, the possible sacrifice demanded of ordinary citizens was suddenly brought home. 'He was dignified and moving, brief and sad,' recorded Sir Henry Channon. 'He had barely finished when the sirens sounded.'[95] For millions of people across Britain, that presaged Armageddon.

Would formations of bombers appear immediately, dropping poison gas, destroying buildings and starting uncontrollable fires? Did the siren herald the knockout blow? How would public morale, untested in war for twenty-one years, react to the attrition of the *Luftwaffe*? Across Britain the thousands of men and women in civilian defence services braced themselves for action. Air raid wardens and firemen, ambulance drivers and policemen, the WVS and hospital staff looked to the skies and awaited the ordeal. They were not to know that 'the intruder was only a friendly "civil" from France, flight plan unfiled, heading happily for the aerodrome at Croydon'.[96] Over the following eighteen months the air raid siren would sound, especially at night, with more devastating consequences.

NOTES

1. U. Bialer, *The Shadow of the Bomber* (1980), 2.
2. See G. Douhet, *Command of the Air* (1943).
3. See W. Mitchell, *Winged Warfare* (New York, 1930).
4. J. Fuller, *The Reform of War* (1923), 70. See also Bialer, 102.
5. *Ibid.*, 152–53.
6. R. Titmuss, *Problems of Social Policy* (HMSO, 1950), 4–5.
7. M. Smith, *British Air Strategy Between the Wars* (1984), 61.
8. *Ibid.*, 104. The US Strategic Bombing Survey, 1945, compared strategic and tactical bombing with a cow and a pail of milk. 'To deny immediate aid and comfort to the enemy', tactical attacks would upset the pail. 'To ensure eventual starvation, the strategic move is to kill the cow'.
9. A. Marwick, *Britain in a Century of Total War* (1970), 62.
10. 270 H. C. Deb, 5s, c. 632, 10 November 1932.
11. L. Charlton, *War From the Air* (1935), 147.
12. See W. Gunston, *Fighters*, 1914–1945 (1978), 52–5.
13. 295 H. C. Deb, 5s, c. 859, 28 November 1934.
14. A. Huxley, *Encyclopaedia of Pacifism*.
15. J. Haldane, *Air Raid Precautions* (1938), 7.
16. CAB 23/35, 42(38), 24 September 1938.
17. F. Sykes, *From Many Angles* (1942), 558.
18. Sir Charles Webster and N. Frankland, *The Strategic Air Offensive Against Germany, 1939–1945*, vol. i (1961) (*SOAG*), 31.
19. AIR 5/416, 'Position of the Relative Numbers of Fighters and Bombers Required for Home Defence', 29 June 1923, Enclosure 1A.
20. *Ibid.*, 25 July 1923, Encl. 17A.
21. *Ibid.*
22. *Ibid.*
23. *Ibid.*, 19 July 1923.
24. O'Brien, 19.

25. See Smith, Appendices, 328–5.

26. Cooper, 54.

27. H. Penrose, *British Aviation: Widening Horizons 1930–1934* (HMSO, 1979), 167–8.

28. Pile, 53–7.

29. Interview, Dr W. Penley, Swanage, 17 November 1994.

30. Dr R. Searth, 'The Sound Mirrors at Hythe', *Sanctuary* (MoD Conservation Magazine), No 23 (1994), 14–16.

31. H. Penrose, *British Aviation: Ominous Skies, 1935–1939* (HMSO, 1980), 15.

32. Wimperis to Dowding, 4 March 1935.

33. AIR 41/17, 17.

34. *Ibid.*, 19.

35. *Ominous Skies*, 289.

36. AIR 41/17, 17.

37. *Ominous Skies*, 289.

38. *Ibid.*, 69.

39. See AIR 19/524, 'Fighter Aircraft Deliveries in 1939'; see also AIR 8/218, 'Strength Returns, Metropolitan Force Squadrons, 1938'.

40. AIR 41/14, ADGB, i, Appendix 6, 26 October 1936 (COS 513 [J.P.]).

41. ACAS (114) 169, 27 July 1938.

42. AIR 41/17, 18.

43. CAB 16/134, ADR 145, July 1938.

44. P. Wykeham, *Fighter Command* (1960), 153.

45. R. Clark, *Tizard* (1965), 159–60.

46. AHB Monograph, *Signals* (3), vol. 5, 'Fighter Control and Interception', 14 July 1939, 113.

47. AIR 8/863, also published as a supplement to *The London Gazette*, 11 September 1946, 'Sir Hugh Dowding's Despatch, the Battle of Britain', 4543–71, para. 232.

48. AIR 16/255, AOC-in-C's recommendations for expansion to 50 fighter squadrons. Park to Stevenson, 24 November 1938.

49. AIR 41/17, 11-12. The squadrons were Nos 23, 25, 29, 219, 600 and 604.

50. Pile, 88.

51. BBC broadcast, Home Service, 12 August 1939.

52. O'Brien, 14–15.

53. *Ibid.*, 55.

54. 292 H. C. Deb, 5s, c. 2335–36, 30 July 1934.

55. Statements Relating to Defence, Cmd 4827, 1935.

56. 302 H. C. Deb, 5s, c. 367–68, 22 May 1935.

57. O'Brien, 64.

58. Annual Register, 1936, 27.

59. 317 H. C. Deb, 5s, c. 1144, 14 November 1936.

60. O'Brien, 78.

61. Home Office, *Air Raid Wardens*, Memorandum No 4, 4 March 1937.

62. O'Brien, 96.

63. Kent County Council, *Kent: the County Administration in War* (1946), 67.

64. *Ominous Skies,* 188–9.
65. O'Brien, 107, quoting 1 and 2 George VI, Ch. 6.
66. *Ibid.,* 114.
67. A. Toynbee, *Survey of International Affairs,* vol. i (1938), 194.
68. W. Churchill, *The Second World War. Vol. I: The Gathering Storm* (1948), 244–5.
69. O'Brien, 117.
70. See Home Office Circular, 25 February 1939; Handbook No 8; Handbook No 2.
71. Letter, Home Secretary to Dowager Lady Reading, 20 May 1938.
72. O'Brien, 136.
73. Home Office Circular, 14 February 1938.
74. O'Brien, 147.
75. *Ibid.,* 154, note 1.
76. Home Office Circular, 24 September 1938.
77. BBC broadcast, Home Service, 27 September 1938.
78. 339 H. C. Deb, 5s, c. 359–73, 29 September 1938.
79. 342 H. C. Deb, 5s, c. 2880–92, 21 December 1938.
80. For the effect of bombing on Air Ministry thinking, see Papers of Lord Douglas of Kirtleside, Imperial War Museum, London, Box 2, File 2, 13 June 1963.
81. *The Times,* 31 March 1939.
82. A. Glendenning, *Nineteenth Century Review,* 11 August 1939.
83. O'Brien, 232–3.
84. P. Ustinov, *Dear Me* (1977), 117.
85. Cmd 5374, February 1937.
86. O'Brien, 250.
87. 343 H. C. Deb, 5s, c.1923, 16 February 1939.
88. 340 H. C. Deb, 5s, c. 421–2, 3 November 1938.
89. O'Brien, 270.
90. Women's Group on Public Welfare, *Our Towns: A Close Up* (1943), 1.
91. Ministry of War Transport, *Transport Goes to War* (HMSO, 1943), 28–46.
92. J. Banus and H. Murray, in *North London Collegiate Magazine,* December 1939.
93. O'Brien, 296.
94. BBC broadcast, Home Service, 11 a.m., 3 September 1939.
95. R. R. James (ed.), *Chips: The Diaries of Sir Henry Channon* (1967).
96. R. Hough and D. Richards, *The Battle of Britain* (1989), 66.

CHAPTER THREE

BACKGROUND TO BOMBING

BOMBING RESTRICTIONS

For twenty years after the end of the First World War further widespread fear grew over the new weapon of air power. If it were to be combined with the employment of poison gases, which had killed or maimed thousands of soldiers by 1918, could the aerial threat become as unmanageable as the broom in the hand of the Sorcerer's Apprentice? The equation of war had been revised. No longer was it limited to a contest between groups of fighting men killing or being killed, hundreds of miles from their homes: now their wives and children, together with the elderly, were included as legitimate targets. Governments were compelled to take steps protecting those threatened by bombing, and in this were faced with a dilemma. Should they themselves use aircraft, one of the most powerful weapons in their armoury, to destroy an enemy's industrial resources and to break civilian morale? Or should they persuade other groups to impose a mutual ban on the bombing of civilians near targets far from the battlefield, securing the safety of their own people at the cost of renouncing a potent weapon?

As Bialer shows, during the inter-war period three main sets of proposals were advanced. First, an effort was made to define 'legitimate objectives' of air attack; secondly, plans were suggested to limit bombing to the battle zone; and thirdly, demilitarised areas were named, and these were to be immune from air strikes.[1]

A conference was held at The Hague in 1923. Present were lawyers from Japan, Italy, France, Holland, the United States and Great Britain, their purpose to agree on a code of conduct for aerial warfare that all would follow. Lawyers, however, can dwell in a *de jure* land unrelated to *de facto* actions. For example, in attempting to formulate a code of conduct, difficulty arose over Article 24, which stated that 'aerial bombardment is legitimate only when directed at a military objective.' What constituted a 'military objective'? Obviously, enemy troops, warships or aircraft were military objectives, but what of factories, railway junctions in urban areas or merchant ships carrying supplies? Different nations at varying stages of a war would be likely to amend definitions to suit their own circumstances. 'The heart and the conscience of the combatant', wrote Professor Spaight, the British member of the Commission, 'are the guarantee for fair fighting, not any rule formulated in a treaty or in a manual.' Nations, therefore, would interpret wordings, definitions and consequent actions in the light of their own needs. Bialer comments that, in the long run, 'the juridical, political and essentially logical obstacles to an air convention proved to be insuperable'.[2]

Yet statesmen could foresee dangers building from a lack of discussion. Until the outbreak of the Second World War the British Government therefore attempted—obviously not entirely with altruistic feelings—to reach some international agreement with 'sincerity and consistency'. Politicians in Britain feared that their nation had more than most to lose from extensive air warfare. Subsequently, the disappointments that followed the breakdown of an International Disarmament Conference at Geneva, which opened in 1932 and closed two years later, were particularly marked in Britain. In essence the Conference was bedevilled by the Franco-German rivalry that had been a strong undercurrent in European history over the previous sixty years. The Germans, smarting ever since Versailles under a real or imagined sense of grievance, wanted *Gleichberechtigung* (equality of rights); the French, ever mindful of previous German depredations, intended to keep gains made by that treaty. For the British, who were particularly vulnerable to assault from the skies, an agreement on air disarmament or bombing restrictions would have been beneficial. However, the omens for peace grew less promising when Germany finally left the Conference on 14 October 1933.

Despite this, the British Government sustained the hope that undertakings to restrict bombing would be given through international agreements. For them two alternatives existed: either they could declare unilaterally their acceptance of the rules laid down at The Hague, or they could attempt to convene a new conference of involved nations. Either choice had weaknesses, and, anyway, the Air Staff, which had pinned its faith in the power of the bomber, was opposed to such steps.

Germany, the potential enemy, grew in power under the Nazis. After her armed forces were extended, especially the *Luftwaffe* from 1935, discussions were held in the hope of reaching an understanding. When Lord Halifax met Hitler on 19 November 1937 he was informed that the Germans might re-start negotiations, yet by the following February the *Führer* dashed these hopes. Angry at the reaction of the British Press to the proposed *Anschluss* with Austria, he addressed the *Reichstag*: 'It would be a good thing to limit armaments or prohibit bombing,' he said, 'but it would be better to muzzle the Press'—a remark hardly likely to endear him to the British.[3]

The following month the Germans showed their scepticism of resolutions and conferences. 'Even if the Soviet Union declared itself ready to refrain from the use of bombs,' Ribbentrop told Sir Nevile Henderson, the British Ambassador to Berlin, on 3 March, 'it would be impossible to place any faith in such a declaration.' In commenting on these words, a Foreign Office official believed that the time had come to stop the pretence of there being any chance of agreement on prohibition.[4]

In Britain, the arguments continued over what constituted a legitimate target. For example, on the question of whether German factories should be bombed, the Air Staff approved wholeheartedly. They believed that the Nazi economy would be hit hardest in that way, and this became part of their Western Air Plans. However, some naval staff disagreed because, in the words of the First Sea Lord, 'once the right to bomb outside the fighting zone was allowed, the whole prospect of protecting the civilian would disappear'.[5] In addition, if the Germans were asked to renounce their right to bomb, they might in return demand that the Royal Navy lift a maritime blockade. That would be to Britain's disadvantage in war because the economic stranglehold had been such a potent, yet non-violent, weapon in 1914–18.

In the House of Commons in 1938 Prime Minister Chamberlain laid down principles to which he pledged Britain in an air war. Only military targets would be raided. 'It is against international law to bomb civilians as such and to make deliberate attacks upon the civilian population.' He also announced that legitimate targets 'must be capable of identification'. Care had to be taken in raiding military objectives, 'so that by carelessness a civilian population in the neighbourhood is not bombed'.[6]

A view widely held by airmen was that bombing of civilians would waste resources. 'We may be sure, however, that British bombers will not be used for attacks on civilians,' wrote one at the time of Munich. 'Even apart from humanitarian grounds, which always make a strong appeal to British people, we shall use our bombers to better effect by attacking military targets.' He then explained the possible long-term effects of bombing civilians: 'The wise commander aims always at winning the war, not at making himself spitefully unpleasant to the enemy people.'[7] By 1939, as both Britain and Germany pushed to build aircraft and train men, questions of the legitimacy of bombing remained unresolved, with no further conferences or mutually agreed rules. These would be decided pragmatically, according to the needs of the time, although both sides knew that wanton bombing of civilians could be counter-productive.

As the war opened, with the German invasion of Poland on 1 September 1939, President Roosevelt of the United States appealed to all combatants. He began with a reminder that in recent years thousands of civilian casualties had been caused by the raiding of 'unfortified centres of population'. A continuation of that form of 'inhuman barbarism', he believed, would lead to the slaughter of hundreds of thousands of other innocent human beings. 'I am therefore addressing this urgent appeal to every government which may be engaged in hostilities,' he went on, 'publicly to affirm its determination that its armed forces shall in no event and under no circumstances undertake bombardment from the air of civilian populations and unfortified cities.' He added the rider, ambiguous in its interpretation by the combatants, that 'the same rules of warfare will be scrupulously observed by all their opponents'.[8] The British Government's reply to this 'weighty and moving appeal' was made the same day. They would 'refrain from such action, and confine bombardment to strictly military objectives'. Then came the proviso, added as a form of escape clause, that their actions would be maintained provided that 'these same rules will be scrupulously observed by all their opponents'.[9]

On the other side, on 1 September Hitler told the *Reichstag*, 'I will not make war against women and children. I have ordered my Air Force to restrict itself to attacks on military objectives.' He repeated this intention in his response to Roosevelt on the following day. That was 'a precept of humanity' and 'has always been advocated by me', but again came the proviso that both sides would have to respect the decision. 'It is a natural condition for the maintenance of this command that the opposing air force should keep to the same rules.'[10]

A day later, as they entered the war, the British and French Governments published their own 'Declaration on the Conduct of Warfare'. They opened by reiterating their wish to spare civilians, and also 'monuments of human achievement which are treasured in all civilised countries'. Instructions had already been sent to their commanders, forbidding the bombardment of 'any except strictly military objectives in the narrowest sense of the word'.

Next they spoke separately of operations on land and sea and in the air. For the first, they had decided to exclude, in particular, artillery bombardments of 'large urban areas situated outside the battle zone'. Secondly, at sea, they would observe carefully the rules laid down regarding attacks made by submarines, and on merchant shipping. In connection with air warfare, they reaffirmed 'their intention' to abide by the terms of the Geneva Protocol of 1925, which forbade the use of gases or 'bacteriological methods of war'. They would ask the German Government for a similar undertaking. It is noticeable that their pledge avoided mentioning aerial strikes against civilians, or on targets situated near residential areas. Finally came the safety valve that these statements presumed reciprocation from the enemy, failing which both governments reserved 'the right to take all such action as they may consider appropriate'.[11]

A German note to Roosevelt was transmitted through the Swedish Minister on 16 September. The document emphasised that, ever since the start 'of the action against Poland which Germany has been forced to take', their forces had been instructed not to attack women and children. War would be confined to military objectives, and they claimed already to have observed all of these declarations 'in the strictest manner possible'. This conveniently bypassed two facts related to the invasion. One was Germany's secret agreement with the Soviet Union to dismember Poland after the carefully timed onslaught on that independent state. The second was the deceit used in the Gleiwitz incident as an example of a Polish frontier 'attack' to excuse the invasion.

However, they accused the British Government of breaking their assurances by instituting a naval blockade, which affected women and children. Here was a resurgence of the German fear from the First World War. They also blamed the Polish Government for turning open towns into 'focal points of their military operations' and for encouraging civilians to fight the German Army as *francs-tireurs*. Finally, they claimed that Polish troops had 'employed yellow cross gas', an accusation unproven either then or since.

Then, in the language of diplomacy often employed by combatants, the German Government asserted that their forces would 'wage warfare in a chivalrous and humane manner'. Nonetheless, they retained their right to reply to what was deemed 'any violation of the law'. Again they referred to the British blockade which had been so effective only twenty-one years earlier. Against that threat the Germans would use forces 'which they have at their disposal'; those, in the context of war with Britain, were the aircraft of the *Luftwaffe*, as well as U-boats. Hitler's words here were ill-chosen, bearing in mind that the steamship *Athenia* was sunk without warning by *U30* on the first afternoon of the war, with the loss of 112 passengers.[12]

Consequently, at the start of the war, the matter of which categories of target would be raided from the air was still shrouded in mists. The statements of all involved governments were hedged by qualification and it appeared that, at the smallest pretext, the old adage that all is fair in love and war would be used in the national interest. Of course, no government would declare openly an intention to bomb and terrorise civilians exclusively, with the aim of breaking their morale. All governments, however, appreciated that bombing could, even incidentally, have that effect—as demonstrated for the Germans in the Spanish Civil War and for the British through the policy of aerial policing of dissident tribesmen.

The reality, nevertheless, was that all governments, regardless of public statements issued over morality, barbarism, restraint and principles, were constrained by two technical factors. Firstly, no air force possessed at the time an infallible method of navigation guaranteed to place aircrews over a target which could be clearly seen and identified. Secondly, even if aircrews could recognise their aiming-point, they had no bomb sight capable of planting on the target every bomb dropped, nor could they promise that blast would be limited to that area.

BOMBER COMMAND OVER GERMANY

With the division of the Royal Air Force into separate commands in 1936 came an increasing realisation by service leaders and politicians of the need for defence of the home base. Consequently, over the following three years the importance of Fighter Command grew, with the advent of fast monoplane aircraft and of radio direction-finding. Yet the Trenchard 'Bomber Doctrine' continued to govern the planning and overall policy of the Air Staff, as it had from 1918. In their belief, the value of fighter defence was unknown, unproven and mainly a sop to civilians. Only bombers had the power to win wars.

They encouraged a scheme of retaliation, answering aggression with an equal threat, to deter an enemy. Retributive bombing would affect the morale of his civilians, cripple his economy and, by compelling him to employ resources in home defence, limit his opportunities for an offensive. Consequently, after 1936 they intended to expand Bomber Command into a force capable of engaging any adversary. It would act as a type of aerial heavy cavalry, divorced in method and environment from the attrition of land warfare. The Command would also go far in the role of defending the home base, once undertaken by the Royal Navy.

With Britain's traditional reluctance to become embroiled in European quarrels, bearing in mind especially the massive bloodletting of trench warfare, Bomber Command would enable the nation to sustain its independence. Britain's international aims would be supported. Lord Salisbury commented on these in the nineteenth century. 'British foreign policy is to drift easily downstream,' he asserted, 'occasionally putting out a boat-hook to avoid a collision.' Bomber Command was to be that boat-hook.

When Germany was recognised as the potential aggressor, in the words of the Official History, 'until 1938 the doctrine that a counter-offensive was the only reply to the German threat held the field'.[13] Therefore plans were laid by the Air Staff for a bombing campaign to be launched in the event of war. A list of targets was drawn up in the 'Western Air Plans' and by 1938 the three most promising had been identified. First, strikes could be made directly against the German Air Force, its bases and supporting factories. Secondly, the German Army's transport system of road, rail and waterway communications could be attacked. Thirdly, raids could be launched against Germany's war industry and oil supplies, especially in the Ruhr, Rhineland and Saar.[14]

Investigations, however, soon showed that only the last was a realistic aim for British bombers of the time. The Ruhr, with its large proportion of German industry, could be reached and was an attractive target. 'If an early attack were made, before the defences were fully efficient, a crippling blow might be struck at the outset.' A similar campaign against oil supplies 'would effect an equally immediate reduction in Germany's capacity to wage war'. Here was the feared knock-out blow in reverse. John Terraine notes the Air Staff's 1938 estimate that by striking at 26 coking plants and nineteen power stations, with 3,000 sorties in a fortnight, the German war-making capacity would be brought 'to a standstill'. That end could be achieved for the predicted loss of 176 aircraft.[15]

That the industrial might of Germany, a nation of 75 million inhabitants, could be overwhelmed by bombing and the issue of the war settled within two weeks was indeed a sanguine hope. This is appreciated by examining the strength of those RAF bombers able to reach the Ruhr. 'There were . . . in fact only 17 operational squadrons in Bomber Command which could contribute to the strategic air offensive.' The force comprised 77 Wellingtons, 61 Whitleys and 71 Hampdens. In real terms the Command was a Samson with ungrown locks. The new four-engine bombers, planned from 1937, would not reach operational use until 1941.[16] The weaknesses in his Command had been identified by the Commander-in-Chief, Air Chief Marshal Sir Edgar Ludlow-Hewitt, and he never failed to point these out forcefully to the Air Staff. They, however, with a belief in the power of the bomber, were often unprepared to accept them, which earned Ludlow-Hewitt a reputation almost equalling that of fellow C-in-C Dowding at Fighter Command. In Ludlow-Hewitt's view, his men lacked suitably equipped aircraft and training.

By September 1939 even the planners of the great bombing offensive recognised the drawbacks of their schemes. The force at their disposal, 'before the new heavies could get into bulk production', wrote Slessor, the Director of Plans, was inadequate 'whether in technical performance, hitting power, training or ability to sustain operations in the face of war wastage of aircraft and crews'.[17] In 1939 Bomber Command 'was not trained or equipped', noted the Official History, 'either to penetrate into enemy territory by day or to find its target areas, let alone its targets, by night'. At the start of the war the Command 'was above all an investment in the future' which had to be conserved, expanded and trained.[18]

Another worry emerged. If Britain opened a bombing offensive against Germany, the *Luftwaffe* might retaliate. A Joint Planning Committee report in October 1938 pointed out that if the RAF bombed factories producing military supplies, that might provide 'the right of an enemy to attack London, our supply system and seaborne trade'. Even worse was the French fear of retaliatory bombing which would result from RAF aircraft flying over enemy territory from bases in France: 'they dreaded the German reply'.[19] At the start of the war the Chiefs of Staff still did not want to upset the Germans. Such action, they believed, would be tantamount to stirring a hornets' nest. Noting that no knock-out blow had come from Germany, they commented that 'this state of affairs may last for some time if we ourselves do nothing to disturb it'. However, if the RAF were to assault the German homeland, 'it will come to an end and this country will be subjected to bombing attack'.[20]

Consequently, it is interesting to compare the high hopes once cherished of Bomber Command's impact with what happened between September 1939 and the opening of the German Night Blitz a year later. At first, two main targets were selected: units of the German Navy in the area of the North Sea; and German civilians, whose torment was to be showered not by bombs, but by propaganda leaflets in their millions. At the same time, the Command was being expanded, equipped, trained and tested for the later aerial onslaught against Germany which developed from 1942.[21]

Three main bomber types were employed for these incursions. The first was the Armstrong Whitworth Whitley Mk V, originally designed in 1932 as a troop-carrier, then transformed into a bomber two years later. With a wing-span of 84 feet, it had a range of 1,500 miles and a top speed of 230mph. The bomb load was up to 7,000 lb. 'The Whitley was a sturdy aeroplane with few vices, if any,' commented a former pilot. 'It could take a lot of punishment and was a pleasure to fly if a trifle on the slow side.' The crew of six had six .303in machine guns for defence.[22] Second was the Handley Page Hampden, some-times nicknamed 'The Flying Suitcase' because of its remarkable shape. The Mk I had a wing-span of 69 feet and a top speed of 265mph and carried a 4,000lb bomb load. The crew of four had four machine guns for defence, too weak an armament for early daylight raids. The last aeroplane was the Vickers-Armstrong Wellington Mk II, usually known as the 'Wimpey', with an 86-foot wing-span and unusual geodetic construction. The prototype flew on 1 June 1936 and soon it was adopted as a standard bomber, whose two Merlin engines gave a top speed of 270mph. This aircraft, with a crew of six, carried four machine guns and a bomb load of 4,500lb.

New bombs were used by the RAF from 1937. The high explosives had an open cylindrical drum surrounding the tail-fin and were of streamlined shape. Most were 250lb or 500lb general-purpose bombs, but incendiaries were also carried.[23] A major drawback in the early stages of the war was that, through a faulty mechanism, too many failed to detonate on impact. Bomb sights were generally updated versions of those of the First World War and usually called Course-Setting Bomb Sights (CSBS). Most adjustments were made by a bomb-aimer, but for success the aircraft had to maintain a straight and level course during the bombing run. Any small movement in the air would bring wide misses on the ground. In war conditions, with anti-aircraft fire, search-lights and fighters intruding, there was often great inaccuracy.

Neither new bombs nor aiming sights were of any use if aircraft could not locate their destination. Therein lay one of the Command's greatest weak-nesses, because at the outbreak of war navigation generally was so poor that bombers consistently failed to reach and recognise their targets—and difficul-ties suffered by day were greatly magnified at night. The skills needed by trained observers were not sufficiently recognised by the RAF until 1938, and training was often poor. A navigator had to know the wind speed 'and so to check his dead reckoning', noted the Official History. 'It was hoped that he could establish his position by observation of the stars at night, while by day or night he could be assisted by wireless fixes from ground stations.'[24] The difficulties experienced by a man hunched over a map table, with a small light, in an iced-up bomber under fire on a cloudy night were hardly allowed for.

Ludlow-Hewitt wrote to the Air Ministry at the end of 1937 suggesting that civil airlines had made great progress in providing navigational aids, homing devices and direction-finding equipment. These, however, were 'at present far from being available to Royal Air Force pilots'.[25] Therefore, even before the war, the Command had a high accident rate. At the start of hostilities 'it became quite obvious that not only the North Sea was taking its quota', wrote one pilot, 'but also the Irish Sea when aeroplanes overflew the country in bad weather'.[26] The phrase used by many airmen was that their navigators flew 'by guess and by God'.[27]

Nevertheless, in September 1939 Bomber Command entered the war with an unquenchable spirit, which was maintained for six years. At the start, like the *Luftwaffe*, they overestimated the power in battle of the unescorted bomber when tackled by the new generation of fighters. The theory that a bomber formation could use its concerted defensive firepower to restrain attacks from German fighters was soon shown to be sadly awry.

During the first three months, a series of daylight strikes was aimed at German naval units, but losses were heavy. The Germans had made progress with their own *Freya* radar and bombers could be detected at some distance. Wellingtons, Blenheims and Hampdens took part in these early raids but encountered difficulties over navigation and ineffective bombs.

The opening raid on Wilhelmshaven on 4 September 1939 cost seven of the 29 aircraft involved, while on the 29th five Hampdens were lost from the eleven which raided the Heligoland Bight. Apart from heavy, accurate AA fire, German interceptors were guided to the attackers and showed in combat the superiority of the fighter over the bomber. On 14 December half of the Wellingtons raiding the Schillig Roads were destroyed, but the final nail in the coffin of Bomber Command's daylight raids was hammered in four days later. In attacking Wilhelmshaven, twelve of the 24 Wellingtons were lost, while three others crash-landed on their return. A casualty rate of 62.5 per cent was too high to be sustained, so day operations were called off—a turning-point in the history of the Command, which then concentrated mainly on night operations for the remainder of the war. A German pilot's report stated that approaching Wellingtons from the frontal beam 'can be very effective if the enemy aircraft is allowed to fly into the cone of fire. The Wellington is very inflammable and burns readily'.[28]

Until the following spring, aerial activity over northern Europe was limited. Weeks of freezing temperatures brought ice and snow to provide the worst winter experienced since 1881. Bomber Command operations continued on a reduced scale, taking two main forms. One was 'Gardening', the laying of mines, mainly off the German coast. The other was 'Nickelling', the dropping of millions of leaflets across the German mainland. Both were night operations, when crews hoped for the safety of darkness in the fashion followed by the *Luftwaffe* over Britain a year later. At that time German night defences were not as efficient as they later became, first under General Kammhuber, then later during the great bomber offensive after 1942.

For a number of airmen the dropping of leaflets was a wasted effort. They argued that German people would be unimpressed; even if they were stirred, the Nazi dictatorship offered little opportunity for dissent. 'Since the outbreak of war,' wrote the British-born Christabel Bielenberg, 'listening to foreign broadcasts was punishable by a minimum of five years' imprisonment, and the maximum penalty was death.'[29] Such an environment allowed small scope for the success of a leaflet which 'measures $8^1/_2$ ins by $5^1/_2$ ins and is printed on poor quality paper'.[30] Nonetheless, some people hoped that propaganda would have an effect. 'The showers of leaflets on strongly defended German territory must have had a moral effect on the German people,' wrote one commentator. 'They will realize that the leaflets could have been replaced by bombs.'[31]

In Britain, several officers who had faith in Trenchard's Bomber Doctrine regretted the RAF's apparent lack of aggression. Sir John Salmond, a former CAS, wrote to Trenchard at the end of 1939. 'If this is the attitude of the Government, namely to wait continually on the enemy's initiative, we shall lose it.' At the top of the letter he pencilled, 'I was very anti-continued confetti-bombing.'[32]

Notwithstanding criticisms, leaflet raids gave bomber crews useful experience in navigating over enemy territory in darkness. Whitleys of No 4 Group flew widely, reaching even Vienna, Prague and Berlin. They suffered few losses. Many sorties were made between 10 November 1939 and 16 March 1940. A pilot said that they produced 'valuable and much-needed experience of long-distance night flying', which provided 'excellent training as flights of ten and twelve hours' duration'.[33] A particular drawback was the severe weather, with temperatures often −30°C at 15,000 feet. Navigation was mainly a matter of observation, and this was referred to by a Group Commander as 'a never-ending struggle to circumvent the law that we cannot see in the dark'.[34]

'Nickelling' was abandoned on 6 April 1940, just three days after Ludlow-Hewitt was replaced as C-in-C Bomber Command by Air Marshal Portal, an airman more wedded to the Trenchard Doctrine. On the 9th, the 'Phoney War' ended abruptly. German forces, like a great Kraken, invaded Norway and occupied Denmark. Over the next five weeks British bombers appeared to be caught regularly on the back foot. Their interventions in the Norwegian Campaign were largely ineffective. When the Western offensive opened on 10 May, matters grew worse. The light bombers of the Advanced Auxiliary Air Force suffered tremendous losses during low-level daylight attacks on advancing German troops and their communications. By 12 May the AAAF had lost half of its bomber strength, while two days later at least a further 40 aircraft were destroyed. Once again, daylight bombing against powerful AA defences and fighters was shown to be suicidal.

Thus at the War Cabinet meeting in London on 15 May, Bomber Command was allowed, at long last, to start the bombing campaign envisaged from prewar days. Raids were to be made on the Ruhr and on oil targets in western Germany. These could well bring retaliatory attacks on Britain, but Dowding of Fighter Command was confident that his squadrons would contain them. British raids would be made at night, when losses would be comparatively small.

Koch suggests that Bomber Command on its own initiative may have started these raids earlier, on the night of 11/12 May.[35] This was true, but understandable in the circumstances, where operations against German targets had previously been agreed should that nation invade the Low Countries. In simple terms, Germany had launched unprovoked aggression and Bomber Command responded. The Germans, well experienced in propaganda, soon falsely accused British aircraft of attacking the city of Freiburg on 10 May, when in reality the bombs had been dropped by their own Heinkel 111s.

A night offensive over the *Reich* built up during the rest of the summer, and between 11 May and 24 September Bomber Command made raids on all 137 nights. At the time the Command was the only instrument of war capable of tackling immediately an aggressor of apparently unremitting power and unbroken success. As Churchill explained to Beaverbrook on 8 July, only one factor would defeat the enemy—'an absolutely devastating, exterminating attack by very heavy bombers from this country upon the Nazi homeland'.[36]

The RAF did not set out intentionally to bomb civilians. 'Moral effect, although an extremely important subsidiary result of air bombardment, cannot in itself be decisive,' stated an Air Staff note to Portal on 21 July. 'There must be material destruction as a primary object.'[37] The general policy was to assault centres of communication and supply, especially oil. Many of these were in built-up areas and, given the contemporary weaknesses in locating targets and aiming bombs, residential districts inevitably were hit.

This problem affected both air forces, and the Germans had a similar experience in their Western Campaign. In principle they struck at military targets, but, under the exigencies of war, areas containing civilians suffered. An example was Rotterdam on 14 May, where 800 were killed in what were intended to be raids on defences. Other cases occurred in France. A British officer noted in his diary on 10 May that there were 'some heavy civilian casualties down the road this morning by the railway at Tergnier. A sad affair. The target was legitimate enough for all that.'[38] In another case, Horne wrote that the *Luftwaffe* had no policy of strafing civilians on roads, yet, either from mistaken identity or from personal malevolence, incidents did occur. 'Many reliable witnesses testify to the fact that refugee columns *were* machine-gunned and bombed in open country.'[39]

From the end of June Bomber Command's efforts were spread over a far wider area than the *Luftwaffe*'s, at least partly losing the value of concentration of force. British aircraft had to participate in the efforts to defeat a proposed seaborne invasion, by bombing shipping in ports along the Channel coast. This aspect of Bomber Command's contribution is often overlooked in what is usually termed 'The Battle of Britain', where Fighter Command's sterling defence more readily caught the public eye and imagination.

The bombing offensive over Germany between May and September brought a strong reaction from the German population. In a year of victories it was difficult to accept that an enemy apparently on the verge of defeat could hit back. The inhabitants of inland towns and cities far from the battlefront suddenly found themselves in the firing line, much to their discomfort.

Koch wrote of their feelings. A report dated 20 June spoke of 'strong hatred of England', which called 'time and again for revenge'. The people of Danzig demanded 'the complete destruction of London' as a reprisal. On 4 July another report admitted that 'all areas concerned report an increased nervousness, particularly disquiet and depression among women and children, a general drop in morale at the workplace as a result of over-tiredness'.[40] There were casualties among civilians and some damage, although on nothing like the scale suffered, and to be suffered, in Britain. As Irving shows, in a six-month period from May to November, 975 German civilians were killed, only half the number of those who died in road accidents—a fact which gave satisfaction to Milch, the Inspector of the *Luftwaffe*.[41] In the same period the *Luftwaffe* killed 15,000 British civilians.

Bomber Command's effort from June to September was a reminder to the German people that the fight was unfinished. 'At present, the warnings are causing a loss of output whose consequences are far graver than those caused by the actual bomb damage,' stated a Goering Order on 15 August. 'In addition, the frequent air raid warnings are leading to nervousness and strain among the population of Western Germany.' By invading neighbouring, smaller, neutral nations, Germany had seized broad swathes of Europe. Her victories, widely acclaimed by her own citizens, brought suffering and hardship to millions in the occupied lands. Those people had little sympathy for the Germans when Bomber Command began to exact retribution from a nation which had spread so much misery among others.

NOTES

1. Bialer, 109–10.
2. *Ibid.,* 111.
3. *Ibid.,* 117.
4. FO 371/21656C, 1524/42/18.
5. CAB 55/13, Limitation of Armaments Sub-Committee, July 1938.
6. 337 H. C. Deb, 5s, c. 937–8, 26 June 1938.
7. Major F. Robertson, 'What of the Air Menace?', *Flight,* 22 September 1938.
8. AIR 41/40, Appendix A1.
9. *Ibid.,* Appendix A4.
10. See F. W. Koch, 'The Strategic Air Offensive Against Germany: The Early Phase, May–September 1940', *Historical Journal (HJ)* 34, 1 (1991), 122.
11. AIR 41/40, Appendix 3.
12. *Ibid.,* Appendix A4.
13. *SOAG,* i, 87.
14. *Ibid.,* 94.
15. J. Terraine, *Right of the Line* (1988), 81.
16. See *SOAG,* iv, Appendices 38 and 39.

17. J. Slessor, *The Central Blue* (1956), 205–6.

18. *SOAG*, i, 118 and 134.

19. *Ibid.*, 99.

20. CAB 66/1, W,P, (39), 19, Air Policy Report by COS Committee, 11 September 1939.

21. COS Memo, 31 August 1939.

22. T. Sawyer, *Only Owls and Bloody Fools* (1982), 60.

23. For details of bombs, see Cooper, 108–14.

24. *SOAG*, i, 112.

25. Terraine, 83.

26. Sawyer, 26.

27. *SOAG*, i, 112.

28. C. Bekker, *The Luftwaffe War Diaries* (1969), 101.

29. C. Bielenberg, *The Past is Myself* (1968), 60.

30. 'Leaflets Over Germany', in *The Aeroplane*, 5 April 1940.

31. *The Aeroplane*, 14 September 1939.

32. Papers of MRAF Sir John Salmond, RAF Museum, Hendon, B2638. Letter, Salmond to Trenchard, 30 November 1939.

33. Sawyer, 25.

34. *SOAG*, i, 206.

35. Koch, 127.

36. Beaverbrook Papers, Historical Collection 184, House of Lords Record Office (HLRO), BBK D/414, vol. i, 8 September 1940.

37. *SOAG*, i, 150–1.

38. Anon, *Diary of a Staff Officer* (1941), 4.

39. A. Horne, *To Lose a Battle* (1969), 398.

40. Koch, 133.

41. D. Irving, *The Rise and Fall of the Luftwaffe* (1973), 112.

CHAPTER FOUR

ON THE GERMAN SIDE

PRE-WAR

Although the main German Night Blitz opened in September 1940, the *Luftwaffe* had launched raids in darkness since the start of the war a year earlier. These assaults had been part of the German bombing plan since pre-war days. For many German leaders there were two crucial factors to be borne in mind from the First World War. The first was the wide success of the U-boat campaign in exerting a stranglehold on Britain's seaborne supplies, a campaign that had not been easily broken. The second was the Allied blockade that had played a vital part in Germany's defeat in 1918—and the determination that it should not happen again.

A study produced in 1944 by the German Air Historical Branch (8th *Abteilung*) commented that 'from the experiences of the 1914–18 war, it was to be expected that in any future war the final decision would no longer be fought out on the ground'. Instead, 'the enemy would try to break down the economic strength of the *Reich* and the morale of the people . . . the Allies succeeded in doing this in the First World War by an economic blockade'.[1] Those testing and unhappy days for Germany were remembered by Hitler, who, speaking of the forthcoming struggle with Russia, said, 'I need the Ukraine so that they cannot starve us out as they did in the last war.'[2] At the level of ordinary civilians, one woman recollected the effects of the blockade in Berlin in 1918: 'Now one sees faces like masks, blue with cold and drawn with hunger,' she wrote, 'with the harassed expression common to all those who are continually speculating as to the possibility of another meal.'[3] The Germans had a vivid appreciation of the power of economic warfare.

Planning for this form of struggle was prompted by the two European crises of 1938, in February over Austria and in August over Czechoslovakia. On each occasion General Felmy, commander of *Luftflotte II*, was ordered to examine possible British targets. Suggested points included ports in southern England, factories in or near London and airfields in East Anglia. However, in September Felmy published a memo which was forthright but whose pessimism angered Goering. 'With the means available,' Felmy believed, 'we cannot expect to achieve anything more than a disruptive effect . . . Whether this will lead to an erosion of the British will to fight is something that depends upon imponderable and certainly unpredictable factors.' Here was an honest man giving a considered, if unwelcome, opinion: 'a war against England with the means at present available appears fruitless'. Felmy explained that, for raids to be successful, bases would be required in the Low Countries, because bombers would otherwise have to fly from Germany with a bomb load of only 1,200lb and their range would not exceed 425 miles.[4]

In mid-October 1938 Hitler instructed Goering to inaugurate a large construction programme with a 500 per cent expansion of the *Luftwaffe* over the following four years. Goering met Milch to discuss the possibility of an air war with Britain, while on 26 October a full conference was held at Karinhall to lay plans. Two main economic targets were listed. The first was shipping, naval and merchant, which was to be engaged with mines, torpedoes and bombs. The second was a series of mainland targets, to which 30 *Geschwader* were allocated. Jeschonnek, the Chief of Staff, wanted Heinkel 177s for the task, but work on this heavy bomber, essential for the prosecution of attacks on economic targets, was severely curtailed at that stage. The subsequent German assault on Britain, by both night and day, suffered accordingly.

By 1939, as war drew closer, the Germans laid more definite plans for an aerial conflict with Britain. In conversation with Mussolini on 15 April, Goering showed his great faith in the potential of the Junkers 88 as a weapon of economic warfare: 'This bomber has such a long range that it could be used to attack not only England herself, but also . . . towards the West, to bombard the ships approaching England from the Atlantic.'[5] However, the *Luftwaffe* was still experiencing difficulties in production and technical development: as late as August a report on supplies showed that there was aviation fuel available for less than four months of war.

AT WAR

From the first day of the war one British fear was shown to be unfounded. This was that hostilities would open with a knock-out blow against London and other cities. Pre-war predictions of raids made by hundreds of bombers dropping thousands of bombs to cause massive casualties and break public morale were greatly exaggerated.

There were two main reasons why the knock-out blow was never attempted. First, the Germans had not intended to launch it and certainly lacked the bombing strength necessary. Secondly, from the start of hostilities the *Luftwaffe* was busily occupied in Poland, where *Luftflotten I* and *IV* played a prominent part. Their main task, as a tactical air force, was 'the elimination, stage by stage, of each and every obstacle which might frustrate the freedom of movement of the ground forces'. As far as Britain was concerned, Hitler's Directive No 1, issued on 31 August 1939, set out the role of the *Luftwaffe*. It was to defend German territory. Then it was to 'dislocate English imports, the armament industry, and the transport of troops to France'. Another task was to attack warships, 'particularly battleships or aircraft carriers', but raids on the British mainland were 'to be avoided in all circumstances'. Any decisions on attacking London, he stated, were 'reserved to me'.[6]

Soon after the outbreak of war, *Luftwaffe* Intelligence staff presented recommendations for attacks on Britain's economy 'due to the temporary postponement of the offensive in the West'. German war aims, they suggested, must be 'to strike at Britain with all available weapons, particularly those of the Navy and the Air Force'. Britain's overseas trade should be hit, both through shipping and by attacks on ports. 'Our aim must be to reduce imports to a level below the rate of consumption, so that reserves will eventually be exhausted', and that was permissible from political and moral standpoints because 'Britain's immediate war aim is the encirclement, and hence the starvation, of Germany'.[7]

Another Intelligence document spoke of hindering 'the flow of imports, and thus to dislocate the whole enemy supply system'. There were to be attacks on naval vessels and dockyards, on fuel installations and on food supplies. At this stage of the war, the Germans believed strongly in the effectiveness of assaulting Britain's economy. 'Raids must be constantly repeated—by day and by night.'[8]

In reality, a long period of general inactivity followed; this period is popularly known as the 'Phoney War' or, in German terms, the *'Sitzkrieg'*. Little action was seen on land across the Franco-German frontier, or at sea, apart from the attrition brought about by U-boats or in isolated encounters such as the Battle of the River Plate. Most German air activity was concentrated over the North Sea, involving a few strikes against units of the British Fleet. These were permitted by Hitler's Directive No 4, which stipulated that the *Luftwaffe* might 'operate in the German Bight and in the Western declared mined areas and in direct support of naval operations against English and French ships'.[9]

This happened on 26 September. Two British battleships, together with two battlecruisers, the aircraft carrier *Ark Royal* and several other vessels, were sighted near the Great Fisher Bank and attacked by four Junkers 88 dive-bombers. Although the attacks sank no ships, the Admiralty was worried by the vulnerability of units off the East Coast. Concern deepened on 16 October when dive-bombers struck at warships in the Firth of Forth, hitting three vessels. During the following day, bombers raided Scapa Flow, discovering that Royal Navy units had already been moved to the Clyde, on the Scottish west coast. The strength of the German air arm had been proved. 'By two or three boldly executed strokes, and at a total cost of four aircraft,' commented one historian, 'the German Air Force and the U-boat service between them scored a resounding strategic success.'

Throughout the rest of the winter, the German campaign of mining off the East Coast interrupted shipping trade. A number of mines were laid by U-boats, but many were sown by aircraft. This was done at night by Heinkel 115 seaplanes, employed particularly when the deadly magnetic mine was intro-duced. Thousands of tons of shipping were sunk in estuaries from the Thames to the Humber and the problem was not solved until the advent of the 'de-gaussing' system. Overall, the end of 1939 and the dawn of the new year were marked by little enemy air activity: more explosions and fires in the United Kingdom had at the time resulted from a small IRA campaign.

A deciding factor in all forms of warfare during the winter of 1939–40 was the climate. Atrocious weather descended across Europe, with ice and snow, to produce the most testing conditions. On 20 January, parts of the River Thames froze and 20 degrees of frost were recorded in London. These conditions lasted throughout January and February and were followed by heavy flooding during the subsequent thaw. A girl in Kent noted in her diary that on 29 January her father took over twelve hours on a train journey home from Yorkshire. 'Conditions were terrible. Trains stopped. Deep snow everywhere. 3ft in Yorkshire—worst since 1814.'[10] Active warfare was brought largely to a halt.

At this point in February, No 60 Signals Group was formed in Fighter Command 'to take over the technical and administrative control of the radar chain'.[11] The Group did sterling work in the development of systems of Raid Intelligence and helped to hone the system which operated so well during daylight raids later in the year. There were, nevertheless, still great difficulties of detection in darkness.

The RAF's worries over night air defence were shown early in March 1940, as the weather improved. Air Vice-Marshal R. Peck, who had a special interest in the subject, wrote to the Chief of the Air Staff asking for a special committee to be formed. There was need, he said, because of 'the magnitude and urgency of the position of night interception'.[12] Newall agreed and a letter, sent to Dowding on 10 March, suggested that the problem 'should be urgently examined by a committee on a higher plane than formerly'. Consequently, the first meeting of the Night Interception Committee was held four days later and its stated purpose was 'to explore every practical avenue in order to discover a solution of the night fighter interception problem and to institute action to this end'. The agenda for the meeting was accompanied by an appendix entitled 'Present Position and Suggested Methods of Interception', on which Dowding pencilled many comments. On the day before the conference, the Air Ministry sent him extra notes concerning systems of Airborne Interception, but the C-in-C gave them a frosty reception. Prickly additions like 'Not understood' were marked in red crayon beside several items.[13]

In the chair at the first meeting was Air Marshal Peirse, the Deputy Chief of the Air Staff. Among others present were Joubert, Tizard and Watson-Watt, in addition to Douglas, Assistant Chief of the Air Staff, Dowding, and Quintin Brand, who was to lead No 10 Group in the daylight Battle of Britain and had wide experience of night flying during the First World War. The presence of these men showed the importance of the problem for the RAF. Peirse predicted with accuracy that at some stage 'our good defences would force [the enemy] to adopt night bombing'.[14]

A second meeting followed a fortnight later and three others were held before the opening of the German offensive in the West and the Dunkirk Evacuation took precedence over other matters. In May the Chiefs of Staff learned that 'our defence against night attack is still far from effective'. In spite of wide discussion there appeared to be little progress towards holding off the bomber under cover of darkness.[15]

The German invasion of Denmark and Norway led to no sudden increase in air activity over Britain, although the *Luftwaffe* flew some sorties by day and night. In one of these, on 30 April, a minelaying He 111 crashed at Clacton-on-Sea, killing two civilians and injuring 150. These were the first civilian casualties to be suffered on the British mainland since the start of the war.

While the Allies were experiencing reverses in the Norwegian Campaign, the German *Blitzkrieg* opened in the West on 10 May. Holland, Belgium and Luxembourg were invaded and soon *Panzer* divisions moved through the Ardennes to attack the French and British armies. Dissatisfaction with Chamberlain's leadership led to his replacement by Winston Churchill on 10 May. From that day the aerial threat to Britain, both in daylight and at night, grew closer and more intense.

Although the strongest *Luftwaffe* effort was experienced over the Low Countries and France in daylight, some bombers visited Britain by night. 'Apart from operations in France,' Hitler wrote on 24 May, 'the *Luftwaffe* is authorised to attack the English homeland in the fullest manner, as soon as sufficient forces are available.' The attack, he ordered, would open with 'an annihilating reprisal for English attacks on the Ruhr'.[16] The first bombs to fall on England since the First World War were dropped over Kent on 10 May, while on the 25th bombs landed at Middlesbrough. From 6 June several raiders made incursions by night, while others continued to lay mines round the coast. 'Single bombers appeared simultaneously at many points along the coast,' commented a writer, referring to the opening attack. 'Some penetrated well inland. Raid warnings were sounded, anti-aircraft guns and searchlights went into action, and fighters were heard in most instances.'[17]

The first major raid by German aircraft as part of the *Luftschlacht um England* arrived during the night of 18/19 June. He 111s of *KG 4* flew from a French airfield to attack various parts of the country. Bombs fell in East Anglia, the North and the South-East. In addition, 'the first bombs on the London area hit plough-land at Addington in Surrey'.[18] In full moonlight, five bombers were shot down by Spitfires and Blenheims, probably because they flew too low and were picked out by searchlights. Although what the Germans would have termed 'legitimate targets'—aerodromes and oil installations—were hit, so too were civil buildings. A church, houses and a school were struck, killing ten civilians and injuring 24 others; only one military casualty was reported.

During the period from 5 to 30 June, thirteen airfields, sixteen industrial plants and fourteen port areas were hit in night raids. Among these targets, the ICI works at Billingham was bombed, as were steelworks at Middlesbrough and Scunthorpe. By the end of the month the *Luftwaffe* had lost eleven bombers in these attacks, but RAF defences had also suffered: ten fighters, six of them Blenheims, had been brought down, with the loss of five pilots and five air gunners killed.[19]

German leaders then were optimistic that the British Government would sue for peace. From the end of the Dunkirk Evacuation, about 5 June, to the collapse and surrender of France on the 22nd, Hitler believed that Churchill would seek terms. After the signing of the armistice at Compiègne, the German leader, still confident, continued to relax his efforts. Moreover *Luftwaffe* formations, whose commitment had contributed so much to the Western Campaign, had suffered losses and they required time to regroup and re-establish their strength, before starting the main onslaught against Britain. However, the rejection of Hitler's offer on 19 July was a great disappointment to the Germans, who were thereby confronted with two problems. First, they had missed the opportunity of attacking the British at their most vulnerable time, immediately after Dunkirk. Secondly, as the British would now be defeated only by invasion, or through the power of aerial bombardment, the burden of war fell on the *Luftwaffe*.

Therefore, from July, as the daylight Battle of Britain developed, the German night offensive grew. Bombers from *Luftflotte II*, under Kesselring, and *Luftflotte III*, under Sperrle, were stationed across the Low Countries and France, available for action. Goering had explained their tasks on 30 June: 'So long as the enemy air force remains in being,' stated his Directive, 'the supreme principle of air warfare must be to attack it at every possible opportunity by day and by night, in the air and on the ground.'[20]

The greatest efforts were made in daylight, yet night raids were extensive. The attacks provided aircrews with good flying and navigation practice by night, especially using radio aids. They also were guaranteed to cause trouble both for the British defences and for civilians, whose sleep was disturbed by sirens. The Germans referred to these raids as *Störangriff*—dislocation and nuisance raids. Several assaults in early July were aimed at railway targets, affecting civilians. In response, public morale was helped if local authorities made rapid repairs, clearing streets of rubble. 'It was shown also that the presence of good defences'—which referred to AA guns or balloons—'helped to keep up spirit, based largely upon the idea that they were "hitting back".'[21]

There were only four nights in July when German raiders were not over Britain. The Home Secretary reported that between 7 and 14 July, 960 high-explosive and 534 incendiary bombs had fallen, killing three people and injuring 61.[22] This pattern continued through the following month. For example, a Heinkel 111 of *KG 4* crashed in Scotland at 1.30 a.m. on 8 August while returning from a minelaying operation at Belfast.[23] On 10 August night sorties occurred over South Wales, Cornwall and Devon. Altogether, 43 high-explosive bombs were dropped, many on Swansea, where seventeen civilians were killed and eight injured. Two nights later 54 people died, with 218 injured, while on the 13th, following intensive day activity, aircraft of the specially trained *Kampfgruppe 100* bombed the Nuffield factory which produced Spitfires at Castle Bromwich.

'The raid was something of a freak,' wrote Telford Taylor, 'for night bombing remained on both sides a game of blindman's buff'—a comment made before the writer appreciated the German use of radio beams.[24] Goering maintained faith in the usefulness of these strikes. 'Our night attacks are essentially dislocation raids,' he wrote on 15 August, 'made so that the enemy defences and population shall be allowed no respite.'[25]

His recognition of the importance of night raids was again shown four days later. Apart from detailed instructions regarding day sorties, he laid down that attacks on the British aircraft industry should be carried out at night. 'It would appear desirable for the purpose of night operations to allocate to units areas which they will come to know better during each successive raid,' he believed. Within the area, a list of target priorities should be made, and 'there can no longer be any restriction on the choice of target'. He excluded only London and Liverpool, whose fate would depend on his orders. That night over 60 people were killed or injured in raids.[26]

From then until 7 September the *Luftwaffe* stepped up attacks in darkness, in conjunction with the daylight onslaught against Fighter Command in the south of England. Until 25 August, 'no urban area had suffered attack by night from more than twenty aircraft',[27] but then the major attacks started. These were registered in German records as raids in which at least one hundred tons of high-explosive bombs were dropped, and were concentrated on a few cities. They included Birmingham, Coventry, Liverpool, Plymouth, Bristol and Swansea. For four successive night strikes against Merseyside, the *Luftwaffe* employed 100, 137, 109 and 107 aircraft respectively. On the 28th they used 103 tons of high explosives and 6,800 incendiaries, with even greater numbers being dropped on the two succeeding nights. Attacks on the 31st led to long periods of air raid warnings across Britain; these varied, for example, from six hours in Liverpool and Central London, to five hours in Norwich and Birmingham and four in Manchester and South Wales.

Units launching these raids came from *Luftflotte III* in north and north-west France. Included in them were *KGr. 100* and *KGr. 606*, both pathfinder or 'fire-raiser' units, which prepared the way for aircraft of KG 27, KG 51 and KG 55, all of which were then specialising in night bombing. In the early days of September the *Luftwaffe* was finishing its exploratory phase and was ready to embark on the great Night Blitz. By then many aircrews were acquainted with the areas of operations, with British weather conditions and with AA defences. It was discovered later, from the interrogation of prisoners-of-war, that they had to study 'such landmarks as lakes, rivers, estuaries and arterial roads'. In addition, 'the need for strict wireless discipline was emphasised in order to afford our Wireless Intelligence Service as few opportunities as possible'.[28] *Luftwaffe* preparations were most efficient.

In Britain, casualties were heavy and the damage was considerable, giving civilian defence services in some cases their first taste of war. Doctors, policemen, nurses, firemen and wardens received early practice in the duties which would fully occupy their lives over the following year. During the seventeen nights from 21 August to 6 September inclusive, 471 people, most of them civilians, were killed and 2,316 injured in night attacks. By the latter date, *The Aeroplane* was able to report that 'night raiding was widespread and hardly any of the larger industrial centres and ports of England and Scotland escaped'.[29] This added to the worries of service leaders and politicians, whose greater concern was the main daylight battle then being fought. Martin Gilbert shows that on 31 August the War Cabinet learned that during August, in all attacks on the United Kingdom, 1,075 civilians had died.[30] In total, during the first complete year of the war, and even before the great London raid of 7 September 1940, almost 4,000 civilians were killed or seriously injured in Britain, with thousands of others slightly hurt. In addition, damage was caused to thousands of homes and other civilian buildings. Most of these casualties resulted from bombing, in spite of the stated German restrictions against raiding non-military targets.

Just as worrying for the British defensive system was Fighter Command's lack of success in darkness. During August RAF fighters flew 828 sorties across Britain on 26 nights, searching for the scores of bombers attacking cities. In that time they claimed only four enemy aircraft, of which three were allowed. AA guns apparently did better, with claims of sixteen destroyed. Taking the period between 1 June and 6 September, *Luftwaffe* incursions over Britain, with greater or lesser amounts of bombing, occurred on 77 of the 98 nights.[31] The auguries were grave even before the Germans decided to turn their full attentions to London.

THE BOMBERS

Many British people who lived under the German Night Blitz can still recall the drone of enemy bombers, especially the irregular beat of unsynchronised engines. At the time they knew that the invisible aircraft could at any time spread death, injury or destruction. In most cases they were unaware of the devastation wrought until the following day, when sombre scenes were unveiled. Bombers were seldom visible at night. Occasionally one was picked up by searchlights, or seen burning if hit by the defences, but bombs usually arrived from a hidden source. What were the characteristics of these aircraft? Who were their crews? What types of bomb did they drop?

As Cooper explains, German aircraft manufacturers in the 1930s used 'a necessary deception in view of the Versailles Treaty'.[32] They were forbidden to produce military aeroplanes, therefore companies built aircraft which were ostensibly designed for civil purposes yet were stepping stones in developing machines for war. The policy paid dividends: by March 1936, at the *Luftwaffe*'s Rechlin research station, pilots were already testing Heinkel 111s, Dornier 17s and a Junkers 88.

German intervention in the Spanish Civil War began in August 1936; by the following summer Dornier 17s and Heinkel 111s were in action, helping to attain air supremacy. The war taught engineers and aircrews many lessons about both the design and the employment of bombers, as well as about tactics. 'The *Luftwaffe* gained combat experience in Spain,' wrote Schliephake, 'which could never have been gained by theoretical instruction, however well devised, nor by tactical exercises, however well planned.'[33] However, one of the effects of the conflict acted to Britain's benefit during the Battle of Britain and the Night Blitz. This was the German failure to incorporate a heavy bomber into their air force. The *Kondor* Legion in Spain had shown the value of using aircraft in a tactical role, supporting ground forces. Therefore dive-bombers and medium bombers were developed rather than an aircraft to carry larger loads of high explosives and incendiaries. The aircraft which suffered particularly from this decision was the Heinkel 177. Had this heavy aeroplane been developed in a strategic role, it could have made a considerable difference in 1940. In Suchenwirth's view, 'long-range bombers could have created an entirely different situation'. They had the ability 'to appear anywhere over the British Isles', and anti-aircraft defences would have been 'so thoroughly dissipated by long-range bombers that defeat would have been inevitable'.[34] Considering the strength brought later in the war to the Allied bombing campaign against Germany by Lancasters, Stirlings and Halifaxes, together with Liberators and Fortresses, the *Luftwaffe*'s striking power during the Night Blitz was small.

The largest German bomber employed generally during the campaign was the Heinkel 111. Ernst Heinkel at Warnemünde had been secretly building aircraft with a potential military use since 1923. He had to ensure that the breaking of the terms of the Treaty of Versailles was not uncovered, but it was, in his own words, 'an extremely risky game of hide-and-seek with the Allied Control Commission'.[35] Over the following years he built several types, especially the Heinkel 70, as steps towards the development of the Heinkel 111, designed for medium-range operations. These, it was anticipated, would be part of a short, or lightning, war, in which the German Army would play a prominent role.

In August 1933 Milch visited Heinkel's factory to examine blueprints of the Heinkel 111. After the prototype was tested at Rechlin it was approved as 'the standard bomber of the future; it could carry a ton of bombs and was fast by modern standards'. In May 1936, at Oranienburg, near Berlin, Heinkel built a factory capable of turning out one hundred Heinkel 111s monthly. The first came to the *Luftwaffe* a year later.[36]

By the outbreak of war the P-series He 111 was in general *Luftwaffe* service and was 'a typical Heinkel product, with the elliptical wings and oval, well-streamlined fuselage'.[37] One of these aircraft, of *KG 26*, was the first to fall on British soil when shot down in Scotland on 28 October 1939. The Heinkel 111 had a wing-span of 74 feet and a length of 55 feet and carried a crew of five. Power came from two 1,200hp Daimler-Benz 1601N engines, giving a top speed of 250mph at 16,000 feet. The fully glazed nose provided excellent visibility, but the defences were too weak to contend with RAF fighters during daylight raids. The three hand-operated 7.9mm machine guns had a narrow field of fire. However, the aircraft's greatest weakness was its comparatively small bomb load: not designed for strategic warfare, the bomber carried only 4,400lb.

Occasionally during the Night Blitz the Dornier 17—the 'Flying Pencil'—was used. It was flown both for bombing and reconnaissance. Originally designed as a mailplane to carry half a dozen passengers, the prototype emerged in 1934. Three years later the Dornier 17 proved to be faster than any of Europe's contemporary biplane fighters, which added to the worries of those who feared the 'knock-out blow'. Gradually changes were made to the design, including the fitting of a bulbous glazed area at the front to house the crew of four. By 1940 the Dornier 17Z version was employed in attacks on Britain by both night and day.

The Dornier 17 had a wing-span of 59 feet and length of almost 52 feet. Powered by two Daimler-Benz 600A engines, it had a top speed of 255mph, although daylight formation flying was 75mph less than this. The aircraft could absorb heavy punishment because, as Alfred Price mentions, its air-cooled engines, 'lacking the fragile system of radiators and coolant pipes necessary for liquid-cooled engines, were far less vulnerable to enemy fire'.[38]

The third type of bomber used in the Night Blitz was the Junkers 88, in which Goering and a number of senior *Luftwaffe* officers placed great faith. This was an excellent, versatile aircraft, developed from a specification of 1935 which required a fast, twin-engine bomber. During the war more than 15,000 were built, some seeing service as bombers and others as night fighters. In 1940 the Junkers 88A was in service, powered by two Jumo engines, each of 1,200hp, giving a speed of 286mph at 18,000 feet. With a wing-span of 60 feet and length of 47 feet, the aircraft could carry 5,500lb of bombs. In defence the crew of four operated three machine guns, but the Junkers 88's main protection in daylight raids was its speed, enabling it 'to prove all too often capable of getting away from the Hurricane'.[39] A further point in the Junkers 88's favour was its use as a dive-bomber. Stahl, who flew one during the Night Blitz, noted in his diary, 'My feeling of trust in this magnificent aircraft increases from day to day and hardens into real self-confidence.'[40]

Principally using these three types of aircraft, the *Luftwaffe* opened the intensified Night Blitz. The disadvantages suffered during daylight raids were largely offset at night. In addition, all *Luftwaffe* bombers had one advantage possessed by few of their opponents: they were fitted with self-sealing fuel tanks—a great benefit if hit.

THE BOMBS

Although spared the widely predicted Armageddon of a gas bombardment at the start of the war, millions of Britons suffered attacks from high-explosive and incendiary bombs. They became inured to 'the screech of a bomb, the dull crash of its explosion and the smell of cordite that filled the air a moment later'[41] when a high explosive landed. Or they might hear 'a sound like stones being thrown against the house or a number of slates falling from the roof', when small incendiaries rattled down.[42]

Although German bombers carried smaller loads than those transported by Allied aircraft later in the war, their cargoes were sufficient to cause heavy casualties and widespread destruction. There were several categories of bombs that did the damage. First were the widely used general-purpose bombs of the SC (*Sprengbombe-Cylindrisch*) variety, which comprised about four-fifths of those dropped. Their purpose was to cause widespread damage, especially in urban areas. They varied in weight from 50kg, through the 1,800kg 'Satan', to the 2,500kg 'Max', which was the biggest to fall on Britain in this period. Usually they were made of thin steel, to increase the effects of blast. The 250kg bomb was extensively used, with an overall length of more than five feet and a width of eighteen inches. The charge/weight ratio was 52.5 per cent—guaranteed to damage targets heavily by blast.

Sometimes, to enhance the fearsome effect of bombs, and affect civilian morale, small tubes were attached, giving a whistling or screaming effect as the bombs fell. The device was known as 'The Trumpets of Jericho', 'but we were not impressed,' wrote Roger, 'and instead of calling them bombs any more, we called them "screaming meemies"'.[43] The smaller bombs were carried inside aircraft; those over 500kg had to be held by metal brackets, either under the wings or the fuselage. They were filled with trialen, amatol or TNT. SD (*Sprengbombe-Dickwandig*) bombs were given a thicker casing, with greater penetration against strongpoints. Moreover, as *Splitterbomben* they were anti-personnel explosives, varying in weight from 50 to 1,700kg. They were used less frequently in the Blitz than SC bombs.

Widely feared were the aerial mines, generally known to civilians as 'land mines'. Originally these were magnetic mines used against shipping and sown in coastal waters during the early months of the war with great effect. During the Blitz they were dropped over land targets, particularly in raids on cities, and caused severe damage through their wide field of blast. An impact fuse was fitted and the mine fell by parachute, a measure which angered British authorities because it could not be aimed accurately at a military target. Mines were known to British Bomb Disposal experts as 'Type C' (1,000kg), or 'Type D' (500kg). The *Luftwaffe* also dropped 'Type G' (1,000kg), which had no parachute and was 9 feet 4 inches long. The last named was introduced at the end of the Night Blitz, when the first one fell near Dumbarton, Scotland, during May 1941.

Problems for the defences came not only from explosives which detonated on impact, but also from those set with time fuses. Subsequently, the work of

Bomb Disposal Teams of the Royal Engineers in dealing with unexploded bombs (UXBs) was highly dangerous, demanding a special form of courage. Some bombs penetrated to great depths. One which fell at Enfield on 13 October 1940 burrowed to 26 feet and did not explode until 8 January 1942. The deepest penetration came from an 1,800kg 'Satan' which, including its fins, was 13 feet 6 inches long: it was discovered 64 feet 6 inches below the surface.

The number of UXBs was large. 'At one period, 30 November 1940, I made a check up on outstanding UXBs,' a soldier recollected, 'making a total at that date of 131 to be worked upon. Ilford—40, Barking—22, Dagenham—13, East Ham—30, West Ham—26, and subsequent raids added to this total.'[44] In their work, Bomb Disposal Squads were often troubled with booby-trap fuses, leading to sudden explosions. On 5 November 1940 at Dagenham, for example, five soldiers were killed and seven injured. At East Ham five weeks later eleven men were killed. Parachute mines, used from September 1940 until 1942, were sometimes equipped with booby traps. 'Photo-electric cells were fitted behind little glass windows and connected to the main explosive circuit,' wrote one Engineer officer, so that the removal of the "dome" would allow daylight to enter and so cause the photo-electric cells to operate and explode the mine.'[45]

One of the deadliest weapons was the incendiary bomb. The bombs were usually packed into containers, which were dropped and opened at a given height, scattering the contents over a wide area. For example, a 500kg container held one hundred and twenty 1kg incendiaries; others weighed 2kg. They were made of magnesium, were ignited with a small impact fuse and burned at a temperature sufficient to melt steel. When lodged into the roofs of buildings, especially unattended premises, the resulting fires caused enormous damage. Some were fitted with a small explosive charge which went off after seven minutes and was intended to deter those trying to fight fires. Larger incendiaries included a 50kg phosphorous bomb, and oil bombs weighing 250 or 500 kg. A German report on an airfield raid on 16 August 1940 noted that 'the new 500lb Flam incendiaries also proved effective'.[46]

As the *Luftwaffe* had been developed as a tactical air force, working in close cooperation with the Army, dive-bombing became an important part of aircrew training. This enabled bombs to be placed on targets and paid dividends, for example, when Junkers 87 'Stukas' operated with remarkable accuracy during the Western Campaign. However, these tactics were unsuitable in night attacks, so when bomb-aimers were trying to hit definite targets rather than dropping loads haphazardly across urban areas they used bomb sights. These were sometimes not much advanced on those of the First World War and failed to give accuracy. Some aircraft carried the Lotfe 7D tachometric sight, with a small electric motor moving a gyro-stabilized telescope, which was kept on target by the bomb-aimer. Information was fed into a small type of computer which released the bombs automatically after a run of about forty seconds. At other times the bombs were dropped by button or trigger. Afterwards, at night over cities, the bombers would often circle above, their ominous presence a worry to people below.

The loads dropped varied greatly according to the type of bomber and the distance of the target from the base. A typical load carried by a Heinkel 111 over London might be 32 bombs of 50kg each, two of 500kg and one 'Hermann' of 1,000kg. Another Heinkel might carry two large containers each holding 700kg of fire bombs. A Junkers 88 could carry two or four 500kg bombs fitted externally, while a Dornier 17 could hold an internal load of twenty 50kg bombs. With hindsight, these amounts appear small compared with the loads carried later in the war, yet that knowledge would have been of small comfort to the millions of civilians waiting below. 'They came down with a tearing sound as well as a whistle,' wrote one air raid warden. 'Sticks of four, sticks of six came crashing down, and still the planes circled above, and the homes rocked and trembled.'[47]

AIRCREWS AND TRAINING

Germany, it has been said, possessed a Prussian Army, an Imperial Navy and a National Socialist Air Force. Certainly, the aircrews flying the bombers which failed to overwhelm Fighter Command in the daylight battle and then turned their attention to devastating night raids were among the best recruits into any of the German armed services. 'In the post-war period,' according to an official British assessment, 'Goering had done everything possible to make the German Air Force the élite arm of the *Wehrmacht*.' He had offered special inducements of pay, conditions and opportunities which drew well-qualified and ambitious men to the *Luftwaffe*. Therefore, 'the German Air Force attracted the very cream of German youth to its ranks'.[48]

In addition, by the autumn of 1940, as they opened night attacks on Britain, many German aircrews had great experience of war. Some had already fought in five campaigns, from which they had learned much about bombing. Those with the longest service had seen action in the Spanish Civil War, in the Polish Campaign and then in Norway, before helping to defeat France and fighting in the daylight battles over southern England. RAF pilots had a far narrower experience, their first taste of action generally being in May and June 1940.

Although the Treaty of Versailles had banned Germany from having an air force, there were few restrictions on manufacturing civil aircraft. After the Paris Air Agreement of 1926 the Germans were 'left with complete freedom in the sphere of civil aviation', and thousands of men started to train in gliding clubs and at commercial flying schools. A secret military training centre was set up at Lipetz in Russia, attended by many future officers. Consequently, in September 1939 the *Luftwaffe* comprised some 1,500,000 men, of whom 75,000 were aircrew, with a further 10,000 under training.

Their preparation by then had 'reached a degree of quality not exceeded in any other European air force',[49] and the potential strength of the *Luftwaffe* was both widely known and feared. For all entrants, several months were spent at a Recruit Depot, before a posting on to a holding depot, thence to an Elementary Flying Training School. There the instructors selected those best suited for bombers or fighters, or to be navigators. Prospective bomber pilots then progressed to another school for up to six months, where they had about sixty hours' flying on twin-engine aircraft. Some practice was given in night and blind flying and later at a specialised Blind Flying School, where another sixty hours' practice was carried out, together with work on a Link ground trainer.

Subsequently came further training at another centre, with longer night flights in all weathers. When passed to operational units, most men had trained for between eighteen and twenty-four months and had about 250 flying hours in their log books. The importance of this training was noted by Adolf Galland, in commenting on the change from day to night bombing over Britain. It 'took place without any loss of time. This was possible because the crews, as part of their peacetime training, had received complete instructions and practice in night and blind flying'.[50]

An important difference between the *Luftwaffe* and the RAF was seen in one role . At the start of the war the navigator was the captain of a German aircraft, and the most experienced member of the crew. If the plane ran into trouble he would take over the duties of any other crewman, so his training, at a special Observer School, included piloting, gunnery, bomb-aiming and radio work. The position of navigator changed later in the war.

The Night Blitz was thus carried out mainly by aircrews who had trained at one of the nearly 100 flying schools in the *Reich*. For example, Hajo Hermann joined the *Luftwaffe* in 1936 and fought in Spain, Poland, Norway, Holland, Belgium and France before taking part in the attacks on Britain. The raid on London on the night of 7 September 1940 was his 69th of the war. 'By 18 October 1940 I had already logged 21 "revenge attacks" on London alone,' he claimed later.[51] Peter Stahl, who was part of the force devastating Coventry on 14 November, was at the start of the war 'a blind-flying instructor, introducing young airmen and officers into the mysteries of bad-weather and night flying'.[52] No other air force in the world had as many experienced flyers.

THE ORGANISATION

The RAF and the *Luftwaffe* were dissimilar in one important aspect of organisation. In Britain, from 1936 the service was split into Commands according to the role required from aircraft, for example Fighter Command and Bomber Command. The Germans, however, divided the *Luftwaffe* into a number of *Luftflotten*, or air fleets, each of which was a kind of miniature air force. All contained aircraft with different types, for example bombers, fighters and reconnaissance planes.

When the Germans overran France in 1940, three *Luftflotten* were moved into position to attack Britain. The least important and effective was *Luftflotte V*, under General Stumpff, based in Norway, which played little part in the following combat. *Luftflotte II*, under *Feldmarschall* Kesselring, was stationed in the Low Countries and north-eastern France, while *Luftflotte III*, under *Feldmarschall* Sperrle, was placed in northern and north-western France. In the main, the daylight Battle of Britain was conducted by the two latter air fleets.

However, from September the Night Blitz was launched primarily by *Geschwader* from *Luftflotte III*. In the *Luftwaffe*, a *Geschwader*'s strength was about 90 aircraft, although at any time a number of them were unserviceable. During the winter of 1940–41 most raids were made by *KG 1, 3, 26, 27, 51, 54, 55* and *77*. In addition, the *Luftflotte* employed smaller 'pathfinder' groups, each of about 30 aircraft—the *Kampfgruppe*—of *KGr. 100, 606* and *806*. The great majority of bombers were Heinkel 111s or Junkers 88s, flying from captured French airfields or rapidly developed airstrips. These were at or near such places as Orléans and Tours, Dinard and Orly, Evreux and Villacoublay, while *KGr. 100* operated from Vannes. Bomber crews flew one or two sorties nightly from these bases to raid cities across Britain. Sometimes people on the ground wondered how enemy pilots could find their way unerringly to their targets in complete darkness.

THE BEAMS

Seldom do the events of real life equal those portrayed in novels about espionage or secret intelligence. However, at the start of the Second World War an incident in Norway matched the best fiction, when an anonymous report was sent by 'a well-wishing German scientist' to the British Naval Attaché in Oslo. It included much information on scientific and technological advances made by the German armed services and gave details of devices connected with fuses, rockets, radar and torpedoes. At the time, authorities in the United Kingdom expressed reservations over the 'Oslo Report'. Was it a hoax, or a German attempt to mislead British Intelligence by feeding them a mixture of true and false information? One particular device which was mentioned and not greatly regarded then concerned a ground station sending radio signals to an aeroplane in flight. When the signal was returned, the position of the aircraft could be determined and this information could be passed back to its pilot. If this were done from two stations, he could be guided to a target.

Dr R. V. Jones, a young scientist, was attached to Air Intelligence in September 1939 to explore 'any new applications of science to warfare by the Germans'.[53] Gradually he became interested in the possibilities of using radio beams for navigation and in the *Luftwaffe*'s achievements in that field. His interest quickened at the end of February 1940 when he learned that German prisoners-of-war had been overheard discussing a form of radio aid for bombing known as *X-Gerät* (X-Apparatus). On 3 April the mystery deepened when a piece of paper recovered from a crashed Heinkel 111 mentioned 'Radio Beacon *Knickebein* from 0600 hours on 315°'. Jones discussed the matter with Royal Air Force officers and other scientists and was convinced that the Germans were able to help bomber crews by employing radio aids. After thought and deduction he prepared a report on 23 May. 'It is possible that they have developed a system of intersecting radio beams,' he noted, 'so that they can locate a target such as London sufficiently accurately for indiscriminate bombing.'[54]

At the time Jones did not appreciate how correct he was and how advanced German plans were . The nature and purpose of the *Luftwaffe* was to be mainly an aggressive, tactical air force employed in an offensive role. However, during the Spanish Civil War, at night, or in bad weather, the *Kondor* Legion had experienced difficulty in locating objectives. Consequently German scientists experimenting with radio aids for navigation spent time on beam systems to guide bombers towards targets. They did not neglect a defensive radar system, but it played a lesser part in their work until late 1941, when the RAF's bomber offensive intensified over Germany.

In the early 1930s the Lorenz company developed a radio beam system intended to help civil aeroplanes to locate airfields in bad weather or darkness. From 1933 Dr Hans Plendl, a scientist, evolved from this a contrivance which allowed a bomber to fly along, or parallel to, one beam; this was crossed at intervals by three other beams, emitted from another station. These gave the distance from the target, and the navigator, by activating a clock installed in his aircraft as he received signals from the last two beams, allowed bombs to be dropped automatically and exactly over the target. This was the *X-Gerät*, which had a range of about 180 miles. In November 1938 the *Luftwaffe* began training a special unit for operating bombing by beams, and a year later it became known as *'Kampfgruppe 100'*. Its 25 Heinkel 111s were specially equipped with *X-Gerät* and played an important part in night operations over Britain from the summer of 1940.

Another system, developed by the Telefunken company, was simpler than *X-Gerät*, with a range of 270 miles, although it was less accurate. This was *Knickebein* (Crooked Leg) and used only two Lorenz beams. One was the approach beam, along which the bomber flew, while the other was the cross beam, intersecting over the target. *Knickebein* could be easily picked up on the Lorenz blind-approach apparatus fixed in all *Luftwaffe* bombers, so no extra devices were required. At the start of 1940 the *Luftwaffe* had three *Knickebein* transmitters in position, the nearest at Kleve, close to the Dutch border. After the Western Campaign later in the year, *X-Gerät* and *Knickebein* apparatus was installed in parts of northern France and Holland, facing the British Isles. The Germans were ready to open a campaign of accurate bombing.

By October the Germans had a third, even more sophisticated device ready. The work again came from Dr Plendl, who produced the *Y-Gerät* system, which 'by itself contained all the equipment necessary to direct a bomber to its target'.[55] A single beam was employed, and through a series of radio signals sent between the ground station and the bomber, the aircraft's position could be assessed accurately. When the aircraft was over the target, the crew were instructed exactly when to release their bombs.

Therefore, both before and during the intensified Night Blitz, British defences were confronted by complicated forms of German technology which posed grave threats. These were the problems which Jones and other scientists had to solve if the nation were to survive.

On 12 June Group Captain Blandy, Head of the RAF's Signals Intelligence Service, showed Jones a copy of an intercepted German message which contained the words 'Knickebein' and 'Kleve'. Jones knew that the message was for Groups flying Heinkel 111s and he therefore investigated the radio equipment carried in a Heinkel which had been shot down earlier. He searched for a special device which could pick up *Knickebein* signals, but a prisoner-of-war was overheard to claim that no matter how hard the British searched, they would never find it. However, Jones suspected that signals were received on the ordinary Lorenz blind-landing receiver and his thoughts were confirmed by another scientist. Thus, any bomber could use *Knickebein*. His fears were expressed to Lindemann, scientist and friend of Churchill, who, after some early doubts, came to appreciate the accuracy of Jones' estimates.

The British authorities reacted rapidly to the potential danger and Air Marshal Sir Philip Joubert was appointed by the Air Ministry to prepare counter-measures to what was recognised as a growing threat. On 16 June a meeting of the Night Interception Committee was held to discuss the evidence of German beams. When asked to recommend measures against them, Dowding replied briefly, 'Jam!'[56] However, in view of his later reputation within the Air Ministry for being slow to cooperate and respond to the Night Blitz, it is interesting to read letters exchanged between him and Tizard. On 17 June Dowding referred to the previous day's meeting as 'a rather curious affair'. It had been called 'to discuss some rather nebulous evidence about German long-distance navigation by Lorenz Beam'. Then came the admission, noted by his critics: 'I also said that the subject did not appear to be particularly apposite to the Night Interception Committee'—which was a bad misjudgement, begging a question. If German beams were not apposite to a committee set up to explore night defence, whose responsibility were they? [57]

Tizard's reply also showed an apparent unawareness of the threat. 'I am disturbed about the way certain people seem to panic suddenly,' he stated. 'The result of these sudden committee meetings is that people go off at half-cock and no one seems to have a clear-cut responsibility.' He finished by agreeing with Dowding that 'this matter has little or nothing to do with the Night Interception Committee'.[58]

Jones was called to a meeting in the Cabinet Room at 10 Downing Street on 21 June. There he disclosed details of *Knickebein* in a story which, in Churchill's words, 'for its convincing fascination, was never surpassed by tales of Sherlock Holmes or Monsieur Lecoq'.[59] Jones was addressing a formidable audience of politicians, senior air staff and scientists, several of whom were, at the very least, amazed by what they heard. Tizard alone showed some open scepticism. Steps were now taken to discover which parts of Britain had beams laid across them. If they could be located, all doubts would be refuted. That evening a specially equipped Anson detected one, about a quarter of a mile wide, near Spalding. Jones's claims were vindicated.

At once, counter-measures were taken and a silent war began between the 'scientific wizards' on both sides of the Channel. The Germans had a head-start because their apparatus had already been produced and established, with bomber crews trained in its use. On the British side there was a rush to devise equipment for interfering with the enemy's systems. The magnitude of the dangers facing the United Kingdom from a night 'beam war' were increasingly appreciated, as the ability of the RAF and ground defences to respond to such attacks was limited. In addition to the somewhat passive defence of tackling beams, steps had to be taken to improve a more active form of defence, in which guns, searchlights and radar-controlled fighters could locate and destroy enemy bombers. Much work lay ahead, and the results of the next few months could well settle the outcome of the war. On 28 June Jones produced a paper, 'The Crooked Leg' (*Knickebein*), setting out all that was known of the beam. He expressed his concern: 'It shows that the German technique is well developed—almost beyond what we thought possible; if they can place an aircraft to within 400 yards over this country, they may well have an extremely accurate system of RDF.'[60]

To counter *Knickebein* beams, which were codenamed 'Headache', Air Commodore O. G. Lywood, of the Air Ministry's Directorate of Signals, set up a special unit in early July. It was known as No 80 Wing. The operation, under the immediate command of Wing Commander E. Addison, had to improvise jamming equipment. For example, some electro-diathermy sets were commandeered from hospitals and adapted to emit a jamming noise over *Knickebein* signals at short range. Addison also had a number of modified Lorenz blind-approach receivers which gave out dot-and-dash signals similar to those of *Knickebein*. By using them, false beams could be laid to divert enemy bombers.

In addition, much of the technical work of producing equipment to confuse the Germans was undertaken by the Telecommunications Research Establishment (TRE), at Swanage, in Dorset. There, experiments were led by Dr Robert Cockburn, a young physicist. 'The British wizards were working day and night', later wrote a night fighter pilot, 'building a type of scientific radio jammer, code-named "Aspirin" and designed to swamp the *Knickebein* signals.' However, several months elapsed before their device was ready.[61]

In the meantime, No 80 Wing took another step towards the goal of confusing the German signals. A system of Masking Beacons, called 'Meacons' was set up to intercept enemy beacon signals and repeat them. 'If this is done,' Lindemann told Churchill on 10 August, 'the wireless operator in the German machine cannot distinguish between the signals from his beacon and the echo signal from our station, and his direction-finding is set at nought.'[62] The first 'Meacon' operated at Flimwell in Kent on 24 July, and by 18 August nine were working. By that time the Germans had some 80 beacons installed from Norway, through Germany, to northern France, although only a dozen were used at any one time.

The contest between those employing and those intercepting *Knickebein* beams was well under way even before the intensified Night Blitz opened. In many ways the Germans had squandered the element of surprise by using it too widely for practice flights in advance of the main campaign, thereby giving the RAF an opportunity to learn something of its mysteries. However, the more complicated *X-Gerät* system provided greater problems when brought into action during August, as did the *Y-Gerät* later.

At that time the monitoring Y-Service picked up unusual signals which were unconnected with *Knickebein* and were soon known as 'Ruffian' to the RAF. Their origins were traced to Cherbourg and Calais and they were recognised as navigation beams. They were, in fact, signals from *X-Gerät* stations. On 11 August the special *X-Gerät* unit, *KGr.100*, with about 30 Heinkel 111s, was moved from Germany to Vannes in Brittany. Two nights later it attacked the Nuffield factory at Castle Bromwich, near Birmingham, which was about to produce Spitfires. Although the reason was unknown at the time, the bombing was remarkably accurate at night, with eleven bombs landing on the main target.

One reason why the Germans pressed ahead with *X-Gerät* was explained later by a bomber pilot. 'For in more and more instances had it been found that the radio beacons for *Knickebein* were being subjected to intensive interference

93

and were useless for navigation,' he admitted. 'The British were getting cleverer and cleverer at breaking into our radio–navigation system.'[63]

During the rest of August the skilled crews of *KGr.100*, their Heinkels decorated with a Viking ship emblem, used *X-Gerät* to fly a number of sorties over Britain. These culminated in the heavy night raids made on Liverpool at the end of the month. As the *Luftwaffe* prepared to change the main effort from daylight attacks to the night campaign early in September, it possessed beam systems capable of leading bombers accurately to targets across the United Kingdom, in spite of British counter-measures. However, the new campaign was opened against a target that could be easily approached without the guidance of beams. This was the area that British authorities had recognised as particularly vulnerable ever since the air raids of the First World War, because of its closeness to mainland Europe and the fact that the Thames Estuary pointed towards its heart. Thus on 7 September, in a raid of Wagnerian style and size, almost a thousand aircraft of the *Luftwaffe* launched the heavy attack on London's Dockland, followed by a night of further destruction and terror. The new strategy struck first at the very heart of the British Empire.

NOTES

1. AHB Translation VII/10, AHB 6, 21 November 1946, 'The Course of the Air War over Central and Western Europe'.
2. A. Hillgruber, 'England's Place in Hitler's Plans for World Dominion', *Journal of Contemporary History (JCH)*, 9, 1 (1974).
3. Evelyn, Princess Blücher, *An English Wife in Berlin* (1920).
4. Irving, *Rise and Fall*, 64.
5. *Ibid.*, 75.
6. H. Trevor Roper (ed.), *Hitler's War Directives* (1964), Directive No 1, 31 August 1939, 3–5.
7. AHB Translation, vol. 2, No VII/30, 'Proposal for the Conduct of Air Warfare against Britain', 22 November 1939.
8. AHB Translation, vol. 2, No VII/26, 'The Course of the Air War against England', Luftwaffe 8th *Abteilung* Report, 22 November 1939.
9. Trevor Roper, Directive No 4, 25 September 1939.
10. Diary of Miss Beryl Cleveley, 29 January 1940.
11. AIR 41/17, 17.
12. Wykeham, 155–6.
13. AIR 16/427, Enclosures 1A, 3B, 4A, 4B, 4C, 4D, 4F.
14. *Ibid.*, Minutes of First Meeting, Enclosure 8B.

15. AIR 41/17, 4 May 1940, 9.
16. Trevor Roper, Directive No 13, 24 May 1940.
17. 'The Unceasing Offensive', *The Aeroplane*, 14 June 1940.
18. *Front Line*, 6.
19. AIR 41/17, 53.
20. Goering Directive, 30 June 1940.
21. AIR 41/17, 38.
22. Ministry of Home Security, Weekly Appreciation, 7–14 July 1940.
23. The tailplane of this aircraft is in the North-East Aircraft Museum, Sunderland.
24. T. Taylor, *Breaking Wave* (1957), 137.
25. Goering Directive, 15 August 1940.
26. Goering Conference, Karinhall, 19 August 1940.
27. AIR 41/17, 44.
28. *Ibid.*, 48.
29. *The Aeroplane*, 6 September 1940.
30. M. Gilbert, *Winston S. Churchill: Finest Hour*, vol. vi (1983), 264.
31. AIR 41/17, 47.
32. Cooper, 72.
33. H. Schliephake, *The Birth of the Luftwaffe* (1971), 44.
34. R. Suchenwirth, *Historical Turning Points in the German Air Force War Effort* (New York, 1968), 43.
35. Schliephake, 15.
36. Irving, 45.
37. 'Aeroplanes of the Luftwaffe', *The Aeroplane*, 21 September 1939.
38. A. Price, *The Hardest Day* (1979), 24.
39. Hough and Richards, 47.
40. P. Stahl, *The Diving Eagle* (1984), 44.
41. Mrs R. Henrey, *London Under Fire 1940–45* (1969), 36.
42. Peter Elstob, quoted in A. Price, *Blitz On Britain 1939–1945* (1977), 104.
43. G. Roger, *The Blitz* (1990), 74.
44. H. Hunt, *Bombs and Booby Traps* (1986), 16.
45. *Ibid.*, 29.
46. W. Dierich, *Kampfgeschwader 'Edelweiss": The History of a German Bomber Unit 1939–1945*, (1975), 99.
47. Nixon, 17.
48. Air Ministry, *The Rise and Fall of the German Air Force*, Pamphlet No 248 (1948), 28.
49. *Ibid.*
50. A. Galland, *The First and the Last* (1955), 95.
51. H. Hermann, *Eagle's Wings* (1991), 66.
52. Stahl, 11.
53. See R. V. Jones, 'The Electronic War', in W. Ramsey, *The Blitz: Then and Now*, vol. i (1987), 282–93.
54. R. V. Jones, *Most Secret War* (1979), 131.
55. *Blitz*, i, 293.

56. AIR 41/17, 26; also letter to author, Professor R. V. Jones.
57. AIR 16/427, Encl. 77A, 17 June 1940.
58. *Ibid.*, Encl. 79A, 19 June 1940.
59. W. Churchill, *Second World War. Vol. II: Their Finest Hour* (1948), 340.
60. *Secret War*, 150.
61. P. Townsend, *Duel in the Dark* (1986), 53.
62. A. Price, *Instruments of Darkness* (1977), 34.
63. Dierich, 102.

CHAPTER FIVE

CHOOSING LONDON

LONDON VERSUS BERLIN

Why did the Germans not open the intensified Night Blitz on Britain earlier than 7 September 1940? There is a widely accepted, yet not entirely accurate, view that the attacks started and developed as a type of retaliatory tennis-match, fuelled by revenge, especially between Hitler and Churchill. In A. J. P. Taylor's opinion, 'Hitler felt that he must retaliate for the sake of his prestige'.[1] This resulted from a blunder made by one or more German bomber crews on the night of 24 August. In this story, *Luftwaffe* bombers flew towards targets at Thameshaven and Rochester, but several lost their way and bombs fell in the City of London. According to Richards, the bombs landed, 'to be exact, in Fore Street, near the Barbican',[2] while a magazine reported that 'for the first time in this War, the Germans sent night bombers to raid London on August 24 ... The London raid began soon after 23.00 hours and a serious fire in the City was started.'[3] Thus the centre of the capital was hit by aerial attack for the first time since 1918.

Ishoven reported the cause as 'faulty navigation', although 'standing orders by Hitler himself forbade such attacks'.[4] Irving offers several views. In one, a single bomber 'overshot its target' and 'a stick of bombs fell inside Greater London'. He asserts that no one was killed, but that a hundred people lost their homes 'in the working-class East End'.[5] Koch, who takes a critical look at Irving's claims, notes that elsewhere Irving mentioned 'a squadron' bombing London in error, killing nine civilians, 'a mistake which caused Goering to punish the culprits'.[6] In the widely acclaimed film *The Battle of Britain*, an offending aircrew are ordered back to Berlin for disciplinary treatment.

The next night, at Churchill's prompting, a force of British bombers was dispatched to Berlin. The Prime Minister, always searching for an occasion to show that the RAF had the power and will to hit back at a time when they were suffering an onslaught against Fighter Command aerodromes, wanted also to exact retribution for the bombing of London. Therefore Hampdens and

Wellingtons of Bomber Command made the long and hazardous flight of over 500 miles to the German capital. Because of poor weather and inaccurate navigation a number failed to reach the target, and those that succeeded caused little damage. Further raids followed and, according to the German Naval War Staff Diary of the 28th, a bomb close to the Görlitzer railway station killed ten civilians.[7] In Richards's words, 'the same medicine was administered several times during the next few nights'.[8] Colville, one of Churchill's secretaries, wrote on 26 August that, on learning that Bomber Command's next target was to be Leipzig, the Prime Minister was dissatisfied. He sent a minute to Newall, the CAS, ordering that 'now that they have begun to molest the capital, I want you to hit them hard, and Berlin is the place to hit them'.

These raids were small in overall effect, but German pride had been dented. Shirer, an American newspaper correspondent in Berlin, noted that 'the Berliners are stunned. They did not think it could ever happen.' Goering had promised that enemy aircraft would never bomb the *Reich*, but 'for the first time the war has been brought home to them'.[9] Christabel Bielenberg, British-born and married to a German, related that she left Berlin with her children at the time because of 'the advent of British bombers'. A side effect of the raids, she recollected, was that since Berliners were regarded 'by the rest of Germany as a very cocky lot, the RAF were accompanied on their nightly visits by a certain amount of *Schadenfreude*' from other parts of the country which had already suffered raids. And yet the damage caused 'had proved barely exciting enough to justify the bus fare for a family outing on a Sunday afternoon'.[10] The significance of the raids, however, was that they were an uncomfortable reminder that the war was not yet won. In the words of Briggs, they were a demonstration that 'Germany was not invulnerable (as her leaders had led her people to suppose) and that Britain was neither down nor out'.[11]

For Hitler, the consequence was definite. Since 17 August he had been at the Berghof but on the evening of the 29th he returned to Berlin. According to the War Diary he did this 'on account of the British air attack of last night'.[12] Milch, Inspector General of the *Luftwaffe*, joined him on 3 September and the *Führer* asked for an increase in the production of heavy bombs, obviously for use against cities.[13] Hitler now opened a campaign of words at Britain, for which Telford Taylor believed that he had two reasons: first, he wanted to blame the British for what they were about to receive; and secondly he wished to satisfy the desire of the German civilian population to exact revenge for what were, in comparative terms, very small raids.[14]

The opportunity arose on Wednesday 4 September at the Berlin *Sportpalast*. The *Führer* arrived at a mass rally organised to begin a winter relief campaign and addressed an audience containing many civilians, especially nurses and social workers. With his customary skills of oratory, Hitler issued a mixture of innuendo and threat, suggestion and promise, to excite his listeners and boost morale. He claimed to have waited three months without responding, in the hope that 'they might stop this mischief', but Churchill had taken that as a sign of weakness. His audience would now understand that Germany would answer in increasing measure each night. 'And if the British Air Force drops 2,000 or 3,000 or 4,000 kilograms of bombs, then we shall drop 150,000, 180,000, 230,000, 300,000, 400,000, one million kilograms.' He reached a crescendo, bolstered by his faith in what the *Luftwaffe* could achieve. 'When they declare that they will attack our cities, then we shall wipe out their cities.' He called the RAF bomber crews 'night pirates' and then struck a note which has added to the theory of night bombing as a contest of revenge and retribution, especially between him and Churchill: 'The hour will come when one of us will break, and it will not be National Socialist Germany.'[15]

Facts show at least an element of truth in the assertion that both sides desired revenge, with the two leaders determined to meet force with force. Nonetheless, it is incorrect to view this as the sole, or main, reason for the change in German strategy which brought London into the front line. In reality there were deeper causes, linked directly to the daylight Battle of Britain.

THE REAL REASONS FOR THE BLITZ

When interviewed after the war, General Deichmann, leader of the Karlsruhe study into the wartime activities of the *Luftwaffe*, offered military reasons as the prime motive force for the opening of attacks on the British capital. In this, he disagreed with Chester Wilmot's opinion, which gave reprisals ordered by Hitler 'for British attacks on Berlin'. He also differed from the view later advanced by 'Beppo' Schmid of *Luftwaffe* Intelligence that 'only political considerations prompted these attacks'. In Deichmann's opinion, 'military reasons were predominant'.[16]

It is therefore necessary to examine what had happened in the daylight battle by the early days of September. After Goering's conference of 19 August, the *Luftwaffe*'s policy had been to bring extreme pressure on Fighter Command's airfields in No 11 Group, using formations of bombers heavily protected by fighters. This changed approach brought results from the grinding attrition exerted on Park's squadrons over the succeeding fortnight. For example, on 30 August German airmen flew 1,345 sorties over Britain, a total that rose next day to 1,450. On that day the RAF lost 39 fighters, while during the first six days of September Fighter Command had a further 98 machines shot down and 43 pilots killed. By then No 11 Group were enduring the heaviest burden, with several squadrons down to half or three-quarter strength. On 7 September Dowding and Park met in conference with Douglas, the DCAS, to plan a revision of the method by which squadrons were replaced in the line, so great had the strain been over the previous fortnight.[17] The Germans did not know the extent of Fighter Command's losses, which were overestimated by Schmid's Intelligence department, yet they sensed that the pilots and aircraft of No 11 Group were locked in an aerial wrestling grip from which they could not easily escape.

Consequently, according to Deichmann, several days before the opening of the daylight and night raids on the British capital, 'Feldmarschall Kesselring asked me if the RAF fighter forces were by now sufficiently weakened for us to mass-attack the most important targets in London without too great a risk to our bomber-formations.'[18] In this way, Kesselring and his commander-in-chief hoped to attract the bulk of the RAF's remaining fighter force to the defence of the city. There, German aircraft would have the best chance of destroying them and achieving final victory. After that would come the overwhelming of other units of the RAF, preparing the way for a seaborne invasion. In Goering's opinion, if total success were achieved by the Luftwaffe, there well might be no need for landings, as the British Government would be compelled to seek peace.

Basic faults in Luftwaffe strategy and tactics thus far had led to failure to win the daylight battle. Fighter Command, not needing to win the battle, only not to lose it, had held on. In spite of the determination of German bomber crews in launching raids against airfields or aircraft factories, or in being used as bait to attract British fighters into contest with Bf 109s, the outcome had not been resolved by the early days of September. The RAF, fighting with equal determination and great courage within a carefully planned defensive system, had proved to be the biggest and most efficient air force ever engaged by the Luftwaffe. There would be no more easy successes comparable with those gained in Poland, Norway, the Low Countries and France.

These factors were exacerbated by poor German Intelligence. A survey of British fighter strength on 17 August estimated that only 300 fighters were left at Dowding's disposal, a number reckoned to have been severely reduced over the following three weeks of unrelenting assault.[19] This handful of machines was the force which the *Luftwaffe* was about to demolish. It is small wonder that Goering invested such faith in the great afternoon raid on 7 September, followed by the opening of the Night Blitz. Here was to be the final crushing of Dowding's forces, which explains why Deichmann claimed that the change of strategy was 'necessary for military reasons if a decisive victory was to be won'. He stated that *II Fliegerkorps* and *Luftflotte II* wanted mass attacks 'even if air superiority had not been achieved', because of 'the general situation of the war in the air'.[20]

There was, however, a more pressing need for the Germans to change the bulk of their campaign from day to night raids. This was the extent of their bomber losses from mid-July to the end of August. According to the Quarter-Master General's Department of the German Air Ministry, by 30 September *Luftwaffe* bombers had suffered a 69 per cent casualty rate during daylight raids. This total comprised 621 aircraft destroyed and 334 damaged; when this number is added to the 724 bombers destroyed or damaged during May and June, the rate of attrition suffered by aircrews is obvious.[21] 'The losses suffered by our bomber units must be terrible,' wrote a German pilot stationed in Denmark on 25 August, a comment supported by several factors.[22] The first was the peril of the double crossing of the Channel, especially the return flight. The second was that men shot down over Britain, if escaping with their lives, inevitably became prisoners-of-war, with no chance of return. The third was the weak defensive armament of bombers confronted by eight-gun Hurricanes and Spitfires. Interviewed in 1945, Werner Junck, who commanded *Luftflotte III*'s fighters during the battle, claimed to have advocated 'at an early date in the Battle of Britain that night attack be substituted for day attacks. This was finally done because of the severe losses in daylight raids.' He called the battle 'a sort of air-Verdun, in which the Germans were at a disadvantage'.[23]

By the start of September, German hopes that the *Luftwaffe* alone would defeat Britain by a daylight offensive were looking forlorn. The only realistic assault, by means of a seaborne landing followed by a series of land battles, all protected by the *Luftwaffe*'s air umbrella, became increasingly unlikely. Suitable tidal conditions for an invasion to be launched by the middle of the month were narrowing in number. A mutual distrust of commitment between the German Army and Navy brought delay which left the burden of war in the hands of Goering's aircrews. Yet, on the British side, the suspicion that the raids on London were the forerunners of seaborne landings occupied the minds of military leaders, politicians and the nation generally. One result of the bombing on 7 September was the issuing of the invasion code-name 'Cromwell' at 8.07 p.m. as landings were believed to be imminent.[24]

A change from day to night attack would provide bomber crews with a cloak of darkness in crossing the Channel and reaching targets. The strain and fear of fighter attacks would be removed. In the opinion of Noble Frankland, 'the only opportunity for a sustained air offensive was therefore under conditions in which Messerschmitts and Spitfires could not operate effectively; that is, under the cover of darkness'.[25] The pressure on the morale of German fighter pilots by September was considerable, a point made by Steinhoff, who led an escort group of Bf 109s. Bomber crews were affected at least as greatly, as they had less chance of protecting themselves in combat. Weariness from continuous operations, together with heavy casualties, caused a small number of aircrew to be affected by *Kanalkrank*, the German equivalent of 'lack of moral fibre' (LMF).

Two other important aims underscored the *Luftwaffe*'s change to attacks on London, especially by night. They were explained by Bechtle, Operations Officer of *KG 2*, to a German Air Force General Staff conference in 1944. 'Incomparably greater success than hitherto could be anticipated from this policy,' he stated, adding that 'economic war from the air could be embarked on with full fury.' Furthermore, he claimed, the morale of the civilian population could be 'subjected at the same time to heavy strain'.[26] Similar thoughts were expressed by Kesselring in his memoirs. Between 6 September 1940 and June 1941 'our main assignments now were the disturbance of production and incoming supplies with their underlying purpose of slowing down British armament production, and initiating a full-scale economic war'. The matter of civilian morale was covered by the statement that 'the "reprisal raids" were also started'.[27]

Regarding the effects on civilians, by the summer of 1940 there was always the German hope that aerial bombardment would lead to a breakdown in everyday life, with pressure brought on the government to make peace in order to avert anarchy. The Official Narrative refers to the German belief that 'the exertion of sufficient pressure on morale, together with a sufficient measure of destruction, would demonstrate the futility of further resistance and bring offers of submission'.[28] This aspiration had been declared by General Jodl on 30 June 1940: 'In conjunction with propaganda and terror raids from time to time—announced as "reprisals"—a cumulative depletion of Britain's food stocks will paralyse the will of the people to resist, and then break it altogether, forcing the capitulation of their government.'[29] Although Hitler appeared to have reserved to himself permission to bomb 'purely residential areas', he showed fond hopes of what effects the attacks on London might have: 'If eight million go mad, it might very well turn into a catastrophe!' After that, he believed 'even a small invasion might go a long way'.[30]

And yet Hitler's muddled thinking on the distinction between various targets was recollected when Kesselring was interviewed in July 1945 for the United States Strategic Bombing Survey. Hitler had ordered 'that we should not start the bombing of the civilian population, but he did, however, order the bombing of political targets:

'*Question:* What is a political target?

'*Answer:* The government district—the leadership center.

'*Question:* Do you think that you carried out strictly Hitler's orders?

'*Answer:* As a flyer I have to say the following. The order was given and carried out, if possible. That there were times when a bomb has to be released by accident, is well known to every aviator.'[31]

To summarise, the Germans had a variety of motives for turning to attacks on London and opening the main Night Blitz against Britain. They were thereby able to take pressure off the *Luftwaffe*, especially bomber crews, by changing the main assault from the RAF to economic and civilian targets. Also, they made much of the claim that they were doing no more than retaliating for RAF raids on German civilians. Whatever the truth or exaggeration of that, German leaders were not slow to use it as a justification for the Night Blitz

FURTHER LONDON RAIDS, 8–14 SEPTEMBER

After the great raid of 7 September, the Germans maintained the momentum of the London Blitz over the following four nights. On the Sunday evening, bombers returned at about 8 p.m. and commenced a steady onslaught, sustained by 200 aircraft during the next nine hours. Once again Dockland was heavily hit, with many targets still burning from previous attacks, but the raid was extended to cover other districts. Places in the south-east, the north-east and the centre of the city were hit and new fires started, although all except one were under control by the following morning.[32]

On Monday morning the *Daily Telegraph*'s headline was 'Air Attack on London Renewed Last Night', before reporting optimistically that damage in the docks was less than might have been expected. Food supplies, it announced, would not be affected.[33] The *Daily Express* wrote of 'Cockneys in the Fight', comparing their ordeal with that of the Dunkirk Evacuation, before quoting a more hopeful statement from a Port of London official that 'while damage by fire at the docks is considerable, discharging and loading berths are intact, and all services of the port will be maintained'.[34]

On the further side of the Channel that day, the *Luftwaffe* High Command (OKL) laid down guidelines for bomber *Geschwader*. 'By night *Luftflotte III* will carry out attacks with the object of destroying harbour areas, the supply and power sources of the city,' one report stated. London was divided into two target areas, A and B. The former included 'widely stretched out harbour installations', while the latter contained 'the power supplies and the provision installations'.[35] Putting the policy into practice that night, the *Luftwaffe* returned in force, with bombers from *Luftflotte III* flying singly or in small groups all through the hours of darkness. Almost 200 aircraft raided the capital, causing widespread damage. One bomb struck St Thomas's Hospital, while Somerset House and the Law Courts were also hit. Some 370 civilians were killed and 1,400 injured, adding alarmingly to the total of casualties caused in only three nights of raids.

During both the Tuesday and Wednesday nights further attacks on London followed, as well as on other British cities, including Liverpool. However, although damage was caused, there were fewer casualties. Civilian services were emerging from the unexpected shock of the first attack and worked steadily to fight fires, rescue the trapped and care for the injured. They included groups of men and women drafted in from areas outside the capital. The organisation of these services, planned from pre-war days, was exposed to considerable strain in some parts of London because of the intensity of raids on certain boroughs, especially in Dockland. Faults and shortcomings occurred, especially in caring for the homeless, yet in general the system operated satisfactorily and everyday life was maintained—though with difficulty.

LEADERSHIP

During the afternoon of Sunday 8 September Winston Churchill travelled to parts of the East End of London which had suffered heavily over the previous twenty-four hours. The reasons for the visit throw some light on his outlook and powers of leadership at the time. First, the Germans had obviously changed the direction of their campaign on to the capital itself. In doing so they had, at a turn, caused far heavier civilian casualties than had been suffered earlier and had also inflicted considerable material damage. The Prime Minister wanted to see the result of their work, a point reinforced by his personal detective. 'He insisted upon seeing for himself what was going on,' wrote Inspector Thompson, adding that the Prime Minister's interest 'was infinitely greater than his fear of what might happen to him.'[36]

Secondly, having heard from pre-war days predictions of the effects of bombing on morale in built-up areas, Churchill was demonstrating his leadership of the nation by a personal presence at a time of difficulty. For him, the exhortations of communiqués and speeches were not enough. By being present among those who had suffered directly, he intended to boost morale. 'They saw the towering courage that had been Churchill's all his life,' Jones wrote later. 'Everyone knew in that mysterious way that tells true from false that here was a man who would stand to the last; and in this confidence they could stand with him.'[37]

A third reason for the visit stemmed from Churchill's concern at the power and effect of aerial bombing. In his mind rested thoughts not only of the destruction that the *Luftwaffe* could cause in London, but also the effect that Bomber Command might have on German industrial centres. In a message to the War Cabinet only five days earlier, he had asserted that 'we must therefore develop the power to carry an ever-increasing volume of explosives to Germany, so as to pulverise the entire industrial and scientific structure on which the war effort and economic life of the enemy depend'.[38]

Among those accompanying him was General Ismay, the Prime Minister's agent of 'communication on military matters', who recalled the afternoon. One place visited was an air-raid shelter where about forty people had been killed by a direct hit. Others were searching nearby for belongings. The effect of Churchill's presence was immediate: 'They stormed at you as you got out of the car with cries of "It was good of you to come Winnie. We thought you'd come. We can take it. Give it 'em back."'[39] Thompson remembered a similar response from people whose morale was undaunted. 'The cry went up on every side: "We can take it, we can take it—but give it them back."' Churchill promised 'repayment with compound interest'.[40]

Two points are noteworthy here. First, ordinary men and women, in spite of the surrounding tribulations, were pleased that their leader had gone to be with them. Secondly, they wanted retribution. Sir Auckland Geddes, the Regional Commissioner for ARP in south-eastern England, explained their feelings. He wrote: 'It is more than the normal civilian can be expected to stand, to have three or four raids in a single day, each producing its tale of casualties and destruction, with no visible hits back at the enemy.'[41]

Throughout the Night Blitz the majority of people in London and other bombed cities were prepared to bear the burden laid on them. 'Business as usual' was a sign often displayed by shops. One London store sought to take advantage of disaster with a humorous, defiant notice: 'They can smash our windows, but they can't beat our furnishing values.'[42] But most citizens wanted the satisfaction of knowing that Britain was hitting back in kind. No one understood that more than Churchill. Those who seek to demean his achievements fail to comprehend how in 1940 he represented the general spirit of the nation, especially those who had been directly under the enemy's attack. 'Although as a nation we were alone, as individuals we were all in it together,' wrote Jones. 'He felt our temper exactly.'[43] Churchill commented later, 'It fell to me in these coming days and months to express their sentiments on suitable occasions. This I was able to do, because they were mine also.'[44]

The suggestion by some writers that Churchill was a warmonger was refuted by one independent witness, the American J. G. Winant, who saw him at close hand during the Blitz. 'It was said by some that "Churchill enjoyed the war". No blacker lie was ever spoken. No one could have seen him, in the dark days of the war, as I did, and ever doubt his suffering or his caring.'[45]

Ismay recollected that during his visit to the East End the Prime Minister stayed in the area until darkness fell and the next raid started. With some difficulty they drove back to Downing Street, where anxious ministers and assistants were waiting. 'Churchill strode through them without a word.'[46] He had been deeply moved by what he had seen and was now confronted by two major problems. First, he had to promote measures to defend the capital against night bombing; secondly, he had to ensure that the enemy suffered in similar fashion.

A first step in this direction was taken at the War Cabinet meeting of 10 September, when ministers were told that the bombing of London was 'quite indiscriminate'. Consequently, RAF crews flying over Germany were to be instructed 'not to return home with their bombs if they failed to locate the targets which they were detailed to attack'.[47] On the following day Churchill sent Ismay a personal minute showing his continuing concern for the effects of bombing on London's civilians. Ismay was asked to investigate food supplies and distribution, provision being made for the homeless, and exhaustion suffered by Fire Brigade personnel. He was also to report on worries over gas, water, electricity and sewage disposal.

The Prime Minister broadcast later that day, referring to the bombing as 'cruel, wanton and indiscriminate', and as part of the German invasion plan. Hitler hoped to 'terrorise and cow the people of this mighty imperial city', but had failed to appreciate their spirit and 'tough fibre'. In a passage reminiscent of Latimer's words to Ridley at the stake almost four centuries earlier, Churchill referred to the fires burning in the capital: Hitler had 'lighted a fire which would burn with a steady and consuming flame' until Nazism had been 'burned out of Europe'. Such words, attempting to turn the attacker's onslaught to the defender's advantage, were inspirational, even to those who had so grievously suffered.[48]

Another notable visitor to London's East End was the King, George VI. On Monday 9 September he spent three hours in a heavily bombed area and saw the devastation caused to thousands of his people. In some places whole rows of terraced houses had been turned into piles of rubble. He heard at first hand the stories of families who had lost everything except their lives and determination.

After the visit the King, together with Queen Elizabeth, went to Windsor. During that night a bomb fell on the terrace outside the north wing of Buckingham Palace. It exploded at 1.30 a.m. on Tuesday morning, destroying windows in the King's sitting room. According to a newspaper reporter who later visited the site, 'Walls were charred with black smoke and one heavy piece of stone had been blown over the Palace and had landed eighty yards away.'[49] Worse followed on Friday the 13th. When the King and Queen were together in Buckingham Palace they heard a German plane approaching. According to the King's diary, they saw 'two bombs falling past the opposite side of the Palace, and then heard two resounding crashes as the bombs fell in the quadrangle about 30 yards away'. Altogether, the aircraft dropped six bombs, only one of which struck the building itself, damaging the chapel and injuring four people.[50]

Noticeable for the maintenance of public morale, in spite of proximity to the bombing, was the King's decision to stay in the capital. 'The children won't leave without me,' Queen Elizabeth is reported to have said, 'I won't leave without the King, and the King will never leave.' This example of leadership was respected by ordinary people and was an early step taken by the Royal Family to show a spirit of unity in war.[51] Queen Elizabeth stated, after the

Palace had been hit, 'I am glad we've been bombed. It makes me feel I can look the East End in the face.'[52] In Lacey's opinion, 'This was representative monarchy leading its people in battle in a totally new way.' He then referred to 'the dogged, unassuming example' set by the King and Queen.[53]

Consequently, the example of national leaders at a difficult time helped to strengthen public resolve. Writing of the new Blitz, *The Spectator* asserted that 'its immediate object no doubt is to break morale. In that it will fail as other endeavours have failed from which Hitler and Goering are seeking now to divert attention.' Battle was engaged between, on the one hand, the determination of German airmen to succeed and, on the other, the stubborn will of Britain not to be beaten.[54]

THE BRITISH DEFENCES

One factor was immediately apparent from the start of the intensified Night Blitz. The airmen of Fighter Command who had fought so valiantly and to such good effect by day had little chance of locating, intercepting and destroying bombers at night with the equipment then available. Therefore the burden of defence fell on ground forces manning balloons, searchlights and anti-aircraft guns. Balloons and searchlights had both been employed during the First World War. By September 1940 Balloon Command, under Air Vice-Marshal Boyd, controlled Nos 30, 31, 32 and 33 Balloon Barrage Groups, which were generally positioned near large urban areas such as Coventry, Manchester, Birmingham and Liverpool. In daylight they were something of a deterrent to low-flying aircraft, but they were less effective at night when raiders flew above 5,000 feet. The balloons were 62 feet long and inflated with about 19,000 cubic feet of hydrogen, and most were fitted with a Double Parachute Link, which was a great impediment to any aircraft colliding with the cable. At the opening of the Night Blitz, London was protected by 450 balloons flown from mobile winches.

Searchlights also had limitations as a means of defence. Pile wrote that on cloudless nights bombers operated from about 25,000 feet. 'At those heights searchlights were, in my opinion, useless.'[55] Clouds and moonlight also affected the efficiency of lights, of which there were almost 4,000 during the Night Blitz. At the start of the war searchlights were of 36in (90cm) diameter, with a carbon projector, and produced 210 million candlepower. As the battle progressed, some were replaced by a larger light of 60in (150cm) diameter, generating 510 million candlepower, which was controlled by a radar device code-named 'Elsie'. The plan was for this 'master light', in a section of three, to illuminate the enemy, then for the other two searchlights to form a cone round it. However, searchlights were sometimes an inadvertent aid to bomber crews who could then tell the general direction of a target surrounded by beams of light.

At first, the gunners made no more than a desultory defence against the night raiders on 7 September. They appeared to have been taken by surprise by the German change of target. Therefore, during the night raid anti-aircraft guns did not engage the enemy over the Inner Artillery Zone until almost half an hour after the first bombs had been dropped in south London. That night bombers met little resistance from ground defences.[56]

Of the Command's seven AA divisions operating in September 1940, two were immediately concerned with the defence of London. The First Division covered the Metropolitan area, while the Sixth Division was stationed in south-eastern England and southern East Anglia. However, these forces suffered from several grave deficiencies. The first was a shortage of guns, which was experienced over the whole of the United Kingdom. A report produced for the Chiefs of Staff in August noted that 'out of a total of a hundred places which recent examination has shown to require heavy anti-aircraft defence, provision has been made for only about sixty, and those are often of a token measure'. In many cases the number of guns available was 'only some 50 per cent of what is considered necessary'.[57] In mid-1940 the suggested figures of weapons needed for home defence were 3,744 heavy guns and 4,410 light guns, yet on 11 September the whole Command could call on only 1,313 heavy guns. The First Division had 235, of which 199 were situated in the IAZ, and 44 light guns.[58]

The heaviest gun used had a calibre of 4.5in and had usually been set in fixed emplacements since pre-war days. Although efficient against high targets, it was unable to engage those at low altitude, or dive-bombers. Next in size was the 3.7in, which came into service in 1937 and was generally a more successful weapon. It could be employed in either a mobile or a static role and fired a shell weighing 28lb, coming from a complete round which was 3 feet 6 inches long and weighed 49lb. An Army three-ton lorry could transport 89 of these rounds to the site, where troops then had to carry them to the guns.[59] The Command also had a number of 3in guns which had been pressed into use, although in Pile's opinion these weapons were 'known to be quite ineffective against the improved performance of enemy aircraft'.[60] Light weapons consisted of 40mm

Bofors and 20mm Hispano guns. These, although useful against low-flying aircraft in day raids, were able to play only a small part in night attacks.

General Pile's difficulties over positioning guns had been multiplied after Dunkirk when some had been moved from defending urban areas to guarding airfields and factories. At the time the protection of the latter was paramount, but the heavy bombing of London caused guns to be moved south. 'Within twenty-four hours of that night attack, reinforcements were on their way to London,' wrote Pile, 'and within forty-eight hours the number of guns had been doubled.'[61] A great drawback was that the existing system had been based on sound locators feeding information to gun positions which had been set up on fixed lines of approach, especially along the Thames Estuary. The assumption was that the enemy would fly at a constant height in a set direction, at a steady speed, but the German attacks on the nights of 8 and 9 September did not conform to this pattern. A further difficulty was that gun batteries were not small, mobile units. It took some time to site and establish them before they reached a high rate of efficiency.

Another of Pile's problems concerned the quality of his men, some of whom were Territorials. At the start of the war 'many of them were unsuited for any military duty, let alone the highly technical duties of AA'. Of twenty-five men who arrived at one battery, 'one had a withered arm, one was mentally deficient, one had no thumbs, one had a glass eye which fell out whenever he doubled to the guns, and two were in the advanced and more obvious stages of venereal disease'. The situation had not greatly improved a year later because, according to Pile, other branches of the services took the best recruits and he got 'the leavings of the Army intake'.[62]

Yet when the men of the Command were under pressure from 7 September they responded magnificently in the most trying circumstances. Quite a number had come straight from training establishments and had received little practice in working their guns. What is often forgotten in assessing their performance is that, with the start of the Night Blitz, daylight raids on London continued. Consequently, for some batteries there was hardly any respite day or night. For example, on 8 September almost 100 enemy aircraft appeared in daylight over parts of Kent and the Thames Estuary, being engaged by the guns of the Sixth AA Division, before the main night attack on London continued. On 9 September more raids crossed Kent by day and penetrated to the capital, again followed by a night bombardment, then strikes both in daylight and darkness followed from the 10th to the 14th. On the 15th heavy raids occurred

in both morning and afternoon as the *Luftwaffe* attempted finally and unsuc-
cessfully to break Fighter Command. AA gunfire played a prominent part in
that day's fighting and then, after dark, the batteries were in action again as
German bombers returned. The burden laid on gunners was daunting.

On 10 September Pile called a conference of officers to discuss tactics, and
he determined to meet the enemy 'with a barrage the like of which had never
been seen or heard before'.[63] They were told to fire every possible round into
the night sky, even though there were only eleven gun laying (GL) radar sets
available in the whole of London. No searchlights would show, nor would
RAF aircraft appear over London, so skies were left clear for the gunners. Thus
on the night of 11 September the noise and sight of anti-aircraft gunfire
heartened Londoners. Guns that had arrived from other parts of Britain put up
a heavy barrage throughout the hours of darkness. Next day, the *Daily Express*
described a 'terrific London barrage', with 'gunfire louder than the bombs'.[64]
A female warden was more explicit: 'But on Wednesday they brought up the
guns at last,' she wrote. 'There was never such an exhilarating uproar; the heavy
guns boomed and the light ones crashed; they rattled and split the window
panes. It was a splendid and deafening cacophony.'[65] The photographer
George Roger referred to 'the welcome music of the guns'.[66] The fact that few
German aircraft were hit and no attacks were prevented paled beside the
benefits brought to civilian confidence and morale. The guns were used so
heavily that one young officer found that the inner sleeves of barrels had to be
replaced after three days; pre-war Regulars told him that before 1939 they
lasted for three months.[67] AA Command was satisfied, although, as Pile
recalled, the council of one suburb was not. They 'wrote to say that lavatory
pans were being cracked in the council houses by the vibration of the guns, and
would we mind very much moving the barrage somewhere else'.[68]

The odds against hitting an aircraft by night were high. Professor Hill, whose
scientific advice was valued by the Command, pointed out that 'One cubic
mile of space contains 5,500,000,000 cubic yards.' As the explosion of a 3.7in
shell covered only a few thousand cubic yards for about one-fiftieth of a
second, 'the idea of a "barrage" of anti-aircraft shells is nonsense. The word
ought to be dropped; it gives a false impression, and is based on sloppy thinking
and bad arithmetic. Nothing but aimed fire is any use.' To have even the
slightest chance of hitting an aircraft travelling at 250mph, thousands of shells
would have to be fired every second. However, this bald scientific survey
overlooked the reassurance brought to civilian morale by defensive gunfire, as

well as the benefit that bombers were forced to fly higher and some even to turn back from their targets.[69]

DOWDING AND THE AIR MINISTRY

The German change of target quickly exposed the weaknesses of Fighter Command in intercepting the enemy at night. Developments in airborne interception (AI) radar were insufficiently advanced, the Beaufighter was not ready for general service and the whole system of defence in darkness was still in a state of trial and preparation. Consequently, the opening stages of the Blitz were met with little resistance from the RAF. On the night of 7 September two Hurricanes were circling Tangmere aerodrome, 'though they had received no instructions to intercept the enemy' while the Germans were over London.[70]

At once, the lack of response was questioned. Where were the night fighters? Why were bombers not being shot down by Hurricanes and Spitfires? Worrying for service leaders and politicians was the number of civilian casualties, which were far greater than in daylight raids, and also the heavy damage caused in the capital. Consequently, the period between 7 September and mid-November witnessed the final stages of a battle within the top echelons of the Air Staff. Many of the senior officers who had been critical of Dowding's handling of Fighter Command during the day battles now believed that he was failing to show sufficient drive and innovation in countering night bombing. During those weeks the sides drew further apart over the methods required to meet the new threat. The C-in-C asserted that the problem could be solved only by a methodical approach, involving AI apparatus fitted into twin-engine fighters, especially the Beaufighter. The Air Ministry, supported increasingly by scientists and politicians, wanted a swifter and more radical solution, possibly including the use of several day squadrons of Hurricanes, flying at night. By mid-November the impasse had to be resolved and, as all servicemen were servants of the Crown through Parliament, this became the business of senior politicians.

Dowding's response to the problem was cautious. He was not willing to risk single-engine fighters in darkness, working without the benefits of AI. He did, however, immediately put into effect the 'Kenley Experiment'. From 9 September he installed some of AA Command's few gun laying radio-location sets near searchlights in the Kenley Sector, hoping, in his own words, to track 'on the usual line of approach of London Raiders, which commonly make their landfall near Beachy Head'.[71] His expectations of success were not realised. The weather was poor, AI equipment 'proved to be unexpectedly capricious in azimuth' and the Blenheims employed were both slower than many German bombers and 'deficient in fire-power'.[72] The problem remained, and on that night almost 1,800 Londoners were killed or injured.

A meeting of the Night Interception Committee was convened on Wednesday 11 September at the Air Ministry and Dowding set out various methods by which fighters could be operated in darkness. Among his listeners were Sir Archibald Sinclair and senior Air Staff in the persons of Joubert, Douglas, Slessor and Saundby, all of whom were critical of Dowding's efforts for both night and day defence. Dowding's explanations dealt far more with problems than with remedies.[73]

What could be done? Exceptional circumstances called for unusual responses. Lindemann had suggested to Churchill that aerial mines, descending by parachute, should be dropped in the path of bombers approaching London. The operation, known as 'Mutton', was received with little enthusiasm by the RAF, whose leaders and aircrews knew that a more accurate and reliable system of interception was required.

The initiative for new measures came from an unexpected quarter. On 11 September Marshal of the Royal Air Force Sir John Salmond, Director of Armament Production at the Ministry of Aircraft Production, presented a paper on aspects of night fighting to Lord Beaverbrook, his Minister. At that stage Beaverbrook was showing considerable anxiety over the defence of aircraft factories, for which he was responsible. 'All through the summer and early autumn the bombing of the factories continued, while Beaverbrook begged for more protection,' wrote Hollis. 'On August 15th, at Rochester, Short's lost more than three months' output of Stirlings from a heavy attack. On September 4th, Vickers at Weybridge suffered damage equivalent to the loss of 125 Wellington bombers.'[74] It is noteworthy that, on the same day that he received Salmond's recommendations, Beaverbrook also read a paper from Churchill, which explained the purposes of German navigation beams for night bombing. This information gave no comfort to the Minister of Aircraft Production, who could now foresee factories being hit in both darkness and daylight. Next day he noted to the Prime Minister that 'the drain on Hurricanes and Spitfires is very heavy and our reserves have fallen to low levels'.[75]

Therefore Salmond's memorandum was quickly accepted by Beaverbrook. 'He said he would show it to "someone" last night,' wrote Salmond in a letter to Trenchard on the 12th, with which he enclosed a copy of his paper. 'I think you will agree that the matter is extremely important, and I earnestly hope that you will come in on it.' This was, for the RAF's two senior officers, the start of a campaign to improve methods of night air defence, over which both believed that Dowding and Newall were making insufficient effort. 'I have got the names of those who had intimate experience of night fighting and its organisation during the last war,' Salmond noted, adding that 'There will be no dearth of experience to go on.'[76]

On 14 September Beaverbrook wrote to Sinclair announcing that Salmond was to head an investigation into night fighters and requesting the Air Ministry to give all possible help. Beaverbrook, who had fought a number of running battles with Sinclair and the Air Staff over policy, was scoring a point by taking a lead.[77] The Air Ministry's response was immediate and positive. A letter from Newall to Beaverbrook welcomed the move and offered cooperation.[78] At the same time, the Air Council wrote to inform Dowding of developments and requested that 'all matters in connection with air fighting at night' should be investigated. They asked for Quintin Brand, AOC No 10 Group, who had experience of night fighting, to attend Salmond's inquiry.[79]

The Salmond Committee's first meeting was held at the Ministry of Aircraft Production on the 16th. Present were a number of senior officers both from the Air Ministry and from Beaverbrook's Ministry, as well as a Senior Scientific Officer attached to Fighter Command. After accounts had been given of the existing system, changes in the methods of passing on information from RDF stations were suggested to speed up response times. 'At present R.D.F. indications were telephoned to Fighter Command,' stated the minute, 'and thence, after filtering, to groups and sectors.' This system caused delay, which Air Vice-Marshal Tedder claimed was often five or six minutes. Various other criticisms were made both of the equipment used and of the practice of interception; these showed, even indirectly, disapproval of Dowding's system.[80]

At the Committee's second meeting, on the following day, two possible changes in policy emerged from discussion, and these were to lead to controversy with Dowding. First, the view was generally accepted that earlier use should be made of RDF information to bring fighters close to the enemy, which could mean that Fighter Command's filtering system was bypassed. Secondly, the opinion was advanced, particularly by Squadron Leader Max Aitken, who had the double qualification of being a successful fighter pilot and also Beaverbrook's son, that, in the hands of competent pilots, Hurricanes could be employed as night fighters.[81]

It is remarkable that, by the end of the second meeting, no opinion had been sought from Dowding, who had general responsibility for the fighter defence of the United Kingdom. On that day he wrote to Harold Balfour, the Under-Secretary of State for Air, noting that Quintin Brand 'has already been summoned to the enquiry and given his evidence'.[82] The impression is gained that the Committee were investigating independently of the C–in–C; another prominent absentee was Park, AOC of No 11 Group, whose fighters were mainly involved in the defence of London and who was being criticised over day fighting tactics.

What also is remarkable is that the Committee's findings were settled and signed on the 17th, at the end of the second day's gathering, before Dowding had been able to give his opinions. This opportunity did not come to him until the final meeting on the morning of the 18th, when Dowding, together with a general of AA Command, appeared at the headquarters of the MAP. He agreed that a night fighting section of Fighter Command might be formed, but did not wish to increase headquarters staff and 'did not consider any change necessary'. Generally speaking he disagreed with proposals to decentralise control and believed that 'there was a tendency to leave too much to Sector Commanders', a sentiment which ran contrary to the Committee's general feeling. Dowding then explained at some length the methods of night interception possible, with or without assistance from searchlights. In his view, the eight-gun fighter not equipped with AI 'was worthless at night unless searchlights could usefully operate'. He would 'not agree to the suggestion that filtering should generally be delegated to Groups', a recommendation which would bypass his system of control. Yet other Committee members thought this should be done. Their report was then rapidly typed out and sent to both Ministries.[83]

In many ways the Salmond Report, produced in a brisk and businesslike manner, sounded the death-knell for Dowding's leadership at Fighter Command. 'On it I put a private note to Beaverbrook,' Salmond wrote to Trenchard on the 25th, 'to say that I considered Dowding should go.'[84] After Sinclair met Beaverbrook to discuss the recommendations, the Air Council was convened on the 24th and accepted all points. They at once had a copy of the Report sent to Dowding, together with the Council's instructions, which he was required to put into practice.[85]

And yet Dowding still found favour with Churchill, with whom he dined at Chequers on the 21st. The Night Blitz was discussed and there were suggestions of retaliation for the German use of parachute mines. Dowding produced a paper on night interception which the Prime Minister called 'masterly', but Lindemann was disgruntled. In his view, Dowding's suggestions were 'his first admission of a number of facts which have been impressed on him for ages'.[86]

In a letter dated 25 September, Trenchard asked Salmond what he should discuss with Beaverbrook, whom he was to meet shortly.[87] At this stage the differences between Dowding and various other senior Air Staff became apparent. Salmond's reply was trenchant. Beaverbrook, he claimed, would take no part in sacking Dowding because he had worked closely with him and 'has formed a very high opinion of him'. Sinclair was frightened when told, and 'I felt that he was not going to move in the matter.' Newall also came under attack because, at the Air Staff meeting, he had passed Salmond a note asking him not to raise the matter of Dowding there. That was incomprehensible 'as he has told me some days ago how extremely keen he was that Dowding should go'. The C–in–C Fighter Command would not 'accept new ideas on fighting at night', lacked qualities as a 'Commander in the Field', and was now living 'on the reputation he has gained through the successes of the pilots in day fighting'.

Beaverbrook believed that if Dowding had to leave, Newall also should go: 'Personally, of course, I have no objection to coupling them as I think Newall's strategic judgement is completely at fault.' He then listed the CAS's failings over campaigns in Norway, France and Belgium, as well as his failure to help the Royal Navy by reinforcing Malta. Newall was so concerned with the possibility of invasion 'that he will not even tell off a couple of day fighting squadrons to be trained for the night'. He finished by asking Trenchard to raise the cases of Dowding and Newall with Beaverbrook because there was failure 'with these two in the saddle'. Salmond later added a note to his letter, claiming that Churchill had agreed to Dowding's dismissal, 'but it nearly broke his heart'. Then he showed his unwavering determination to achieve change by writing that if the Prime Minister had not agreed, 'I had decided to appeal to His Majesty'.[88]

Dowding was unimpressed by many of the Salmond Report's recommendations. He followed his usual practice of marking points in blue crayon, with a vertical red line added to those which caused him greatest upset. Altogether, three points were approved and ticked. Five received question marks which, for Dowding, meant mild disapproval. Nine were awarded a cross, signifying definite disapproval and, of those, two were decorated with a single red line. No 2, 'The operation of filtering should be transferred from Fighter Command to Group Headquarters in order to reduce delay' had a double red line beside it.[89]

The impression of a minor war between Dowding and the Air Staff is enhanced by reading his replies to Salmond's suggestions, which were sent on the 27th. He had differed from Joubert over the question of filtering in January, and 'the matter has no particular connection with night interception' so he did not wish it to be raised again. The proposal to appoint an Air Commodore for night operations was 'not practical', another proposal was 'altogether premature' and a third would 'hamper my plans'. Others also were rejected. One was annotated 'I do not know what is meant by this', while another proposal was 'no direct concern of mine'.[90] Dowding's letter brought retaliatory comments, possibly from the pen of Mr (later Sir) Maurice Dean, a civil servant in the Air Ministry. These suggested that urgent needs had been neglected and that Dowding was pert and obstructive.[91]

Disagreements continued over the following weeks, as the Air Ministry and the MAP pushed hard to produce more AI equipment and speed up Beaufighter production. On 1 October Dowding was called to a meeting on Night Air Defence at which, once again, his views differed from those of the majority present, who included Sinclair, Newall, Salmond, Douglas and Joubert. Dowding wanted to record 'that, in his view, the proposal to transfer filtering to Groups would not improve the efficiency of night interception'. Joubert, an old adversary on this point, asked for it to be placed on record 'that, in his view, the delegation of filtering to Groups would improve day, as well as night, interception'. The meeting discussed every paragraph of Dowding's letter and the general opinion was that changes in the pattern of defence should follow quickly.[92]

While night bombers had ranged across Britain, and especially over London, during September, only four had been destroyed by fighters. Thousands of civilians were victims of their attacks, and widespread material damage had been caused. 'Our outlook at this time,' Churchill wrote later, 'was that London, except for its strong modern buildings, would be gradually and soon reduced to a rubble heap.'[93] The Prime Minister had to assess whether Dowding was the best leader for night defence. On 3 October Churchill's

Private Secretary wrote that he and Lindemann would like searching questions to be asked of 'the responsible officers' at AA and Fighter Commands. Dowding, he claimed, had the reputation 'of not being receptive to new ideas'.[94] This impression is reinforced by the answer given by Dowding that very day. When asked in a minute what responses should be made to the Air Ministry's request for filtering to be transferred to Groups, he wrote 'NONE, except what Air Ministry specifically orders. D.'[95]

The pressure from Trenchard and Salmond continued, the former claiming that 'I have done all I can in the last two or three days of rubbing in about Dowding.'[96] On the following day Salmond wrote directly to the Prime Minister to put 'the case for a change in the holder of the important position of Commander-in-Chief, Fighter Command'. It was a change that was, in his opinion, imperative and he claimed that other service members of the Air Council agreed. That night over 200 Londoners were casualties of bombing, a factor adding to the Prime Minister's worries.[97]

Churchill's first step was to form a Night Air Defence Committee and, as the problems were so crucial to the national interest, he became Chairman.[98] The first meeting was held on 7 October and Dowding alone appeared to differ from the 'new thinking' of Salmond, Douglas, Joubert, Newall, Watson-Watt, Lindemann and Sinclair. GL radar sets and AA personnel were discussed, together with Beaufighters and AI. The Prime Minister asked Dowding whether he agreed with the recommendations of the Salmond Report and he replied that he had, 'but in some cases unwillingly and under pressure'. When asked to write a report on matters of disagreement he objected in twelve detailed points to the decentralisation of filtering. His refusal to move on the issue was noted particularly by Churchill, who now saw for himself the gap between Dowding and his colleagues.[99]

The Prime Minister's respect for Dowding was still apparent and the C-in-C dined at Chequers on the 13th, reporting his opinion that the Blitz lacked purpose, failing to concentrate on a single target.[100] This assumption, however, was hardly supported on the night of the 15th when a massive raid was launched on London and bombs exploded in Whitehall.[101] Nonetheless, on the following day Churchill took two steps aiming to help Dowding. First, he added his name to those permitted to benefit from Enigma decrypts.[102] Secondly, Churchill read a set of proposals written for him by the Vice-Chief of the Naval Staff, which suggested a different approach to night defence. On the 17th he forwarded to Dowding a copy of the proposals which were 'purely private and for my information', adding that he would 'be glad to hear from you what you think can be done'.

At this point Dowding brought his own cause no benefit. It may have been that he was overburdened with problems of day fighter defence, for which he had to answer his critics at an Air Ministry conference that afternoon. His reply to the Prime Minister fired a series of broadsides at the Admiral's suggestions: on one paragraph, 'I will merely record my disagreement'; on another, 'This paragraph is a little confusing'. The Admiral's suggestion for using fighters was Micawber-like, 'ordering them to fly about and wait for something to turn up'.[103]

The conference held at the Air Ministry on 17 October to discuss day fighting tactics showed deep disagreements over the best methods of interception between, on the one side, Dowding and Park, and on the other, senior members of the Air Staff and Air Ministry.[104] Four days after that, at a second meeting of the Night Air Defence Committee, again with Churchill in the Chair, the Air Ministry ordered Dowding to release three day fighting squadrons of Hurricanes for night fighting. Once more, their differences were shown.[105] Dowding still watched trials of night fighting equipment. 'I am just off on a nocturnal expedition and will ring you when I get back,' he wrote to Beaverbrook on 29 October.[106]

Apart from Trenchard and Salmond, several politicians were unhappy over the responses of the defences to night bombing. The meeting of the Conservative Party's 1922 Committee on 16 October decided to hold a discussion 'in Secret Session on Air-Raid Defence generally, and especially of London',[107] while their vice-chairman wrote to Churchill on 6 November. His committee, he said, were concerned that some RAF personnel had lost confidence in the leader of Fighter Command.[108] Churchill was by now clearly aware of Dowding's intransigence and by early November the Commander-in-Chief's days were numbered.

NOTES

1. A. J. P. Taylor, *English History 1914–1945* (1965), 499.
2. Hough and Richards, 243.
3. *The Aeroplane*, 30 August 1940.
4. A. van Ishoven, *The Luftwaffe in the Battle of Britain* (1980), 89.
5. D. Irving, *Churchill's War* (1987), 406.

6. Koch, 137; see also Irving, *Rise and Fall*, 102, which says that 'one flight of *Luftwaffe* aircraft had strayed over London, killing nine civilians there.'

7. SKL KTB, Part D, Luftlage, 29 August 1940.

8. Hough and Richards, 182.

9. W. Shirer, *Berlin Diary* (1941), 486.

10. Bielenberg, 96.

11. A. Briggs, *The History of Broadcasting in the United Kingdom*, vol. iii (1970), 201.

12. T. Taylor, 342.

13. Irving, *Rise and Fall*, 102.

14. T. Taylor, 157.

15. See *ibid.*, 157–8 and Koch, 138–9.

16. General P. Deichmann, Chief Control Officer of the Karlsruhe Study, 1953–58, 'Reasons of *Luftwaffe* for Changing Over to Mass Attacks on London', Karlsruhe Papers.

17. AIR 16/330.

18. Deichmann, Karlsruhe Study.

19. See AHB Translation, vol. 9, VII/123; also see Price, *Hardest Day*, Appendix C.

20. Deichmann, Karlsruhe Study.

21. W. Murray, *Luftwaffe* (1985), 44 and 57–8.

22. Stahl, 58.

23. US Strategic Bombing Survey, Interviews, 20–24 April 1945.

24. See Gilbert, vi, 774.

25. N. Frankland, *The Bombing Offensive Against Germany* (1965), 55–6.

26. AHB Translation, vol. 2, no VII/26, 'The Course of the Air War against England', 8th *Abteilung*, 7 July 1944.

27. L. Hudson (trans.), *The Memoirs of Field-Marshal Kesselring* (1953), 75.

28. AIR 41/17, 63–4.

29. See T. Taylor, 44–6.

30. See Irving, *Rise and Fall*, 104.

31. US Strategic Bombing Survey, Interview, 7 July 1945.

32. O'Brien, 458.

33. *Daily Telegraph*, 9 September 1940.

34. *Daily Express*, 9 September 1940.

35. OKL Order, 9 September 1940.

36. W. Thompson, *I Was Churchill's Shadow* (1951), 58–9.

37. *Secret War*, 152–3.

38. Churchill memo, 'The Munitions Situation', 3 September 1940, CAB 66/11, WP(40) 352.

39. Ismay, Lord, *The Memoirs of General the Lord Ismay* (1960), 168.

40. Thompson, 63.

41. Sir Auckland (later Lord) Geddes was appointed Regional Commissioner in April 1939.

42. Roger, 167.

43. *Secret War*, 152.

44. For Churchill's sentiments, see Churchill, ii, Ch. XVII and XVIII.

45. J. G. Winant, *Letter From Grosvenor Square* (1947), 98.

46. Ismay, 184.

47. Gilbert, vi, 726.

48. *Ibid.*, 776–9.

49. *Daily Express*, 12 September 1940.

50. Sir John Wheeler-Bennett, *King George VI: His Life and Reign* (1958), 468.

51. C. Hibbert, *The Court at Windsor: A Domestic History* (1964), 288.

52. Wheeler-Bennett, 420.

53. R. Lacey, *Majesty* (1977), 141.

54. Editorial article, 'A Decisive Hour', *The Spectator*, 13 September 1940, reprinted in F. Glass and P. Smedley, *Articles of War* (1990), 126–9.

55. Pile, 145.

56. AIR 41/17, 55.

57. Pile, 144.

58. D.Wood and D. Dempster, *The Narrow Margin* (1961), Appendix VIII.

59. Notes from Captain A. Ellender, formerly RA.

60. Pile, 64–5.

61. *Ibid.*, 149.

62. *Ibid.*, 115.

63. *Ibid.*, 151.

64. *Daily Express*, 12 September 1940.

65. Nixon, 22.

66. Roger, 34.

67. Ellender notes.

68. Pile, 153.

69. *Ibid.*, 173.

70. AIR 41/17, 55.

71. AIR 8/863, 4559, para. 241.

72. *Ibid.*, para. 245.

73. See AIR 20/4298.

74. J. Leasor, *War At The Top* (1959), 115–16.

75. Beaverbrook Papers, BBK D/414, file 1, box 6, docs 68 and 69.

76. Salmond Papers, B2638, Salmond to Trenchard, 12 September 1940.

77. Beaverbrook Papers, BBK D/442, 14 September 1940.

78. AIR 2/7341, 14 September 1940.

79. AIR 16/387, 14 September 1940.

80. AIR 20/4298, 16 September 1940.

81. *Ibid.*, 17 September 1940.

82. AIR 2/7341, Encl. 6A, 17 September 1940.

83. AIR 20/4298, 18 September 1940.

84. Salmond Papers, B2638, 25 September 1940.

85. AIR 16/387 and AIR 2/7341, both 25 September 1940.

86. J. Colville, *The Fringes of Power: Downing Street Diaries 1939–1945* (1985), 245 and 248.

87. Salmond Papers, B2638, 25 September 1940.

88. *Ibid.*, 25 September 1940.
89. AIR 16/387.
90. AIR 2/7341, 27 September 1940.
91. *Ibid.*
92. AIR 20/4298, 1 October 1940.
93. Churchill, ii, 309.
94. See Gilbert, vi, 823.
95. AIR 16/387, 3 October 1940.
96. Salmond Papers, B2638, 4 October 1940.
97. *Ibid.*, 5 October 1940.
98. See Pile, 165–6.
99. CAB 81/22.
100. See Colville Diaries, 265.
101. See Wykeham, 170–2; also see AIR 41/17.
102. See Gilbert, vi, 849.
103. AIR 16/676, 16 and 17 October 1940.
104. See AIR 2/7281, 1 November 1940.
105. CAB 81/22, 21 October 1940.
106. Beaverbrook Papers, BBK D/28, 29 October 1940.
107. Minute Book of the Conservative Party 1922 Committee, 1938–43, Bodleian Library, Oxford.
108. PREM 4/3/6, 6 November 1940.

CHAPTER SIX

HARD TIMES:
SEPTEMBER AND OCTOBER

FURTHER SEPTEMBER RAIDS

After the initial nights of the London Blitz, the remainder of September was marked by an overall change in *Luftwaffe* strategy. There was a gradual decline in the number of daylight attacks, especially by large formations of bombers, and an increase in night bombing, chiefly over London. For the Germans, the two large daylight operations carried out on 15 September were salutary reminders that the RAF had far more fighters than *Luftwaffe* Intelligence had predicted and that the British defence was resolute. During daylight on that Sunday 56 German aircraft were destroyed and the hopes of aerial supremacy, a prerequisite for seaborne invasion, were denied to the *Luftwaffe*.

A few further determined efforts were made by bombers in daylight, particularly on the 18th, 25th, 27th and 30th. None succeeded. In the words of Galland, after the failure of the onslaught on the 27th, 'Goering was shattered. He simply could not explain how the increasingly painful losses came about . . . I answered him that in spite of the heavy losses we were inflicting on the enemy fighters, no decisive decrease in their numbers, or fighting efficiency was noticeable.'[1] Tactics had to change.

The new scheme in daylight was to employ fast Junkers 88s, or Bf 109s and Bf 110s adapted as fighter-bombers, escorted by other fighters, to fly at great height and speed and drop small loads. These sorties had no more than a nuisance value, far removed from Douhet's vision of crushing an enemy's resistance through the power of bombing, which had been the benchmark of air forces since pre-war days. In darkness, however, the scale of attack increased sharply right across Britain, but primarily over the capital. 'The exertion of sufficient pressure on morale together with a sufficient measure of destruction' would, in the belief of many German leaders, 'demonstrate the futility of further resistance and bring offers of submission'.[2] Therefore during September the *Luftwaffe* flew 6,135 night sorties over Britain. The style of raid differed greatly from the day battle. 'At two-minute intervals, usually taking off from midnight onwards,' stated one *Gruppe* history, 'all crews who had been trained for night operations . . . attacked Liverpool, Birmingham, Manchester and, from September 8th onwards, London.'[3]

Their success was accentuated by the comparative failure of the defences. By the end of the month Fighter Command comprised 52 day and eleven night squadrons, with a further $4^{1}/_{2}$ forming, yet in that period only four German planes were destroyed by aircraft.[4] Anti-aircraft guns grew in numbers, firepower and accuracy, but the *Luftwaffe* appeared able to bomb targets at will. The raids 'were all quite routine, like running a bus service', wrote a German pilot. 'The London flak defences put on a good show—at night the exploding shells gave the place the appearance of a bubbling pea soup', but few aircraft were hit. His own plane 'never collected so much as a shell fragment' and the few night fighters they saw never detected them.[5] This point was appreciated in Britain, and not only by the Air Staff. 'Air defence at night proved disappointing,' stated *The Aeroplane*,[6] while a writer in *The Spectator* remarked, 'The hard fact has to be faced that no effective protection against night bombing at present exists.' AA guns and balloons helped, but planes could not be brought down 'except by something better than a fortunate chance'.[7]

There was need for research, suggested a journalist a week later. 'Are we studying the possibilities of a special night interceptor ?'[8] Another writer, with uncanny vision, or access to secret information, believed that 'already there is some reason to suspect that the German bombers are being directed over England by radio beams focused from France, Belgium or Holland'. He then proposed that, as the Standard Telephone Company owned the rights to the Lorenz system, 'we have the apparatus to discover, counter and turn to our own use that stratagem of the enemy, if the suspicion should prove well founded'. In his view, the need for defence against the night bomber was greater than any 'since the Danes came marauding in England'.[9]

Raids were made countrywide, although in September London was the main destination. Air raid warnings sounded across the United Kingdom and, for example, on the night of 11 September, bombers flew over Hull, St Helens, Warrington, Cardiff, Plymouth and Marlow. Liverpool, which had suffered at the end of August, was raided again on 17, 18 and 19 September, as well as on the 21st, 23rd, 26th, 27th and 29th. In one Kentish rural district, just 25 miles from the capital, people lived under the Red Alert for 300 out of the 700 hours, day and night, of the month.[10] ▬

London's special burden was shown every night. At daybreak on the 8th, according to the Ministry of Home Security, the power stations at Battersea and West Ham were shut down and several railway lines in East London made unusable. Also, 'Victoria Station was blocked and only restricted services were operating from there, while all trains into London Bridge were stopped'.[11] On the night of the 11th the Red Alert lasted from 8.20 p.m. until 5.30 the following morning. In spite of AA Command's massive barrage, when 13,500 rounds were fired in the IAZ, there were hits on Woolwich Arsenal and the Surrey Commercial Docks. After the great day raids on the 15th, the *Luftwaffe* returned for seven hours at night, hitting, among other places, Shell Mex House and starting fires in Battersea, Brixton and Camberwell. The following night 170 bombers were over Britain, 130 of them raiding London, which was deluged by 200 tons of bombs. 'Flakes of glass were lying in heaps down Regent Street much as snow lay in heaps this last February,' wrote a civilian. 'The windows of the Galéries Lafayette, Hamley's, Jaeger [and] Dickens and Jones, are all blown out.'[12]

On the 17th, 350 tons landed on the capital, which was more than the total weight dropped across the whole of Britain during the First World War. The worst destruction was caused in the southern and eastern boroughs, for example, Southwark, Poplar and Bermondsey, as well as in the City. By then, Oxford Street also had suffered, with John Lewis's store burned out and others, like D. H. Evans's and Bourne and Hollingsworth's, suffering considerable damage.

On the 20th a magazine reported that St Paul's Cathedral 'was for a time menaced by a one-ton bomb which failed to explode', that an incendiary bomb had started a small fire in the House of Lords and that 'the Law Courts were also damaged'.[13] During the last ten days of the month the onslaught continued. A gas works was hit in Stepney on Friday the 20th and Holborn Viaduct and St Paul's stations were closed, while a UXB at Hendon blocked trains from St Pancras. At midnight on the 22nd, according to one observer, London looked like Dante's Inferno. Within 24 hours, shelters were hit in East Ham and at the Clarnico factory, Poplar.

Darkness on the 26th brought widespread attacks across Britain south of a line from Liverpool to the Humber, but, once again, London was a special target from 8 p.m. to 3.30 a.m. Bombs fell particularly in the north and west of the city, and the Houses of Parliament were hit. Railway lines were affected in the south, as well as LMS routes from St Pancras. More fires were started in

Dockland and the Royal Small Arms Factory at Enfield was bombed. Forty-eight hours later factories and hospitals were damaged, together with Selfridge's in Oxford Street. The month ended with 175 bombers raiding Central London.

By then an American correspondent had noted in her diary that 'Several hospitals have been hit more than once. St Thomas's, on the river opposite the Houses of Parliament (which presumably were the target) is a tragic sight, its wards ripped open by bombs.' She also said that big stores in the West End suffered heavily.[14] A report on the 27th mentioned that shops in Oxford Street had been struck, as well as the East End and south-east London. 'Much damage was done, as well, in the suburbs, particularly in the south-west.' Fire and destruction were spread widely across the capital—and this was still only the opening phase of the Night Blitz.[15]

According to German records, at least 250 tons of bombs fell on each of ten nights in September; in that time London received 10,000 high explosives, apart from thousands of incendiaries.[16] Such a large and prominent target so near the *Luftwaffe*'s bases in northern France and the Low Countries could barely be missed. Some aircraft flew by beam, but for most the navigational aids provided by moonlight, the Thames Estuary, burning fires or the lines of railway tracks, with the centre of their web in the heart of the capital, were sufficient guides. Few of the bombs dropped, either in aimed or in random attack, could fail to inflict damage. Altogether in the month 9,980 tons of bombs fell on England and Wales, mostly at night and mainly on the metropolis. This figure compared with 9,820 tons which had been dropped, generally in daylight, during the previous three months.[17]

What of the German side? In spite of previous heavy losses in daylight raids, many German airmen grew in confidence while bombing in the safety of darkness and still believed that their attacks could lead to victory. 'One cannot imagine that a town or a people could endure this continuous crushing burden for long,' wrote a pilot after bombing London on 9 September. He claimed that local French people around an aerodrome at Abbeville 'boundlessly admire our military achievements. In their eyes we are still heroes, and it is touching how well they look after us.' The response of Londoners to such news would have been unprintable.[18]

Generals Halder and von Brauchitsch, still hopeful of a successful invasion, signed 'The Secret Dossier on the Military Administration of England' on the 9th, planning with Teutonic thoroughness the governing of Occupied Britain.

All firearms and wireless transmitting apparatus were to be surrendered and German penal law would be introduced. The sixth point of a manifesto to the population of Britain warned all civilians 'against resistance to the German forces. The death penalty will be ruthlessly inflicted.' Another directive, chilling in implication, ordered that all men capable of bearing arms and aged between seventeen and forty-five should be interned, 'in so far as local conditions do not render exceptions necessary and should be removed to the Continent as speedily as possible'. The exchange rate was set at 9.6 Reichsmarks to the pound, a ratio which, although unattractive in 1940, would be more compelling to present-day Britons.[19]

To sustain the confidence of the German public, Eugen Hadamovsky, of the *Reichs* Propaganda Ministry, recorded a broadcast from a bomber attacking the capital on the night of the 11th. 'We can see an endless chain of lights, in fact it looks as if London were lit up by one gigantic system of illumination,' he reported. However, it was not 'an illumination ordered by Churchill. Unheard by us, without respite, the most ghastly scenes must be occurring down there, beneath our machines.'[20]

His master, Dr Josef Goebbels, a wizard of propaganda, insisted next day that 'great care must be taken to maintain our assertion that our attacks are aimed solely at military installations'. If civilian targets were hit in the process, 'that is due to the fact that many military installations are situated in the built-up areas of London'.[21] This juxtaposition was common to many urban sprawls which developed throughout the Industrial Revolution in Britain—and, as Goebbels would later discover, in Germany too.

Of the three German armed services closely following the *Luftwaffe*'s efforts during the transition from daylight attacks to night bombing, the most reluctant was the *Kriegsmarine*. Both Army and Navy were sceptical of each other's efforts and plans for conquering Britain, yet each appreciated the extent to which their schemes depended first on the success of the *Luftwaffe*. Thus a Naval Staff report on 10 September underlined the often disregarded role of Bomber Command in preventing 'Sealion'. 'British bombers, however, and the minelaying forces of the R.A.F. are still at full operational strength,' it stated, before adding that 'the operational state which the Naval Staff gave us as the most important requisite for the operation has not yet been achieved: clear air superiority in the Channel and the extinction of all possibility of enemy air action in the assembly areas'.[22] On the same day, the SKL War Diary reported that Hitler 'regards the great assault on London as possibly decisive for the war' and that 'the systematic and prolonged bombing of London can provide an enemy attitude which might make Sealion unnecessary'.[23]

The High Command of the Armed Forces (OKW) took a more optimistic view in a report dated 14 September. They had heard from their Military Attaché in Washington about the mood of the people of London. 'The will of that population is considerably affected by lack of sleep', a weakness which was 'having the greatest effect on morale'. He reported further that 24 docks were burned out and four gasometers destroyed. 'The railway stations Sherrycross [sic] and Waterloo and several underground stations are damaged.'[24]

However, the events of the daylight battles on the 15th changed the mood, because Fighter Command remained unbroken and the pressure of Bomber Command threatened the invasion fleet. Consequently, in Cosgrave's words, 'Hitler was now compelled to make his first retreat in his career as a war leader'—an event of great consequence.[25] The Naval War Diary acknowledged pessimistically on the 17th that 'the enemy air force is by no means defeated; on the contrary, it shows increasing activity'. After predicting poor weather, the note added a point which, in retrospect, was one of the war's most important: 'The Führer has therefore decided to postpone Operation Sealion indefinitely.'[26]

OCTOBER RAIDS

'Londoners have been encouraged during the past week,' an American journalist noted on 6 October, 'by the very definite slackening of night raids over the city.' The anti-aircraft barrage was fiercer, she wrote, 'but the bombing of central London was noticeably less'.[27] Such optimism, however, was transient as the Blitz continued throughout the month, with some particularly heavy raids, especially on the capital, causing further heavy casualties and great damage. Two examples from many illustrate this. In the case of people's homes, during the first six weeks of night attacks on London, there were 'about 16 thousand houses destroyed, or damaged beyond repair, about 60 thousand seriously damaged but repairable, and another 130 thousand slightly damaged'.[28] On the nation's railways, whose hub lay in the capital, the months of September and October brought the worst damage, with an average of forty incidents daily. To show the difficulties for workers there, in October 'marshalling yards in the London area experienced an "alert" almost every night, with the result that out of 382 hours of darkness, shunting had to be carried on in complete darkness for 299 hours'.[29]

One reason for the slackening intensity of the raids in the first week was poor weather, which, nonetheless, only reduced and did not prevent them. They still occurred on every night, with the beam system helping crews to their targets. The Official Narrative points out that on eleven nights during the month 'when the weather was indifferent and we could reasonably have expected a respite from the bombing, the German Air Force was carrying out raids on a large scale'. A powder factory at Waltham Abbey suffered a 'precise attack' on 6 October, when the weather was 'tempestuous'. This was 'a striking example of accurate bombing from a high level in circumstances which were unpropitious'.[30]

Concern over the *Luftwaffe*'s use of beams was considerable among those who knew of them. They were, wrote Churchill at the end of September, 'a deadly danger, and one of the first magnitude'.[31] When Dowding wrote a report on enemy activity throughout October, he called the navigational aids 'so effective that he will be able to bomb this country with sufficient accuracy for his purposes without even emerging from clouds'. The Germans, he stated, could fly in bad weather, when RAF fighters were grounded, and that was 'a most depressing fact'.[32] The weakness of the defences was shown, for example, on the night of 2 October, when night fighters flew 33 sorties but made no interceptions.

In spite of the comparative easing of night bombing, 170 bombers flew over the metropolis on the 4th, dropping parachute mines at Woolwich and Enfield and damaging Willesden Power Station. The next night a bomb struck the Tower of London, while 48 hours later, apart from hitting a cinema and a school in Liverpool, the *Luftwaffe* landed a bomb on No 145 Piccadilly, the former home of the Royal Family.

Speaking in Berlin on 7 October, Goering advanced a five-point plan for war against Britain. Two of those points related to London, which was to be progressively and completely annihilated, while the civilian population was to be demoralized. To these ends, the present air operations were 'merely an initial phase'.[33] Stahl, who bombed London that night from his Junkers 88, wrote that *Luftwaffe* tactics had changed. There were to be larger formations at night 'in exactly the same manner as the British have already tried experimentally over Germany. There is even some talk of retaliation.'[34]

Next day, Churchill told the Commons of casualties from bombing. 'We expected to sustain losses which might amount to three thousand killed in a single night and twelve thousand wounded night after night.' Hospital arrangements had been made for a quarter of a million casualties 'as a first provision'. In reality, there had been altogether about 8,500 killed and 13,000 wounded. Although the Prime Minister pointed out optimistically that these figures were lower than expected, the fact remained that civilians were suffering heavily in total war. A further burden was the destruction of homes, especially 'the number of small houses inhabited by working folk'. London, Liverpool, Birmingham and Manchester might have more to suffer, but he promised that they would be rebuilt.[35]

That night was windy and rough, yet bombers still got through and only one was shot down. Over London there was a heavy AA barrage, but nearly 300 fires were started, including one conflagration at Chiswick and a major fire at Hay's Wharf. St Clement Danes church was struck. On the 9th at 6 p.m. a bomb penetrated the roof of St Paul's Cathedral, leaving a hole 25 feet by 12 feet, then destroying the High Altar. The Royal Courts of Justice were also damaged and the Strand was blocked. German claims referred publicly to legitimate targets being struck. 'Very heavy damage was caused in the docks in the bend of the Thames,' announced an OKW bulletin on the following day. Bombers had also destroyed railway installations in central London, it announced and 'numerous extensive conflagrations were observed'.[36]

Goering was now intent on increasing the pressure of bombing on the capital. He looked ahead several days to the middle of the month when there would be a full moon and ordered heavy raids to be made then. People in Britain came to recognise their added danger at the time from what became known as 'a bombers' moon'. And yet on the 12th they received an unknown benefit. 'The *Führer* has decided that from now on until the spring,' announced General Keitel in circulating Hitler's decision, 'preparations for Sealion shall be continued solely for the purpose of maintaining political and military pressure on England.' The threat of invasion was finally lifted from the additional burden of bombing.[37]

The following week, with a waxing moon, witnessed some of the heaviest raids of the Blitz, bringing massive damage and many casualties. Dowding and the new CAS, Air Marshal Sir Charles Portal, dined with Churchill on the 13th and discussed the bombing. Dowding claimed that the *Luftwaffe* had been 'almost exclusively lacking in purpose' by failing to concentrate on detailed objectives. They also speculated on why there had not yet been a mass night raid on one small part of London, 'with incendiaries and then high explosive'.[38] By then bombs had hit both the War Office and the National Gallery and, while their discussions were in progress, night fighters flew 22 sorties, all unsuccessful. A tragedy also occurred that night at Stoke Newington, where 154 people died in a basement shelter below a block of flats which collapsed.

On the 14th, in clear moonlight, there was widespread further damage and the Carlton Club was hit. Altogether, some 200 Londoners were killed and 2,000 injured in varying degrees. Bombs also landed on St James's Church in Piccadilly and on the Treasury building, opposite Downing Street.

The heaviest raid came on the next night. 'The night was so light', wrote Stahl in his diary, 'that from our altitude of only 3,500 metres we could see every detail on the ground.' He noted that searchlights and AA guns were used in great numbers—but could not stop a devastating attack.[39] Pile reported that his batteries fired 8,326 rounds, but only two bombers were destroyed and two others damaged. He believed that 235 aircraft had taken part, but later research shows that the Germans had employed about 380 planes, the main role being played by *Luftflotte III* in 'a more intense raid than ever before'.[40]

The first plots appeared on British screens by 8 p.m. and raids continued against the capital until 4.45 next morning, made by aircraft flying from France and the Low Countries. The latter came in through the areas of Harwich and the Thames Estuary while the former crossed the south coast of Kent and Sussex. Bombs were dropped mainly from 15,000 feet—although some of the later aircraft flew 3,000 feet higher—and soon their effect was felt below. Railways were hit particularly badly, with rolling stock derailed and five main line stations, including St Pancras and Victoria, being cut off. Trains were wrecked at Willesden and Waterloo. The Underground also was blocked at five points, one where the Fleet sewer was hit and its contents spilled into a tunnel on the Metropolitan Railway. Destruction ranged across London as over 415 tonnes of high explosives fell, together with eleven tonnes of incendiaries, which started almost 900 fires. Morley College and Stationers' Hall received hits, Oxford Street and London Bridge were blocked and homes, hospitals, shelters and power stations were struck. With the coming of morning, as the bombers droned back to their bases, fires still burned and 213 civilians were dead, while 915 had been injured.

Subsidiary raids were made elsewhere by the *Luftwaffe*, the heaviest on Birmingham, which was bombed by 22 aircraft. Almost 200 casualties were caused as houses and factories were hit in the great industrial city by the crews of *KGr.100*, by now very skilled in employing beams to arrive over their targets.

The Blitz on the capital continued nightly, without break, for the rest of the month and was accompanied by lesser, though heavy, attacks on other cities, especially Birmingham. Poor weather did not prevent Heinkel 111s, Dornier 17s and Junkers 88s flying over London, although on some nights the scale of the raids was reduced. Nevertheless, on the 19th 174 civilians were killed, and almost 400 casualties were suffered on the following night. On the 25th a novelty appeared in the form of a few aircraft of the Italian Air Force, which took part in a raid on Harwich.

A disturbing feature of the raids was the continued inability of the defences to hold off the rain of bombs. German pilots flew with a confidence bordering on disdain against guns and fighters which still could not locate them with accuracy. By then, many *Luftwaffe* aircrews were highly experienced and competent in night bombing, whether by beams or other means of navigation. On 18 October Goering sent a message to his men. 'In the past few days and nights you have caused the British world enemy disastrous losses by your uninterrupted destructive blows,' he claimed. The *Reichsmarschall* added that their 'indefatigable, courageous attacks on the heart of the British Empire, the City of London, with its eight and a half million inhabitants, have reduced British plutocracy to fear and terror'.[41]

Although his claims of 'fear and terror' were exaggerated, the defences were faced with problems of awesome proportions. On the night of 16 October five bombers were brought down, but there were few further successes. Dowding reported four days later that the newly introduced Beaufighters were having trouble with their airborne interception radar and with their performance. For example, on the 19th the four Beaufighters available to No 219 Squadron were all found to be unserviceable by the evening. Such factors help to explain the readiness of the Air Staff to order the use of Hurricane day fighters for night defence, in spite of several unsatisfactory features. In the opinion of Douglas, the Deputy Chief of the Air Staff, 'So strongly had Dowding come to believe in his radar-equipped fighters that he had become a little blinded, I felt, to the more simple hit or miss, trial and error, use of single-engined fighters.'[42] Such thoughts also occurred to some pilots of Fighter Command. 'We were after all fighters whose duty it was to defend Britain by night as well as by day,' wrote a member of a Hurricane squadron. 'The day battle had been won, but London was still being cruelly and ceaselessly assaulted night after night. Nor were provincial cities spared.' The challenge had to be taken up, or the capital 'would be reduced to a rubble heap'. Some of those men who had fought so bravely and successfully during the day battle had almost a sense of guilt at being unable to tackle the enemy in darkness.[43]

During October 6,334 civilians were killed and 8,695 seriously injured, and it seemed that the burden stretched far ahead. 'The solution of a defence against the night bomber has still not arrived,' reported a writer. 'Development must be long, but we can hope that the several promising lines of research will result in greatly improved defence by next Winter.'[44] By then, people on both sides of the Channel were asking themselves how and when the campaign of night bombing would end.

The United Kingdom's tenacity, determination and courage were increasingly appreciated on the further side of the Atlantic. Churchill foresaw that in the long run Britain could never hope to win the war alone. Only the power of the USA offered salvation, first through military aid, then through intervention. The Prime Minister pinned great faith in gaining support from his mother's homeland. Even before the war he examined the effects that aerial bombing in Europe might have on the distant Americans. 'Of these grievous events, the people of the United States may soon perhaps be spectators,' he wrote in June 1939. Then they might be 'infuriated by a revolting exhibition. In that case we might see the spectators leaving their comfortable seats and hastening to the work of rescue and of retribution.'[45]

As wartime bombing became a reality in London's skies, a number of American correspondents sent back reports to the United States. These were published and broadcast widely, and they 'aroused widespread admiration on the other side of the Atlantic'.[46] Ed Murrow, of CBS Radio News, told his audience on 10 September that the British people were angry. The Germans hoped that Londoners would demand a new government which would seek peace, but 'it's more probable that they'll rise up and murder a few German pilots who come down by parachute'. Not once, he said, 'have I heard man, woman or child suggest that Britain should throw in her hand'.[47] Helen Kirkpatrick sent reports back to the *Chicago Daily News* and Mollie Panter-Downes wrote for the *New Yorker*. To these were added the opinions of other reporters and photographers who showed the staunch resistance of the British. 'The gent has taken off his clothes and put on his birthday suit,' Churchill observed jauntily to Roosevelt in a telegram on 4 October, sensing the receding fear of immediate invasion. 'But the water is getting colder and there is an autumn nip in the air.' In spite of the Blitz, matters generally appeared to be improving.[48]

Later in the year, especially after Roosevelt's re-election in early November, help from the United States increased. And yet some Americans had reservations. For example, Charles Lindbergh campaigned assiduously on behalf of the Isolationists. Worse still for Britain, the US Ambassador in London, Joseph Kennedy, was convinced that the Germans would win and that his own nation should not be drawn into the conflict. The British 'are in a bad way', he wrote to Roosevelt on 27 September. 'I cannot impress on you strongly enough my complete lack of confidence in the entire conduct of this war.' He believed that 'to enter this war imagining for a minute that the English have anything to offer in the line of leadership or productive capacity in industry that could be of the slightest value to us would be a complete misapprehension'.[49] Fortunately for Britain, these opinions were outweighed by those of Americans who recognised what Britain's stand against dark forces represented for the free world.

The Blitz evinced great concern from British politicians when devastating attacks were made on ordinary people to whom they were answerable. In turn, this concentrated attention on the role of the RAF, both in attempting to thwart the raids and in their own policy of bombing. Not only was Churchill determined to have the best night defence possible, but he was also anxious to strike back at the enemy. In that way, the power of Bomber Command's theory of the offensive could be put into practice and the desire of most British people for retribution could be met.

In spite of the Bomber Lobby's belief in Trenchard's dedication to striking at the enemy, when Churchill asked for an aerial offensive 'to be spread as widely as possible over the cities and small towns in Germany within reach', the Vice-Chief of the Air Staff demurred. He claimed that Bomber Command's strikes were 'planned and relentless', whereas the *Luftwaffe*'s bombing was 'sporadic and mainly harassing'.[50] Churchill replied on 6 September that, while he agreed with the main policy, he believed that 'on two or three nights in a month a number of minor, unexpected, widespread' raids should be launched against 'the smaller German centres'. A catalyst in the discussion arrived when the Germans started to use parachute mines. Then the Prime Minister asked Sinclair 'to let me have your proposals forthwith for effective retaliation upon Germany'. He claimed that squadrons wished to drop mines or large bombs on the enemy, 'but that the Air Ministry are refusing permission'. Three days later, in a note for the COS Committee, Churchill wrote that his inclination 'is to say that we will drop a heavy parachute mine on German cities for every one he drops on ours'.[51]

On 19 September the War Cabinet asked for parachute mines to be dropped on Berlin, but still the Air Staff hesitated because the mine was an inaccurate weapon. If the German capital had to be raided, they suggested that specific targets, for example gas works and power stations, should be aimed for. However, Portal, then C-in-C Bomber Command, had already requested of his somewhat sceptical colleagues on 11 September that twenty German towns should be warned by wireless that one of them would be bombed in retaliation for any indiscriminate *Luftwaffe* attack on a British town. It was not until 23 September that a heavy raid was mounted against Berlin, with a force of 119 bombers.[52]

Once again, in raiding distant German targets, the RAF were at a disadvantage compared with the *Luftwaffe*. Geographical distance and difficulties of navigation made flights both long and hazardous, while accuracy of attack could not be guaranteed. This gave the German propaganda machine opportunities of launching accusations against Bomber Command. Disregarding the extent of casualties and damage caused in Britain by indiscriminate bombing, on 20 September a German broadcast referred to an RAF raid on the previous day during which nine people had been killed at a children's hospital. 'Murder upon murder is the password of the British warmongers. Churchill is letting loose his airmen against the civilian population of Germany,' claimed the speaker. The British had attacked 'places marked with the Red Cross as sanctuaries of Christian love'. There should be 'retribution and harsh retaliation', which was 'only in its initial stage'.[53]

In reality the RAF at that point was still attempting to strike at specific targets, for example oil depots, rather than follow the *Luftwaffe*'s practice over London of unloading bombs randomly across a wide urban mass. The RAF's first 'area' raid of the war, with the centre of a town as its target, was not unleashed until 16 December 1940. Mannheim was then attacked after Coventry had been devastated a month earlier.[54]

FINDING THE ENEMY

What might be termed 'the electronic war' continued with great intensity during September and October. On the British side, however, although advances were made, there was no breakthrough enabling the defences to achieve immediate success. Scientific theories and technological devices had to be painstakingly created and examined, tested and amended. Only then could new systems and equipment be offered to the fighting services. They, in turn, would have to submit them to conditions of war. And yet there was progress in two areas of operation.

The first lay in the defensive field of countering German beams, where the *Luftwaffe* had the advantage of being able to choose targets at will. They could still, by employing either *Knickebein* or *X-Gerät*, lead bombers with great accuracy across the darkened skies of Britain. No 80 Wing, under Wing Commander Addison, used radio countermeasures against *Knickebein*, which were code-named 'Headache' by the RAF. To meet it, 'Aspirin', devised by Dr Cockburn and his team at the TRE, Swanage, was introduced early in September, to send confusing Morse dashes along German beam frequencies. By early October there were fifteen 'Aspirin' sites and a variety of 'Meacons' in operation.

At the same time, No 80 Wing began to use 'Bromide' jammers to interfere with *X-Gerät* signals, which were code-named 'Rivers', later known as 'Ruffians'. 'I had recommended on 11th September that similar counter-measures to those which we were employing against *Knickebein* should be developed against the X-beams,' wrote Jones, adding that 'Robert Cockburn had the development in hand.' He believed, however, that the device 'did not seem to have much effect on *KGr. 100*, which continued to bomb more or less as it pleased'.[55] According to Price, the jammer had been 'hastily conceived' and radiated signals 'at the 1,150 cycles note used by *Knickebein* instead of the 2,000 cycles actually used by the *X-Geraet*'. There was still a great deal to be done.[56]

The second field of research and development concerned the more active defence offered by night fighters. This was the story of a search to bring defending aircraft with some certainty close to attackers in order to shoot them down…the antidote in which Dowding had placed his faith. Progress was made over the two months to overcome the difficulties of unreliable equipment, lack of training for crews, and fighters which were inadequate both in numbers and performance.

In July 1940 the RAF had asked the TRE to provide twelve Ground Controlled Interception (GCI) stations, half of them by Christmas. Their range was about 50 miles and each had a CHL aerial transmitting to a receiver screen (skiatron) a spot of light. This indicated the enemy aircraft and could estimate its distance from the Controller's station.

September and October were months of trial and error for Fighter Command. When Hurricanes, Spitfires and Defiants were put up without the benefit of the latest RDF equipment, few contacts were made with incoming bombers. Those who flew the more specialised Blenheim night fighter, with its AI Mk III, experienced annoyance when detection apparatus failed or because the aircraft lacked the speed and firepower to catch and destroy the enemy. 'With autumn and winter, the night raids became more intensive,' wrote one navigator, 'and we realised that it was up to us to stem the tide.' The frustration, he said, led to many suggested schemes, and his squadron was 'beset with such things as airborne searchlights, showers of magnesium flares, air-sown minefields dangling on parachutes and other menaces'.[57]

The change came with the introduction of the new Beaufighter, with its 'higher powered transmitter giving greater range and a much improved receiver which made it possible to track targets to a minimum range of 140 yards'.[58] When the first of these machines arrived at No 604 Squadron at Middle Wallop at the end of September, aircrews were impressed. 'There she stood, sturdy, powerful, fearsome,' wrote one airman, admiring the heavy armament. 'Four, solid great cannon, firmly set in place just below floor level! Their massive breeches gleamed with an evil beauty.'[59]

Because of a variety of early troubles, however, it was not until the second half of November that the Beaufighters of his squadron had success. By then, the *Luftwaffe* had flown thousands of sorties over Britain at night, virtually unopposed. The gravity of the situation was expressed by Churchill to the War Cabinet Defence Committee on 31 October. 'Our power of survival depends on the maintenance of life in this island,' he declared, adding that this called for 'continued superiority in air defence and the successful countering of night bombing. That we must keep our sea lanes open goes without saying.' The responsibility of the air defence forces was formidable.[60]

THE CIVILIAN RESPONSE

In view of the vast amount of prediction and preparation concerning night bombing, especially with regard to the effects on civilians and their defence services, it is rewarding to explore what happened at ground level. In general terms, citizens realised that the anticipated war for which they had braced themselves a year earlier had arrived at last. Action of the most violent kind had been brought to their doorsteps. They were now in the front line of fighting just as closely as any soldier, sailor or airman facing the enemy. Being unequipped with weapons, however, they had to rely on courage and determination alone.

In London during September a common feature was the fatigue brought on by lack of sleep. 'For Londoners there are no longer such things as good nights,' wrote a correspondent on 14 September. 'There are only bad nights, worse nights and better nights. Hardly anyone has slept at all in the past week.'[61] A female warden in Finsbury remembered that the first fortnight of the Blitz was exhausting. 'Every night and all night there were raids. On the evening of the 11th the "red" came up at 8.5 p.m. and the final "white" at 9.15 the next morning.' At the end of the fortnight, in her estimate, 'I had done 78 hours of raid duty in the first week and 102 in the second'.[62]

People in bombed areas found themselves close to death and injury, through those they knew and loved. Disaster could strike quickly and unexpectedly. The photographer George Roger spent an evening with a girl who was 'petite, just five feet two inches of radiant happiness and pretty as a picture'. After walking her home, he telephoned about midnight. 'There was no reply. The line was dead. Anxiously I walked the mile to her house. It was no longer there.' He recollected that a few hours earlier they had been dancing. 'I could still smell the scent of her hair.'[63]

The response of most citizens was magnificent. The savagery of the bombing, reckoned one writer, 'is matched, and defeated, by the heroism it evokes, the heroism of the common men and women who know from the first moment the sirens sound at night that they are potential victims'. He went on to praise those who were serving as 'fire-fighters, wardens, shelter wardens, St John and Red Cross staffs and all the rest'.[64]

A surprising feature was that casualties were not as great as the Air Ministry's gloomy pre-war estimates. A year before the war, the Ministry of Health believed that between one and 2.8 million hospital beds would be needed for air raid casualties, according to their length of stay. The Home Office predicted that so many coffins and graves would be required that there would be mass burials and the burning of bodies in lime. Failing that, 'Twenty million square feet of seasoned coffin timber would be needed each month at a cost of approximately £300,000.'[65]

Although such predictions were vastly exaggerated, casualties were heavy at the start. For example, on the night of 9 September 370 people were killed and 1,400 injured. Forty-eight hours later, 235 died and 1,000 were injured. This threw a great burden on to the medical branch of the civilian services and also on to doctors, nurses and hospitals. During September there were 9,472 casualty admissions to hospitals, especially from the thickly populated areas, whereas earlier, in May, the number of civilian air raid casualties in hospitals was under 100. Those hurt and detained during all of the mainly daylight raids of June, July and August totalled only 1,858.

The general injuries, too, brought a new dimension to staff who had worked in hospitals in peacetime. There were far more cases of crushing and broken bones, as well as many with cuts caused by flying glass. As hospital buildings situated in the middle of urban areas themselves received bomb hits, staff worked under great difficulties. Some patients were soon evacuated from London to provincial hospitals, but services still had to be provided for those who stayed behind, usually through the Emergency Hospitals.

At the site of bombing, a First Aid Party would soon appear as people were drawn from the rubble by the rescue services. Each party consisted of four men and a driver, all of whom had often had experience in, for example, the Red Cross or St John's Ambulance organisations. On reaching the scene, they had to make the first decision on treatment—whether to take the casualties to a First Aid Post, treat them on the spot or send them to hospital. Later, an 'Incident Doctor' was dispatched to accompany these helpers.[66]

Ambulance drivers were women volunteers who needed a special blend of bravery and skill to negotiate roads during night raids. Often 'craters, fires, trailing wires, boulders or hoses might be in her path'.[67] They drove with an attendant, then had to carry the badly injured—or corpses—to hospital. At a First Aid Post were a doctor, a trained nurse and several auxiliaries, who were usually responsible for an area containing about 15,000 people. 'They took what the ambulances brought them'[68] and at the height of the Blitz, from September to November, saved thousands of lives through their prompt care. Nor should it be forgotten that their work was done without one great medical benefit which did not arrive until later in the war—penicillin.

No one in the ARP services worked harder or closer to danger than the firemen, both regulars and auxiliaries. During the first 22 nights of the Blitz they were called out to deal with about 10,000 fires in London alone. On each of three nights—7, 18 and 24 September—they had to tackle more than 1,000 blazes. This was a scale of raiding exceeding anything they had experienced. The incendiary bomb was small, but if allowed to take hold in buildings it could cause far more damage than high explosives. Some of the greatest trouble came from uninhabited business premises or warehouses, where there were no fire-watchers to move in quickly and deal with the small, deadly bombs. Even the Fire Watchers Order of September 1940 was inadequate in that respect because it applied only to premises where more than 30 people worked or to warehouses of more than 50,000 square feet.[69]

'Most of us had the wind up to start with,' admitted one fireman. 'It was all new but we were all unwilling to show fear, however much we might feel it. You looked around and saw the rest doing their job.'[70] They learned quickly and, although faced with fires of massive proportions, rapidly evolved methods of tackling blazes, cooperating with firemen drafted in from other areas and also working with the other rescue services. The new experience was, of course, vastly different from any training exercise. 'To begin with, they got wetter than they had ever thought a man could be!' and were soaked to the skin in five minutes. Wet and frozen, some men then worked for fifteen arduous hours without respite. Their bravery was second to none.[71]

The workers closest to the general population were the air raid wardens; they were, in many respects, the hub of the civil defence organisation. Their tasks, as laid down before the war, included being guides and helpers, allaying panic, helping the homeless, directing people to shelters and reporting such incidents as the fall of bombs or the location of fires. 'It was not until after the raids had started that I became aware of the multitudinous things a warden needed to know,' one admitted later. The tasks included remembering the names of residents in each house and which shelter they went to, knowing the whereabouts of danger points, hydrants and cul-de-sacs, and learning the telephone numbers of rest centres and police stations.[72]

Usually there were six wardens at a post, responsible for about 500 people. All incidents were reported by telephone to the local control centre, which then organised action. In this way, wardens were both the eyes and the ears of ground defence. When rescue parties arrived, they had to be directed to the exact site of an incident. Wardens also had to offer confidence to those in their care. 'He must infect them and every citizen on the ground with his own steadiness,' both before and after action. This impression of the warden setting an example came through strongly, although many had, before the Blitz, been treated 'with anything from cool indifference or mild amusement to active suspicion as a Nosey Parker'.[73]

About one-sixth of the wardens were women, who served with a dedication and ability that drew general respect. One, recorded as 'Mrs A.', was a district warden in charge of seven posts, which controlled 250 wardens catering for 25,000 people. Although in 1939 there were some reservations over a woman having such authority, her example soon triumphed. She claimed not to be brave. 'When the warning goes or a bomb falls, my inside turns over and I have to get a grip of myself'—an emotion felt by most wardens.[74] Another woman, who had found training to be 'waiting broken by antics' and 'tedious', welcomed the opportunities offered under fire. 'We are conscious, as never before in our lives, of fulfilling a definite, direct and essential function.' She was part of a front-line service 'in action every night in the defence of London' and would not exchange her job for any other.[75]

Naturally, under the stress of bombing there were some faults and failures. 'In an actual raid, when it was generally pitch dark, when there were incidents in all directions, when the telephones broke down,' wrote a warden, there was 'frequently a waste of both personnel and time'. Nevertheless, few civilian defence workers failed to match up to their duties when the time came.[76] Mistakes more often resulted from weaknesses of preparation and organisation. In some London boroughs, for example, after extremely heavy bombing there were few plans for evacuating, feeding and rehousing the homeless. Shelter accommodation was not properly organised. According to one wartime writer, 'It was more than bricks and mortar that collapsed in West Ham on the seventh and eighth of September 1940, it was a local order of society which was found hopelessly wanting.' This was, she believed, 'as weak and badly constructed as the single-brick walls which fell down at the blast'.[77] In Titmuss's opinion, the confusion was sometimes followed by 'a temporary loss of balance among elected representatives and officials and by temporary paralysis of the executive machinery', which he put down to 'ignorance and inexperience'. The crucial factor is that it was, considering the length of the Blitz, no more than temporary.[78]

Much discontent was centred on public air raid shelters. Criticisms did not apply to the Andersons, which had been issued to householders and stood up well. If properly sited and covered, they 'were usually undamaged by 50kg bombs falling 6 feet away or 250kg bombs falling 20 feet away', and their occupants then had no greater injuries than shock.[79] Andersons saved thousands of lives. However, public shelters at first brought some trouble. In the summer of 1940 it was anticipated that these would be occupied for a short period only, but with the advent of all-night raids people started to use them as dormitories. The flimsy surface shelters and those in reinforced basements often had little light or ventilation, and no sanitation. Some flooded or leaked. In these constructions, hundreds at first took cover and, although usually safe from the threat of bombs, they were soon faced by health hazards. The authorities had been so preoccupied with the primary task of making shelterers safe that they had paid little attention to the amenities.[80] Nonetheless, it would be wrong to think of every shelter in these terms, and a good many of them, especially through the initiative of their occupants and wardens, were clean, dry and safe.

The Government took rapid steps to investigate conditions. Within a few days a committee was established under Lord Horder, the Chief Medical Officer of the Ministry of Health. He, together with a Chief Engineer, a Chief Warden and a representative of the WVS, inspected shelters across London and produced a constructive report by the end of September.[81] Elsewhere, Government ministers and Members of Parliament went to see for themselves.[82] They, with local authority officials and representatives of voluntary societies, visited shelters night after night, as well as Tube stations, rest centres, warehouses and railway arches, where people were taking cover. In the metropolis, special commissioners were appointed to investigate the problems of bomb damage, the clearance of debris, public utilities, shelters and homeless people. It would be remiss and inaccurate, while acknowledging the deficiencies, to overlook the considerable efforts made to bring relief and reorganisation. Extreme cases, of course, make news and receive publicity. The most notable occurred on 15 September when about 100 people, led by a few communists from the East End, which had taken the bulk of the bombing thus far, waited by the Savoy Hotel. When the siren sounded they pressed inside and made for the hotel's underground shelter, where they were allowed, albeit unwillingly, to enter. Several American journalists who were present reported the incident, which was received with some satisfaction in Germany.[83]

Wide use was made of Tube stations as shelters, offering as they did considerable protection from bombs. Since pre-war days the authorities had not wanted people to adopt a 'shelter mentality', which would achieve the enemy's aims by causing absence from work and the adoption of a defensive frame of mind. Nonetheless, Churchill, who had been advised that the use of Tubes as shelters was undesirable, took up the matter on 21 September. In a memo he announced his approval of using 'not only the stations but the railway lines' and asked how many people could be accommodated underground. He required 'a short report on one sheet of paper' and enquired if it were true that three-quarters of a million people could be taken in the Aldwych section alone.[84] On the same day the *Daily Mail* reported that the Aldwych to Holborn Tube line 'may shortly be converted into the city's largest air raid shelter'. It referred to the previous night 'as Tube stations were packed with multitudes seeking safety from the raids'.[85]

By then the authorities were powerless to stop the thousands who flocked nightly to the Tube, and to surface and basement shelters, searching for safety. It was estimated that the peak total of shelterers was reached about the end of September, when between 120,000 and 160,000 went to Tube stations every night, apart from those in other public shelters. However, considering the size of London's population, the figures show that many thousands went to other places, or stayed put. A. J. P. Taylor noted that 'six Londoners out of ten slept at home even during the worst days of the Blitz'.[86] The census, taken in November 1940 among the 40 per cent of the population who used shelters, showed that 4 per cent slept in Tube stations and 9 per cent in public shelters, while 27 per cent used their own domestic protection, usually an Anderson.[87]

Some of the greatest difficulties for local authorities occurred days, or even weeks, after bombing. Rest centres had been set up, but with the provision for people to stay only a few hours. Therefore the food offered was mainly bread and tea, while there were few amenities and poor sanitation. Small and inadequate sums of money were offered to those who had lost furniture, clothes or even their complete homes. Stocks of clothing soon ran out. Those who were unable, or unwilling, to move away to relatives or friends were in great distress. After that, those from bombed homes had to be resettled, but few preparations had been made. Some families existed in limbo for several weeks. By the end of September over 25,000 people were in rest centres in the London region and 14,000 of them were in the 'desperately overcrowded centres run by the London County Council'.[88] On 17 October the LCC's centres contained 19,000 homeless, 40 per cent of whom had been in a centre for more than ten days. After six weeks of the Blitz only 7,000 people in the London region had been rehoused by the authorities, and yet on 24 October nearly 25,000 requisitioned properties were held for the homeless and more than 12,000 billets were available outside the County of London.[89] Failures of bureaucracy, combined with a general unwillingness to move from a home area, were at least partly responsible for a sorry state of affairs.

Most rest centres were set up in schools and many were of a low standard. Washing facilities were poor, and at one, in Stepney, almost 300 people at night had to use ten pails and coal scuttles as lavatories, which were not emptied until 8 a.m. the following morning. A report on rest centres, written in 1943, remarked on their early days. 'Dim figures in dejected heaps on unwashed floors in total darkness' were fed 'eternal corned beef sandwiches and tea...the London County Council panacea for hunger, shock, loss, misery and illness'.[90]

Who relieved the difficulties from which some local authorities were suffering, at least partly, through their own neglect? In the main, the voluntary services answered the need. 'Excellent unsentimental work is being done in the rest centres of the hard-hit districts by women's voluntary services,' reported an American correspondent at the end of September.[91] There were, at the start of 1940, over half a million unpaid workers in the WVS. 'We have all types and ages,' said Lady Reading, their founder. 'One fine thing is the way young women have sacrificed leisure or money to work for us.'[92] The work was dedicated, as was shown in a Mass Observation report. This spoke of their helping with transport, operating mobile canteens for ARP workers and firemen and evacuating the homeless. In Stepney, at 1 p.m. in the afternoon of Saturday 21 September, municipal officials went home; the WVS then took over and evacuated 200 people.[93] The WVS was not alone in this work. Among others were 'the Charity Organisation Society, the Society of Friends, the Settlement workers [and] the London Council of Social Service', who all provided help, 'while the official machine was beginning to take effective action'. Occasionally, individuals offered aid on their own initiative, like a lady beetroot seller from Islington who ran a rest centre for 103 people.[94]

An important change to the organisation of civilian defence took place at the end of September. Chamberlain's final illness necessitated alterations in the Government and Herbert Morrison, who had been Minister of Supply, was given a dual role. He now became both Home Secretary and Minister of Home Security, positions which he continued to hold for the remainder of the war. These involved him closely with the Blitz and its effects on the general population. As a former leader of the London County Council and, in Churchill's words, 'in many ways the principal figure in its affairs', he was 'efficient and vigorous'.[95] Morrison understood the problems of the services needed in large urban areas under the stress of bombing.

Finally, the searing experiences of the Night Blitz settled one question which had exercised many minds since the 1920s. Would there be a collapse of public morale when heavy bombing started? Would troops have to be called out to restore order? Would doctors be overwhelmed by an increase in cases of mental disorder? Titmuss was sceptical over the origin of the issue. After examining thousands of government papers from the 1920s and 1930s, he believed that 'it is difficult to find even a hint that this fear of a collapse in morale

Above: With Tower Bridge standing defiantly in the foreground, London's Docklands are seen burning on 7 September 1940. (IWM HU.653)

Right: The Elephant & Castle Underground station in use as a bomb shelter on 11 November 1940. (IWM HU.672)

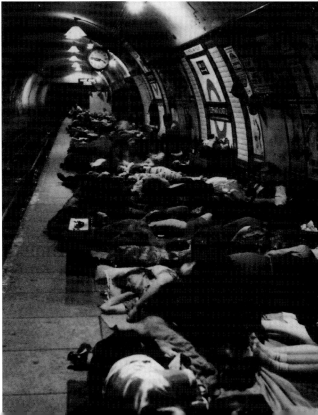

Above: The King and Queen, accompanied by Winston Churchill, survey bomb damage at Buckingham Palace. (IWM AP.89026)

Left: Nurses and babies take part in gas drill. (IWM D.654)

Above: British ports and docks were a special target of German bombing blitzes. (IWM HU.67839)

Right, upper: A stretcher party completes a rescue, 11 November 1940. (IWM HU.1176)

Right, lower: A fire crew fights a blaze in Manchester. (IWM HU.49833)

Above: Of limited practical use but an important ingredient in boosting the morale of the public: a heavy anti-aircraft gun in action against the German raiders. (IWM)

Below: Devastation at the Bank Underground station after a bomb exploded in the ticket hall on 11 January 1942. (IWM)

Right, upper: Ruins in Coventry, November 1940. (IWM)

Right, lower: The results of *Luftwaffe* bombing in Plymouth, April 1941. (IWM)

Left, upper: An Anderson shelter demonstrates its effectiveness following a German raid on 20 March 1941. (IWM HU.48554)

Left, lower: Damage to the railway after a bombing raid in Liverpool. (*Liverpool Daily Post & Echo*)

Above: The Junkers 88 was the *Luftwaffe*'s fastest bomber in 1940, widely used in day and night attacks on Britain. Here an aircraft of *KG 51* stands on a French airfield. The *Geschwader*'s 'Edelweiss' emblem can be seen below the cockpit.

Below: A fire-raiser: a Heinkel 111 of *KGr.100* carries a 2,500kg 'Max' slung under the fuselage. This was the largest bomb dropped during the Night Blitz.

Above: A Dornier 17Z brought down by RAF Hurricanes near Shoreham, Kent, on 15 September 1940. (IWM)

Below: Captured *Luftwaffe* airmen are escorted through a London station. (IWM)

was based on much else than instinctive opinion.'[96] A psychiatric worker in London called the spirit of people 'simply amazing'. There were few cases of mental breakdown, and 'it is impossible to describe the ARP services—which really means to say the ordinary population'. This reinforces Marwick's view that 'civilian morale was toughened by the direct involvement in the war'.[97]

Morale was bolstered also by at least a partial breaking down of the traditional reserve for which the British were noted. Class barriers were eroded. In the main, the working class of the East End suffered more than anyone, and their mettle in adversity was widely admired. The sharing of shelters and hospitals, public transport and 'the terror that walketh in darkness'[98] drew people together in a manner that no form of social engineering could ever have achieved. 'Hitler is doing what centuries of English history have not accomplished,' reported the correspondent of an American newspaper. 'He is breaking down the class structure of England.'[99] Bates noted the same tendency. 'Death is a great leveller; but death by bombing is, in more senses than one, the greatest leveller of all,' he wrote after making several train journeys across Britain. 'It has smashed the silence of the railway carriage.'[100]

Another answer to the question of morale comes from an unexpected quarter. In 1944 Major-General von Rohden signed a study issued by the German Air Historical Branch entitled 'The Douhet Theory in its Application to the Present War'. The paper admitted that Douhet had been wrong. During September and October 1940 there were 49 large-scale and 283 'nuisance' raids flown against London, during which 3,743 tons of high explosives and 14,409 incendiary canisters (AB36) were dropped. 'According to Douhet, a much smaller number of bombs should have sufficed in order to convince the enemy nation of the uselessness of further resistance. In actual fact this expected collapse did not happen.' The writer paid tribute to the spirit of Londoners: 'It would have been wrong to measure the British power of resistance by Italian standards.'[101]

There were a few doubters. Sir Kenneth Clark, of the Home Emergency Committee, believed morale to be poor. According to Nicolson's diary, Clark agreed that 'the spirit of London is excellent, but it would take little to swing this courage to cowardice', especially if the Germans were to make a good peace offer.[102] This, however, was a belief not widely shared and one not reflected in everyday behaviour. In the East End, a Civil Defence officer wrote, there was an immense weariness, but with it went ' a dogged determination to go on, no matter what it cost'.[103] The attitude was epitomised, even in a small

145

way, by the salesgirls of John Lewis's store in Oxford Street, who 'served lingerie to customers from an improvised counter on the pavement, with the wreckage of the store behind them'.[104] London became, in Britain as well as for Occupied Europe and neutral states, a symbol of strength and dogged resistance. 'Greatness, an uncomfortable greatness was thrust upon it during the winter of 1940–1,' reckoned one historian, adding that 'most Londoners were probably quite unaware of the fact'.[105]

The King, in a broadcast on 24 September during which he announced the institution of the George Cross and the George Medal for 'men and women in all walks of civilian life', said that, in spite of German depredations, '"there'll always be an England" to stand before the world as the symbol and citadel of freedom, and to be our own dear home'.[106] This was a theme reinforced by Churchill in Parliament a fortnight later. He spoke of the losses both in casualties and destruction, which were exceedingly heavy. Then he added a sentence which summarised the morale of an unbroken nation. 'Neither by material damage nor by slaughter will the British people be turned from their solemn and inexorable purpose.'[107]

The fourth service, Civil Defence, had proved itself under fire. Though unarmed, by early November it had learned quickly, earning the right to stand beside the armed services in the line of battle.

NOTES

1. *First and Last*, 45–8.
2. AIR 41/17, 63–4.
3. Dierich, 100.
4. AIR 41/17, Appendix 1B.
5. See Price, *Blitz on Britain*, 100.
6. *The Aeroplane*, 13 September 1940.
7. *The Spectator*, 13 September 1940, in *Articles of War*, 126–9.
8. 'The Need For Research', *The Aeroplane*, 20 September 1940.
9. 'The 56th Week of the War in the Air', *The Aeroplane*, 4 October 1940.
10. Beryl Cleveley's diary, September 1940.
11. AIR 41/17, 56.
12. G. Beardmore, *Civilians At War* (1984), 87.
13. *The Aeroplane*, 20 September 1940.
14. M. Panter-Downes, *London War Notes 1939–1945* (1972), 103.
15. In the early stages of bombing, the greatest damage was caused in eastern and southern areas of the capital.

16. See O'Brien, 390.
17. AIR 41/17.
18. Stahl, 63.
19. Milch Papers, RAF Museum, Hendon, Microfiche 565, IV/58/3, 'The Secret Dossier on the Military Administration of England', 9 September 1940.
20. E. Gombrich, *Myth and Reality in German War-Time Broadcasts* (1970), 9.
21. W. Bolke (ed.), *The Secret Conferences of Dr Goebbels* (1970), 12 September 1940.
22. See F. Hinsley, *Hitler's Strategy* (1951), 74–5.
23. SKL War Diary, 10 September 1940.
24. OKW War Diary, 14 September 1940, quoted in M. Glover, *Invasion Scare, 1940* (1990), 175.
25. P. Cosgrave, *Churchill At War. Vol. I: Alone* (1974), 303.
26. SKL War Diary, 17 September 1940.
27. Panter-Downes, 107.
28. R. Titmuss, *Problems of Social Policy* (HMSO, 1950), 276–7.
29. C. Savage, *Inland Transport* (HMSO, 1957), 198–201.
30. AIR 41/17, 50.
31. *Churchill*, ii, 597, Churchill to Ismay, 26 September 1940.
32. AIR 41/17, 49–50.
33. *Narrow Margin*, 385.
34. Stahl, 71.
35. See *Blitz*, ii, 173.
36. German radio broadcast, OKW bulletin, 10 October 1940.
37. *Narrow Margin*, 388.
38. *Colville Diaries*, 265.
39. Stahl, 76.
40. Pile, 175.
41. *Narrow Margin*, 396.
42. W. Douglas, *Years of Command* (1966), 103–4.
43. *Duel in the Dark*, 95.
44. *The Aeroplane*, 22 November 1940.
45. Winston Churchill in the *News of the World*, 18 June 1939.
46. N. Gelb (ed.), *Scramble* (1986), 79.
47. *Ibid.*, 235.
48. Premier Papers 3/468, ff. 94–5; see Gilbert, vi, 825.
49. Gelb, 251.
50. *SOAG*, i, 221–2.
51. Churchill, ii, 321–2.
52. AIR 41/40, 118.
53. See Gombrich, 10. The children's hospital was at Bethel.
54. *SOAG*, i, 215.
55. *Secret War*, 189.
56. *Blitz on Britain*, 103.
57. W. Gunston, *Night Fighters* (1956), 45–6.

58. *Blitz on Britain*, 103.
59. *Night Fighters*, 46–8.
60. CAB 69/1, Minutes of 39th meeting.
61. Panter-Downes, 98.
62. Nixon, 32.
63. Roger, 76.
64. *The Spectator*, 13 September 1940, in *Articles of War*.
65. Titmuss, 13.
66. See *Front Line*, Chapter 15.
67. *Ibid.*, 152.
68. *Ibid.*, 153.
69. O'Brien, 592.
70. *Front Line*, 26.
71. W. Sanson, *Westminster in War* (1947), 121.
72. Nixon, 10.
73. *Front Line*, 143–4.
74. *Ibid.*, 145-46.
75. *The Spectator*, 8 November 1940, in *Articles of War*.
76. Nixon, 31.
77. D. Idle, *War Over West Ham* (1942), 6–7.
78. Titmuss, 257.
79. O'Brien, 505.
80. *Ibid.*, 507.
81. *Ibid.*, 512-13.
82. Titmuss, 257.
83. See V. Lynn, *We'll Meet Again* (1989), 72.
84. *Churchill*, ii, 310.
85. *Daily Mail*, 21 September 1940.
86. Taylor, *English History*, 502.
87. Marwick, 298.
88. Titmuss, 396.
89. *Ibid.*, 276.
90. *Ibid.*, 261.
91. Panter-Downes, 104–5.
92. *Woman's Own*, 24 February 1940.
93. *We'll Meet Again*, 153.
94. Titmuss, 262–3.
95. *Churchill*, ii, 326.
96. Titmuss, 18.
97. Marwick, 297.
98. Psalm 91, v. 5.
99. *New York Herald Tribune*, 21 September 1940.
100. H. E. Bates, 'Fellow Passengers', *The Spectator*, 18 October 1940.
101. AHB Translation, vol. i, No VII/11, 9.

102. See I. McClaine, *Ministry of Morale* (1963).
103. R. Bell, *The Bull's Eye* (1943).
104. Roger, 140.
105. Titmuss, 268.
106. BBC Broadcast, Home Service, 24 September 1940.
107. *Hansard*, 8 October 1940.

CHAPTER SEVEN

CHANGE OF ATTACK:
NOVEMBER AND DECEMBER

THE COVENTRY RAID

On twelve of the first thirteen nights of November enemy bombers flew over London, continuing their general assault with a further 1,539 sorties. In addition, raids were made on other areas, especially the Midlands. Attacks on the capital varied in intensity, being generally lighter than those of previous months, yet heavy damage was still caused. On the 2nd a large fire was started at Barker's, Kensington, while five nights later the GEC factory at Erith was struck and a heavy bomb brought down a block of flats in Southwark. In a bad incident on the 12th, one bomb penetrated to Sloane Square tube station, where hundreds of people were sheltering, causing 79 casualties.

During this opening period of November railway targets were hit. St Pancras, Kensal Green and Bricklayers' Arms suffered on the 7th, and several Southern Railway tracks were destroyed or damaged three nights later. This brought anxiety to the Government as congestion grew. Delays followed in transporting urgent war supplies, as well as coal to London and southern England. In the Willesden yard on the night of the 6th, during a long Alert in which there was intense AA fire, only 146 wagons were shunted, yet a week later, with no Alert in that area, 502 wagons were shunted in a similar period. Strikes against economic targets threatened more harm to the nation than the promiscuous bombing of cities aiming to break morale.[1]

The Germans now changed their general bombing pattern. 'By the middle of November the attempt to bring about the collapse of the British will to fight on by dislocating the capital had failed,' Hinsley believes. Over the subsequent six months the *Luftwaffe*'s 'attack was extended to the chief industrial and communications centres, ports in particular'.[2] These raids served a double purpose. First, they aimed to prevent Britain from making good her losses, then they were intended to check the expansion of war production. Air Intelligence predicted on 18 October the *Luftwaffe*'s resolve to launch massive night operations using some 600 bombers. On 11 November signals from Enigma, as well as a conversation with a *Luftwaffe* prisoner-of-war, showed that the new attacks would hit industrial centres. The pathfinder unit *KGr.100* would open the raid with showers of incendiaries, then the bulk of the force would bomb the burning target area.

Under the code-name 'Moonlight Sonata', the Germans planned several raids on the industrial Midlands. British Intelligence soon reasoned that Target 51, *'Einheits Preis'*, was Wolverhampton and Target 52, *'Regenschirm'* was Birmingham. However, although the word *'Korn'* appeared, it was not known whether this represented another target, a jamming device or a reference to a different context. The *Luftwaffe*'s obvious intention was to launch heavy raids during the period of the full moon in mid-November, yet their exact destination remained unknown. Would it be the Midlands, or would the Germans possibly return to London? The scene was thus set for one of the most dramatic and devastating attacks of the war, one that was to have deep effects in both Britain and Germany. It was, according to the Official Narrative, 'an occasion of singular importance in the history of air warfare'. For the first time ever, air power 'was massively applied against a city of small proportions with the object of ensuring its obliteration'.[3]

Since 1940 a number of people have wondered why Coventry was chosen. The answer lay in its importance as a thriving industrial city. Longmate shows its growth as 'a centre of skilled engineering and the metal trades' from the mid-nineteenth century.[4] The city contained factories producing machine tools and vehicles, aircraft and synthetic fibres. 'Shadow factories' were built and there were many small workshops manufacturing vital war material. In terms of its reputation as a centre of industrial excellence, the Germans viewed Coventry as a legitimate target in their attempts to break Britain's economy. This was the city code-named *'Korn'*.

What they ignored was the city's historical geography, where 'factories, small workshops, shops, flats and houses of all kinds were mixed up together around the ancient centre'. Close to the Cathedral were 'not merely small manufacturing businesses but large concerns which almost anywhere else would have been confined to a non-residential district'.[5] No accurate assessment of the great Coventry raid can be made without an appreciation of this background.

Raids were made on the city before November 1940. Between mid-August and the end of October, during seventeen attacks, 198 tons of bombs fell, killing 176 people and injuring 680.[6] These raids were often regarded as a nuisance, interrupting sleep, but at that time most of the nation's attention was given to the capital's ordeal in the south.

Since 1945 some critics have suggested that Churchill knew well beforehand from Ultra that Coventry was to be the target of a huge raid. He then had to decide whether to order the evacuation of the city, but chose not to because the Germans thereby would have realised that their most secret codes had been broken. These accusations, made by two particular writers, are unsupported by evidence and far from the truth. In war, an attacker has the advantage of laying plans which the defender must attempt to counter. There was no lack of conscientious effort on the British side from airmen, scientists and politicians to have the defences well prepared. 'While the Germans had been perfecting their preparations,' commented Longmate after an exhaustive study of the operation, 'the British Air Staff had not been idle.'[7] Their response, aimed principally through radio countermeasures, was code-named Operation 'Cold Water'. And yet, despite their hopes, there were sometimes errors of coordination and wrong conclusions were drawn. No more could be expected from a group of people who could only surmise, estimate and deduce the enemy's intentions.

On the morning of 14 November Churchill received a memo from the Air Staff. This predicted a forthcoming raid 'probably in the vicinity of London, but if further information indicates Coventry, Birmingham or elsewhere, we hope to get instructions out in time'.[8] At about 1 p.m. German wireless traffic and beam transmissions showed that the operation would take place that night. Two hours later, the RAF's No 80 Wing discovered that the X-Gerät beams intersected over Coventry.

The beams might have been better understood and countered had full advantage been taken of the crash of one of KGr. 100's Heinkel 111s at West Bay, Dorset on 6 November. The aircraft, carrying the full beam apparatus, 'was potentially a unique prize'. However, a disagreement over salvage between the Army and the Royal Navy led to the Heinkel's becoming waterlogged before scientists could examine its precious equipment. 'This failure to save the aircraft intact,' Jones believed, 'may have contributed to the disaster eight days later at Coventry.'[9]

On the 14th, countermeasures against the beams were soon taken, but through error the jamming was put on 1,500 cycles per second instead of the 2,000 cycles used by the Germans that night. Consequently, during the raid

Luftwaffe aircrews could distinguish comfortably between their true beam signs and British attempts at jamming. Whether or not *KGr. 100* would have found the way to the target even if the beam signals had been successfully suppressed is a point of debate.[10]

According to one of Churchill's secretaries who was with him, the Prime Minister was being driven through London on his way to Oxfordshire that afternoon. He opened an Ultra message which announced an imminent very heavy attack on an unnamed target. Churchill felt sure that it would be London again and ordered the driver to take him straight back to Downing Street for an ordeal he was determined to share. Only later did he learn of the change of target.[11]

The defences of Coventry at ground level, both service and civilian, received no advance warning of the raid. The area of time open to question is the period between 3 p.m., when No 80 Wing discovered the position of the beam, and 7.10 p.m. when air raid sirens sounded in the city. Notwithstanding this, if ARP services, city authorities and AA defences had been warned, say, by 5 p.m. that they were the 'Target for Tonight', it is difficult to estimate what radical steps could have been taken in two hours to save life and property. Decisions that are clear from the safety of hindsight were often blurred at the time by exigencies and emergencies. Little could have been done to hold off the raid. Since the opening strike against London on 7 September, AA guns, searchlights and balloons had failed signally to prevent bombing. Night fighters had been generally incapable of locating or engaging bombers in darkness. Nor should it be forgotten that until mid-afternoon on the 14th the size of the raiding force and the exact target were unknown.

German plans were laid thoroughly. Orders published on the 13th mentioned that all units of *Luftflotten II* and *III* would take part first against Coventry, then later against Birmingham. 'These operations will constitute large-scale attacks against an important part of the English war industry.' They would be opened by *KGr. 100*, whose task was to shower the area with incendiaries, with the main force to follow.[12]

In the case of Coventry, specific sites were marked out. For example, fourteen Heinkel 111s of *II/KG 27* had to aim at the Alvis aero-engine works. The Daimler works were allocated to *II/KG 55* and the British Piston Ring Company to *I/KGr. 51*'s Junkers 88s.[13] Nonetheless, in spite of Longmate's claim that 'the Germans meant to hit military objectives, not to make a "terror" attack on the civilian population', it is difficult in the case of Coventry to separate the two.[14] A *Luftwaffe* Order declared that reconstruction and the resumption of manufacturing would be hindered 'by wiping out the most densely populated workers' settlements'.[15] This objective was reinforced by the announcement that each aircraft would carry two parachute mines. Stahl, who flew a Junkers 88 that night, wrote that the mines he carried 'are shaped like big barrels and are intended to float down on to the target under parachutes'.[16] Obviously there was no chance of aiming these with pinpoint accuracy.

The weather was good, although some mist hung in the Midlands. German meteorologists predicted 'four–seven tenths convection cloud, wind N.W. at 5000 to N.E., 60 k.p.h.' in southern England, while their British counterparts spoke of a cloudless, moonlit night, with little wind. These conditions 'brightly illuminated the night and obviously gave much assistance to enemy crews'.[17] This point is mentioned by Stahl, who wrote of 'a beautiful night with marvellous clouds lit up by the moonlight, which makes night flying a particularly enjoyable experience'.[18]

As planned, the Heinkel 111s of *KGr.100* took off from near Vannes, 150 miles south of Cherbourg, flying north along the main beam. They made landfall near Christchurch on the English coast, then flew towards Salisbury and Oxford. After that they reached the three cross–beams from which they regulated the automatic dropping of their bombs exactly over the target, from 7.20 p.m. The aircraft unloaded over 10,000 incendiaries, quickly starting eight major fires and many smaller blazes in the city. In this they carried out their task efficiently, preparing the way for what was to follow.

The main raid lasted until 6 a.m. the following morning and was made by 304 aircraft from *Luftflotte III* together with 133 of *Luftflotte II*. The arrival and departure of each formation was carefully arranged in a timetabled onslaught, both steady and sustained, with no respite for the victims below. Before long, areas of the city were well ablaze as bombs rained down from heights up to 4,000 metres. Stahl, taking off from Eindhoven, soon saw the target: 'A red reflection is visible beyond the horizon before we even cross the coast.' He added that 'there is no need for navigation now'.[19] Another airman recollected that while his aircraft was still over the Channel, 'we caught sight of a small pinpoint of white light in front of us, looking rather like a hand torch seen from two hundred yards'. As he drew closer to the target, the light grew and 'we were looking at the burning city of Coventry'.[20] A British civilian who was almost fifty miles away wrote, 'I saw all the flames, sky-twinklings of shellbursts, and bomb-flashes of the old days. But the wind brought no sound of the bombardment.'[21]

An immense bomb load was dropped that night. Just over 500 tons of high explosives fell, together with 30,000 incendiaries, mainly across the centre of the city, covering a few square miles. Bombs varied in size from 50kg to 500kg HE, to parachute mines each weighing about one ton. The incendiaries, especially those dropped at the start by *KGr.100*, included a number with explosive charges and caused furious fires, some of which burned out of control. Consequently, although attackers approached the city from different directions, some from the south and south-west, others passing over Norfolk and Lincolnshire, all converged on the target area with almost total accuracy.

Casualties were heavy. A later estimate gave 568 people killed, 863 badly hurt and 393 suffering lesser injuries which required treatment.[22] Some died in their own homes, others in the streets, a few in shelters. A Mass Observation report commented that 'nearly everybody knew somebody who had been killed or was missing', in a city where the bombing had been concentrated on a small area.[23] Casualties would have been heavier but for two factors. One was that for some time, especially since early November when there were seven raids on the first twelve nights, thousands of people had 'trekked' out of Coventry each dusk, either to sleep in nearby towns and villages or in the countryside. The second was that those who had gone to shelters, whether Andersons, cellars or reinforced basements, suffered little from death or injury. Longmate notes that of 79 public shelters holding 33,000 people, very few had been destroyed. Nevertheless, through the intensity of the raid on a city of some 238,000 inhabitants, 'a civilian had a 60 per cent greater chance of being killed or seriously wounded during that one night in Coventry than during the whole six years of war elsewhere.'[24]

The *Luftwaffe*'s main aim had been to destroy or damage industrial premises, and in that they had considerable success. 'At a very rough estimate,' reported the Ministry of Home Security, 'one-third of all factories in the city have been either completely demolished or so damaged as to be out of commission for some months.' Another third had been heavily damaged and the remainder slightly damaged. Among those hardest hit were the main Daimler factory, the machine tool works of Sir Alfred Herbert Ltd, the Humber Hillman works, nine aircraft factories and two naval ordnance stores.[25]

Of the city's houses and flats, one in twelve was either destroyed or made uninhabitable. Almost two-thirds suffered some damage. Also affected were garages, hotels, offices and shops; the city's main store, Owen Owen, was completely burned out. In addition, public services were badly affected, with water and sewage pipes fractured, gas mains and electricity cables broken, roads blocked for trams and buses and railway stations and tracks hit. The Coventry and Warwickshire Hospital and Bond's Hospital were also damaged during the night-long ordeal. The city's most famous architectural casualty of the night was St Michael's Cathedral. Early in the raid the 600-year-old building was struck by several incendiaries. Four fire-watchers battled gallantly to contain them, but 'with the failing of our supplies of sand, water and physical strength', wrote one of them, 'we were unable to make an impression; the fire gained ground and finally we had to give in'. The cathedral was gutted and by next morning only the shell remained, with the 300 foot spire pointing skywards like a finger of accusation.[26]

All of Coventry's ARP services deserved the highest praise for their actions on the night, when the scale of attack was fiercer than ever could have been anticipated. The system of communication soon broke down, but there were many acts of individual initiative and bravery. Wardens and firemen, ambulance drivers and police were under great pressure, yet they all responded well in helping others to stay alive. Later, a special constable was awarded the George Cross while a woman warden and a doctor each received a George Medal. As demands grew on the city's resources, fire, rescue and ambulance workers were quickly sent to help from nearby districts.

What of the defences? Coventry was protected mainly by twenty-four 3.7in. AA guns, together with a dozen Bofors, and they fired 'an average of ten rounds per minute for the eleven hours'. Altogether over 6,700 rounds were fired, nearly 1,400 of them from one four-gun site.[27] The intense barrage was noted by Stahl, who wrote of 'this blazing inferno, punctuated by the explosions of anti-aircraft shells', which seemed 'endlessly long'.[28] The end result of the many efforts of AA gunners was that one Dornier 17 was shot down near Loughborough.

The Official Narrative notes a large effort by Fighter Command, which put up 125 sorties of Blenheims, Defiants, Hurricanes and the new Beaufighters. No 10 Group even employed five old biplane Gladiators. However, with efficient systems of GCI and AI not yet in service, 'no decisive interception resulted'.[29] The difficulties are shown by Price, who wrote of bombers flying 'in long "crocodiles" with an average of 12 miles between each'. They steered at altitudes of between 10,000 and 20,000 feet, up to seven miles each side of the main track. Consequently, 'on the average there was one bomber to 330 cubic miles of airspace'.[30]

For the Germans, the Coventry raid was hailed as a huge success. Broadcasts spoke of inflicting heavy blows on the British, causing havoc and immense fires. A German High Command communiqué referred to 'the utmost devastation'. A new word entered both languages—*koventrieren*, or 'to Coventrate', meaning to devastate a place by aerial bombing.[31]

A number of lessons were learned on the British side, apart from the obvious need to improve service defences. One was that civilian morale was at first affected by the stunning intensity of the raid. 'Coventry is finished' was the reaction of some who were surrounded by devastation and lack of water, food, light and power. Had the Germans sustained raids on subsequent nights, the effects might have been catastrophic. 'Another such raid might well have put Coventry beyond the possibilities of repair', with an accompanying result on public determination.[32] Among the stricken city's first visitors, both Herbert Morrison and Lord Beaverbrook had a less than friendly reception, being closely questioned on the weaknesses of the defences. However, public morale received a great boost on the 16th when the King visited the city at short notice, touring bombed areas and meeting people. 'He had come to see us at once, battered and shabby as the city was,' said one woman. 'It did more for morale than any prepared government talk.'[33]

After mass burials of the dead, the city slowly returned to its work. Factory buildings were patched up, power was restored and, often under the greatest difficulties, the production of war materials was restarted. Some observers noted that immediately after the raid there was little local call for retribution against the enemy. This was a common manifestation when people were too shocked to think beyond their surrounding predicament. Public attitudes would change later. A report from the Ministry of Home Security claimed that 'in the case of Coventry, it seems that the enemy would have caused a grave position in the aircraft industry if he had pursued his attacks.' After inspection they could state that 'there has been no case of damage which could be interpreted as catastrophic to the aircraft and aero-engine industry'.[34] The *Luftwaffe*'s failure to repeat the raid was, in the words of the Official Narrative, 'a curious paradox',[35] and it was to cost the Germans dear. Gradually Coventry turned out an increasing volume of aircraft and machine tools, lorries and engineering parts. This work certainly made a vital contribution to the RAF's power of hitting back at Germany during the rest of the war.

Another beneficial result of the raid was the value of advertising the damage caused to civilians, homes and the cathedral. Not only did the British Press describe Coventry as another Guernica and refer to barbarism, butchery and bullying, but also newspapers in the United States caught the mood: they 'could hardly have been more indignant had the outrage been perpetrated on Detroit.'[36] The raid had an effect on American opinion at a time, soon after Roosevelt's re-election, when Britain was desperately seeking war supplies and help from across the Atlantic.

Those senior officers of the RAF who believed in the power of strategic bombing paid considerable attention to the Coventry raid. They were particularly impressed by one of its effects. The Heinkel 111s of *KGr.100* had acted as 'fire-raisers' to open the attack and did enough damage 'to teach us the principle of concentration', later wrote Sir Arthur Harris, 'the principle of starting so many fires at the same time that no fire services, however efficiently and quickly they were reinforced by the fire brigades of other towns, could get them under control'.[37] The bombing of Coventry, therefore, was an important milestone in the story of aerial warfare.

THE REPLACEMENT OF DOWDING

An unforeseen result of the Coventry raid was the hastening on of the removal of Dowding as Commander-in-Chief Fighter Command. By early November there was strong pressure from a number of service and political sources to replace him with a younger man, closer in outlook to those on the Air Staff who wanted changes made in the role of the Command both by day and by night. Differences between Dowding and the Air Ministry had became patent, especially over the need for an urgent response to counter the Blitz, and no one was more aware of the division than Churchill. Therefore the Prime Minister, together with Beaverbrook, decided that Dowding should go to the United States as an Air Force representative on the mission negotiating with the Americans for vital aircraft and supplies.

Over the years there has been controversy and misunderstanding concerning what happened, but it may be summarised by noting that Dowding was treated correctly, though not with charity nor with the respect he had earned as the creator of Fighter Command. He was interviewed by Sinclair on 13 November and told of the need for a man of his calibre in Washington. Dowding then enquired whether this was a temporary posting which would enable him to return to Fighter Command. When told that he was being replaced by Douglas, the DCAS, Dowding said that he would consider the offer and asked to see Churchill.

His meeting with the Prime Minister took place the next morning, and when Dowding demurred at the offer Churchill told him that it was in the public interest for him to take it. Dowding accepted. Those who wanted him to go were relieved, but Churchill and Beaverbrook looked forward to his work in the United States. That night, as if to expose totally the weaknesses of Britain's night defences, the raid on Coventry took place. The next day, during a conversation with Sinclair, Hugh Dalton, Minister of Economic Warfare, was told that Dowding had 'now got stereotyped, keeps things to himself, and has been losing the confidence both of his subordinates and his equals'. The C-in-C was being moved to the USA, 'where he can do very good work'.[38]

His 48 year-old successor, Douglas, who disagreed radically with Dowding over day fighting tactics and who had been increasingly involved in planning for night defence, took over at Fighter Command on 25 November. From the start he faced problems of great proportions which he well appreciated. On 20 November the *Daily Express* had included some highly critical comments on night defence, suggesting that the nation was being offered 'optimistic dope' by some authorities.[39] Douglas immediately wrote to Beaverbrook, asking that there should be no campaign against him 'over the night bomber business'. In reply, Beaverbrook offered to give all the support he could.[40]

Some of the problems were summarised by Park's dispatch of No. 11 Group's November operations. In his notes he remarked that the enemy's method was to select industrial targets 'and to concentrate his whole force on it for that night'. However, he added later, 'it must unfortunately be admitted that the number of successful interceptions has again been negligible'. In his 'Conclusions', Park touched on the root of the lack of success. There was a great need for training. 'Complicated instruments have been put into service and results have been expected from them at once', but all would be wasted 'unless the personnel are trained'. He also suggested that a night squadron be formed 'with pilots of older age and suitable experience, preferably drawn from Bomber Command'. They should be equipped with Beaufighters and sent to a quiet sector to train, then, on return, to action. That 'should achieve results which are at present beyond the capabilities of the Squadrons now in the Group'.[41]

By the time that Park's report appeared, the figure of the number of civilians killed in November raids had been issued. They totalled 4,588, with 6,202 seriously injured.[42] Although the total was lower than had been feared in pre-war estimates, it underlined the inability of Fighter Command to counter night raids. During the month there were only three victories for night fighters. Here was a contributory, though not the prime, reason for Park's removal from his post as AOC No 11 Group on 15 December. 'Defence against the night raider makes little progress,' complained an aeronautical magazine. 'The situation, as it stands, points to serious lack of foresight in official quarters all the more surprising because of the amount of vision which produced the Hurricane and the Spitfire six years ago.'[43] Yet while the RAF's reply to the problem could offer little immediate comfort, AA Command claimed improvement. 'In September 20,000 rounds had had to be fired at night in order to bring down one enemy machine,' noted the Official Narrative, using Pile's figures. 'In October that figure had decreased to 11,500 rounds and in November had decreased still further to 7,270 rounds.' It then added that, in 1918, 6,000 rounds had been required for a similar success rate.[44]

Glimmers of hope appeared. 'The Battle of Britain had been won,' notes Gilbert, and 'the severity of the Blitz had failed to undermine the morale of the British people'.[45] Nor had any German troops landed in Britain. 'If we can hold on until November,' Colville had written in his diary in June, 'we shall have won the war.'[46] Churchill, who celebrated his sixty-sixth birthday on 30 November, could feel some confidence, although, as he told the Commons nine days earlier, 'We have a long road to travel.'[47]

RAIDS ON OTHER CITIES

From mid-November to Christmas the *Luftwaffe* continued its policy of raiding cities other than London, although the capital received several more assaults. On 15 November bombers revisited London at night and 358 aircraft sustained the raid until 4 a.m. the next day. Even bad weather, with heavy cloud, failed to prevent them from reaching the target because many used beams for navigation. 'We now have a new method,' wrote Stahl of that night, 'that enables us to make the approach flight and achieve aimed bombing through cloud cover.' This was *Knickebein*, and 'if I am accurately on course, I hear a continuous tone in my earphones'. Deviation to the left brought the sound of Morse dots, or to the right produced dashes. The system's value to pilots came when they intersected the cross-beam which 'is indicated by a tone in a different key'.[48] Over 400 tons of high explosives were dropped, with more than 40,000 incendiaries.

They fell widely, damaging, among other places, Westminster Abbey, the National Portrait Gallery and four hospitals, as well as scores of homes. Altogether, 142 people were killed and 430 injured, the casualties being spread across 76 of the 95 boroughs in the London region. Stahl claimed that AA guns, which fired over 9,300 rounds 'were shooting even better tonight than ever before'.[49] They had little success, with one Dornier 17 brought down at Harlow—a scant reward for the defences.

Two nights later, with the intention of hitting Britain's economy, the *Luftwaffe* turned its attention to Southampton. Here was an important south coast port which also housed shipbuilding yards and oil installations, as well as the Supermarine Spitfire factory at Woolston. For centuries ships had carried passengers and cargo to and from its docks, but, apart from a few earlier daylight air strikes, the city had not to date suffered heavily. However, by the end of 1940, in the first devastating attacks from overseas for 602 years, four major raids were launched against Southampton, those on 23 and 30 November and on 1 December being particularly heavy. This was the city's main experience of the Blitz, and it had some important consequences.

On the 23rd, 120 bombers of *Luftflotte III* struck for four and a half hours and the fires started could be seen from the French coast. The prime goal, the dock area, was not gravely damaged, although several ships received hits and, in general, economic and military targets suffered little destruction. However, within the city centre widespread devastation was wreaked on shops, offices and homes, while 70 people were killed and 130 badly hurt.

Exactly one week later the *Luftwaffe* returned for another major raid. Bombing was opened by twelve Heinkel 111s dropping flares, followed by very heavy explosions, including two 1,800kg 'Satan' mines. Then 135 further bombers arrived to start fires which, the Germans claimed, again could be seen from the French coast near the Channel Islands. About 135 tons of high explosives and 21,000 incendiaries rained down, killing or injuring 200 civilians. Damage to port installations and factories was not very great, but the centre of the city suffered extensively, especially by fire: roughly two-thirds of the main shopping district was destroyed.

Luftflotte III returned the following evening for a savage six-hour assault which was virtually finished by midnight . It was made by 130 aircraft. Roughly the same number of bombs were dropped as on the previous night; sometimes the fires still burning helped the Germans' aim. Once again the docks area suffered comparatively light damage, but two factories and a flour mill were hit. About 140 casualties were sustained and destruction by fire in the city was extensive.

The following morning, under the headline 'London Blitz Switched on Southampton', the *Daily Express* referred to the nights of consecutive bombing. A staff reporter spoke of the bravery of 'firemen, wardens, rescue squads and ordinary men and women' who had 'stood up to the blitz'.[50] The city's shelters had given good protection during highly concentrated raids, as a Mass Observation report pointed out. 'Shelters in Southampton are more numerous and adequate than Coventry, and definitely . . . more carefully made.' The investigators also noted that 'opinion is unanimous in praising the A.F.S.', although there were great difficulties over cut hoses and water shortages.[51]

It is here that controversy enters the story. At the time of the Blitz all published accounts took an optimistic view of what had happened. While allowing that heavy damage had resulted, reports referred widely to the indomitable spirit of those who had suffered. A similar approach was adopted in the city's official story, written soon after the war by Bernard Knowles, where the bravery of individuals and the determination of the city to survive were dominant themes. However, in 1973 two reports, both written in 1940, were released into public records and, it was suggested by several revisionist writers, showed a darker side to the civilian reaction to the Blitz.

One report came from three investigators of Mass Observation who were dispatched to Southampton immediately after the raids by the Home Intelligence Department of the Ministry of Information, to assess the response of civilians under attack. Their findings, according to the revisionists, showed that in reality public morale was badly affected by bombing. It was also suggested that those who 'trekked' out of the city each night were regarded by the Civil Defence Committee of the War Cabinet as showing weakness.[52]

The second report was made on 5 December 1940 by Wing Commander E. J. Hodsall, Inspector-General of Air Raid Precautions, who visited Southampton and was highly critical of the organisation of civil defence there. In particular, he blamed the Town Clerk, who was 'entirely unsuitable to cope with emergencies', and the local administration, which was 'apparently riddled with intrigue'. Hodsall's criticisms were taken by the revisionists as placing a different perspective on what really occurred during the Blitz.[53]

A balanced view requires a careful exploration of what happened, not only in Southampton but also in other provincial cities hit by bombing. Then the differences of outlook can be assessed. Is it that the authorities at the time were trying to portray the British people as braver than they really were by banning stories of dissent and criticism? Or is it that some more recent historians, wanting to belittle Britain's role and achievements in the war, are anxious to uncover any evidence showing chaos and a lack of moral fibre?

A closer examination of the Mass Observation reports shows facets of the city's character usually overlooked by those who read only that 'Morale in Southampton has distinctly deteriorated' and that 'the strongest feeling in Southampton today is the feeling that Southampton is finished'. These other facets referred to depression felt by dockers, 'but a lot of cheerful determination also'. The shortage of food which followed the Blitz 'absorbed much of the people's attention' and 'led to much dissatisfaction', but then comes a more optimistic comment. The situation led 'also to considerable amusement and informality. Coventry was something like panic. Southampton was something like a picnic!' In the case of entertainments in the city, 'within Southampton leisure outlets are virtually non-existent'—hardly surprising considering the extent of fire and blast damage. However, 'cinemas and other outlets at the periphery are doing a roaring trade, and are frequently overcrowded'. That certainly would not be the reaction of civilians whose morale had been cracked.

On the matter of 'trekking', a woman described how she and a friend once joined 'hundreds of people—mothers, fathers, children. The men had mattresses on their shoulders, the women were pushing prams', all going into the countryside. But on her return, 'my mother thought it was terrible when I told her. She thought we were like cowards.'[54] Even in the following March another Mass Observation report mentioned 'the many people who still do not sleep in the town' and who 'are more frightened of a blitz'. Yet the same report noted 'a confidence in our strength and conviction that we are stronger and are making progress all the time'. It went on: 'No defeatism was encountered', adding that even if people were tired or worried 'they frequently added some comment on the re-assuring way things were going', which were 'optimistic remarks'.[55]

Several factors need consideration here. It was inevitable that some people under the concussion of explosions and the ferocity of fire were at first stunned. Their morale sagged, but it certainly did not break in the manner predicted pre-war, with mobs rampaging the streets and overthrowing the government—and this in spite of the fact that they were civilians, inexperienced in the business of war, being attacked by servicemen who had been trained to kill.

Secondly, by the same token, although local authorities had made some preparations to meet attacks, they could not prevent them. Nor could they predict every move that the enemy would make. For example, estimates in the 1930s had not allowed for the extent of incendiary-bomb fires. Consequently the fire services, although working to their limits, were sometimes unable to contain the blazes. Again, members of the ARP generally were trained far more to deal with damage to installations and property than for the results of bombing on people. In Southampton, as in many other places, schemes for evacuation, as well as for rest centres and caring for the homeless, either were not fully prepared or broke down under stress.

In war, as in peace, a characteristic not limited to the British nation is to blame national and local government when there are lapses in organisation. Such manifestations had occurred in the 1930s when air raid precautions were being prepared. This certainly happened again under the strain of battle. At least British people, living in a democracy where free speech was not forbidden, could speak their minds without incurring a visit from the *Gestapo*.

As for suggestions that pessimistic reactions to the Blitz were covered up by the Government, it is obvious that no nation during any war is going to parade its shortcomings, thereby feeding the enemy's propaganda. The attitude of showing a brave face in times of adversity was common to every combatant. All involved suffered fear. Those thousands of ordinary civilians who acted with an extraordinary courage were, naturally, held up as examples for others to follow. The fact that some acted with less distinction was known and privately acknowledged but, needless to say, was not widely advertised. A cartoon character of the time was named 'Mr Glumpot', who searched far more for Britain's weaknesses than its strengths. Anyone adopting the 'Glumpot' outlook could have value to future historians but was a hindrance at the time. Hence the reports of Mass Observation were not always considered conducive to sustaining morale in 1940.

Another place on the *Luftwaffe*'s list was Birmingham, Britain's third largest city and, as a centre of industry since the earliest days of the Industrial Revolution, a prime target for an assault on the nation's economy. 'Outside London, Birmingham possessed more "key points" than any other city,' stated an official report. It dominated 'the country's output of non-ferrous metal and machine tools' and was important for 'the finishing of steel goods and the manufacture of guns'. Even the great Cadbury's factory at Bourneville, which still maintained some chocolate production, turned part of its effort to war work. This included the manufacture of aircraft parts, 'including hydraulic pressure bodies, radiator flap jacks, dive brake assemblies and vertical milling machines'. In addition, silversmiths and jewellers 'transferred their skills to the making of component parts for radar equipment, rifles and aeroplanes'.[56] Elsewhere in the city were several 'shadow factories'. Rover ran one at Adcocks Green, Nuffield at Castle Bromwich and Austin at Crofton Hackett. Other factories also turned their engineering output to the production of vital aviation material. All of these works were, of course, legitimate targets in war. Difficulties arise when judging whether their operators, without whose skill and energy the war could not continue, also became legitimate targets either at work or in their own homes.

The city's first bomb from the *Luftwaffe* landed on 9 August and several raids with incendiaries caused damage in the centre of Birmingham at the end of the month. Among buildings hit were the University, the Art Gallery and the Town Hall, while both the Cathedral and the Council House roof were damaged by fire. However, before mid-November there had been no massive raid. Some citizens had the comforting belief that the city's position in central England offered safety.

The first large raid arrived during the night of 19 November, only five nights after the devastating assault on Coventry. According to Price, German beams were jammed successfully by 'Bromide' working on the correct wavelength: 'K Gr 100 found considerable difficulty in hitting the city and only a few small scattered fires were started to the south of it.' The following main force 'wandered aimlessly' before bombing 'over a wide area'. The attack, together with one the next night, 'was a failure.'[57] Other accounts paint a different picture. According to German reports, fires were numerous and appeared to cover the whole city.[58] Another writer estimated that 350 bombers were over Birmingham, with 200 on the following night.[59] In reality, the *Luftwaffe* dispatched about 440 bombers, of which almost 310 struck the correct targets. BSA's factory at Small Heath was hit and 50 workers were killed. Lucas and GEC plants also suffered, as did shops, schools, churches and thousands of homes. Some 450 people were killed and 540 badly hurt. Notwithstanding this, the city's war production, so vital to the national cause, was not badly affected.

On the following night the bombers returned, dropping 118 tons of high explosives and 9,500 incendiaries. Factories were struck, although not seriously, and the Hockley Bus Depot was hit, with over 100 vehicles destroyed or damaged. Further raids followed, so that between the 19th and the 28th almost 800 people were killed and 2,345 injured, with 20,000 civilians made homeless. Another British city was being exposed to aerial terror in full measure, and scenes forever associated with the Blitz were noted. On the night of the 22nd, a nurse walked down Macdonald Street and stood on a bridge from where she could count 60 fires. 'The whole town looked alight, gaunt shells of buildings against the flames—smoke hung down everywhere. Firemen with their hoses stood in the river in a vain attempt to get enough water.'[60]

The third heavy raid in four consecutive nights was launched on the 22nd. The onslaught opened soon after 7 p.m. when three Pathfinder sections arrived almost simultaneously to mark the targets. Eleven Heinkel 111s of II/KG 55 dropped flares, followed by incendiaries; nine of KGr. 100's aircraft used X-Gerät; and five of III/KG 26's Heinkels flew by Y-Gerät. Thus began an eleven-hour raid of great intensity—the heaviest yet—in which 600 fires were started. Bombs destroyed part of the water supply system, so many fire crews drew from canals; three-fifths of the city lost mains water. Supporting fire brigades were sent from Cardiff, Bristol and Manchester to help, yet great damage was suffered in the city centre. Nonetheless, 'the fire services performed the remarkable feat of controlling all fires before the attack was over'. The Luftwaffe were failing in their stated aim of devastating Britain's industrial economy. After the three nights of intensive bombing of Birmingham, of 72 factories struck by bombs, 55 had received 'negligible' or 'slight' damage; 'severe' destruction had been caused at only four.[61]

During December the Luftwaffe selected Birmingham again, but mainly on three nights only. On Tuesday the 4th about 50 aircraft of Luftflotte III dropped a variety of bombs, including 16,000 incendiaries, starting fires which, the Germans claimed, could be seen 100 kilometres away. One interesting feature of this raid had occurred earlier on 26 October. The line of blazes in the city marked the track of the X-Gerät beam followed by KGr. 100 and stretched for about three miles along the urban area. Seven factories were hit, one being the Lucas works, but most damage was once again caused to domestic and commercial property. Altogether there were about 85 casualties, fewer than in previous raids.

During the evening of the 4th the bombers returned, led by five Heinkel 111s of KG 26 operating along Y-Gerät beams. Over 60 aircraft destroyed or damaged many homes, but no great destruction occurred to the city's industries. The Wilton Tram Depot was hit and many vehicles were wrecked, while bombs also fell on railway lines, but there were comparatively few civilian casualties.

Birmingham's last major raid of the year arrived on a moonlit night exactly a week later, when 278 aircraft from both *Luftflotten* launched the longest attack yet suffered by the city. Apart from high explosives, nearly 25,000 incendiaries started widespread fires in both residential and industrial areas, such as the Fisher and Ludlow works and the W. & T. Avery factory. The city authorities reacted swiftly to repair damage and maintain everyday life. Almost a hundred people were killed and 235 badly hurt.

Once again, although destruction was widespread and personal misery came to many families, the German onslaught was not sustained. Birmingham, the heart of industrial production in the Midlands, was no more than marginally affected by the *Luftwaffe*'s attentions. The city continued its work and output, so vital especially to the efforts of the RAF. In the long run, a most important contribution to that came from the University of Birmingham's Department of Physics. There, two young scientists, J. T. Randall and H. A. H. Boot, both of Professor M. Oliphant's team, were building and developing at the time the first cavity magnetron. The device's very short wavelength gave greater control and direction and it was, in Jones's words, a brilliant invention. Their work was 'a phenomenal breakthrough which completely revolutionised radar', and the ingenious small artefact was developed to give the Allies a commanding lead, which they maintained until the war ended. For example, by July 1941 10cm radar was operational with the Navy and by early 1943 the invention was adapted to give H2S radar to Bomber Command.[62]

Bristol, as a target, had a two-fold importance. First, it lay on the west side of England and from early times had been an important trading port. For generations ships had sailed from the city to western Europe and to the New World, and a large area of docks had grown at Avonmouth. Secondly, in the twentieth century Bristol had developed as an engineering centre, including air works, the most important of which was the Bristol Aeroplane Company's factory at Filton. As Britain's sixth provincial city, Bristol was the largest west of London and south of Birmingham, with a population more than twice that of Plymouth. It was also 'the ninth town of the country so far as its number of key points was concerned'.[63]

German bombers had twice earlier attacked the Filton Works. At night on 22 August aircraft of *Luftflotte III* had dropped sixteen tons of bombs, causing considerable damage. Then, on the morning of 25 September, 27 bombers, flying from bases at Dreux, Chartres and Villacoublay and escorted by about 30 Bf 110s, attacked from 11,000 feet. They killed 82 people and injured 170 others, most of the casualties resulting from high explosives striking trench shelters. The damage was considerable at a time when Beaverbrook, as Minister of Aircraft Production, was worried over the safety of his factories. 'Rodney Works damage severe,' commented a Home Security report. 'Aero engines damage severe. Flight sheds damage severe.'[64]

There was, therefore, little surprise, with the change of German bombing strategy, when a major night raid was launched against Bristol on 24 November. This was the first of five raids of varying strength which hit the city by the end of the year. *Luftflotte III* dispatched 148 bombers and most reached the city, where they dropped over 140 tons of high explosives and 12,500 incendiaries in four and a half hours starting at 6.30 p.m. One feature of the raid was the employment of three pathfinder groups during the attack. Fourteen Heinkel 111s of *II/KG 55* opened with flares and very heavy bombs, guaranteed to cause severe blast damage. Then four aircraft of *III/KG 26* arrived, using the sophisticated *Y-Gerät* beam to cross the target area. Some aircraft of *KGr. 100*, on their customary *X-Gerät* beam, completed a pin-point raid.

'We sheltered in the basement of our block of flats,' wrote a BBC producer. 'Bombs came crashing all around us. Suddenly the whole of Bristol seemed to be on fire.' There followed six hours of 'slaughter, desolation and ruin' before the All Clear sounded.[65] However, the raid bore little relation to the stated German aim of striking at Britain's economy. A few factories were hit, but there was little damage overall to the dock area. Some bombs struck the Royal Edward Dock, Avonmouth Docks and a grain silo, but the greatest destruction was caused to the city centre. The central area of Broadmead was devastated and many fires were started. ARP services worked well and a great effort was made to overcome the conflagrations, but there was a water shortage. Altogether, 200 civilians were killed and 689 injured—a dreadful blow to the city.

On the following evening another raid was launched. However, the Germans employed only nine aircraft of *KGr. 100*, with *X-Gerät*, which dropped about 70 small high-explosive bombs and 6,500 incendiaries in less than half an hour. Mercifully only nineteen people were hurt, but damage was caused to a bank, two churches and several houses as well as to buildings of the National Smelting Company. This raid, in general terms, was very small. So also was a raid on the next night, when four bombers were dispatched to bomb

Avonmouth, using *X-Gerät* beams. Little damage was done and, to confuse the Germans, decoy fires were lit outside the city.

There was not long to wait before another major attack. *Luftflotte III* sent 122 bombers on 2 December to strike at Bristol with over 100 tons of high explosives and 22,000 incendiaries, although decoy sites nearby drew 66 bombs. With ARP services working well, casualties were lighter than might have been expected: 31 civilians were killed and 131 badly injured. Much damage, nonetheless, was caused to private and public buildings. The University and the Bishop's Palace were bombed, together with a cinema, several churches and the Bristol Children's Hospital. The *Luftwaffe*'s intention of affecting the economy was, once again, not realised: a granary and a timber yard were hit and the railway line from Avonmouth to Filton was blocked, but the main activities of the port and local factories were barely slowed.

The last raid of the year, four nights later, caused extensive damage in the city, especially to railways and power supplies, but by then the civilian defences were coping well with emergencies. Of particular importance in the overall story of the Night Blitz is the fact that in Bristol morale stood up staunchly to the raids. The telephone service and public utilities were not badly smashed and there was good care for the homeless. After the raid of 2 December Mass Observation investigators saw less damage in the centre of Bristol than there had been in either Coventry or Southampton, both of which were smaller cities. There was 'nothing like the dislocation of everyday life and the multiplied personal discomfort,' they reported, 'which still dominates the whole life of Southampton'. Moreover in Bristol, unlike Southampton or Coventry, 'the working classes, in particular, have overwhelmingly "stayed put"'.[66]

'Measured by number and weight of attacks,' remarked an official wartime publication, referring to Merseyside, 'this must rank as Hitler's target Number One outside London'.[67] Liverpool was Britain's most important port on the west coast, with installations stretching for over six miles. On the Birkenhead side of the river were some two miles of granaries, power stations, dry docks and gas works. As this area received thousands of tons of supplies from across the Atlantic, it became a prime target for the *Luftwaffe* and had been raided at night from earlier in the year. 'In their ordeal Liverpool, Bootle, Birkenhead, Wallasey and the rest learned fresh solidarity as Merseyside.'[68] By the end of September bombing of the Liverpool area had already killed 327 people and injured 590 others. October raids added to the toll, with a further 303 casualties. Therefore, as the Night Blitz was turned to provincial cities, civilians in the north-west knew that an ordeal lay ahead.

The first major raid arrived on the night of 28 November and lasted for eight hours from 7.15 p.m. Eight Heinkel 111s of *II/KG 55* opened the attack, dropping flares and bombs to mark the target for over 300 following bombers from *Luftflotten II* and *III*. More than 350 tons of high explosives, accompanied by 30,000 incendiaries, rained down on the area, causing widespread destruction to private and commercial property and killing almost 300 people. In the worst incident a parachute mine hit a school in Durning Road, trapping several hundred people in a shelter situated below the building. Of these victims, 164 died and 96 were seriously injured. Although public utility services were badly hit and the telephone system was damaged, there was comparatively little destruction in the dock area, which was ostensibly the *Luftwaffe*'s main aiming point.

The next large raid came some three weeks later, on 20 December. 'It was a heavy attack, with many hundreds of deaths, widespread fires, and a good deal of civilian damage.'[69] The first bombers flew in at 6.36 p.m., with an onslaught led by *KGr. 100* and *II/KG 55*. Over 200 aircraft dropped 27,000 incendiaries and 205 tons of high explosives, starting many fires in the main dock areas, where timber yards and several warehouses blazed. The Dock Board and Cunard Buildings, the Central Police Office, the Municipal Buildings and the Town Hall all burned. Part of the Adelphi Hotel was severely damaged when a parachute mine exploded in Copperas Hill. Bentinck Street was the site of the worst incident when a bomb struck a railway viaduct used by civilians as a shelter: 42 people were killed and rescue services took two days to free the last of the 48 survivors.

Heavier raids were made by 300 aircraft of *Luftflotte III* on the following night. Altogether over 280 tons of high explosives and 33,000 incendiaries were showered on Liverpool and Birkenhead, the attack being opened by *KGr. 100*. The Germans believed the raid to have been highly successful. Serious fires burned in the King's, Prince's, Canada, Brocklebank and Gladstone Docks, although the port's capacity to take trade was soon restored. The Liverpool to Leeds Canal was breached, its waters flooding the LMS Goods Station at Canada Dock. Flying at 6,000 metres above the city , a *Luftwaffe* pilot watched the conflagration. 'The fires below are quite something,' he wrote later, 'and Knoetsch, who has never seen anything like it before, is shouting for joy.'[70] His two mines were added to the explosions on the ground.

Much damage was also caused to housing, shops, churches and hospitals, and in the Anfield district 74 people were killed when a shelter received a direct hit. Altogether the two nights' raids cost the lives of 702 civilians. This happened in spite of Pile's belief that 'aimed fire by means of radar sets' from his guns 'seemed to be more successful than it was in London'.[71]

The brief statement in an aviation magazine that on the night of 27 November a 'town in the South-West of England' had been raided described what had been a major attack on the city of Plymouth.[72] Over 100 aircraft from *Luftflotte III* raided in good weather, and, after dropping more than 100 tons of high explosives and 6,000 fire bombs, reported conflagrations in Devonport and other parts of the city. Although oil tanks at Mount Batten were ignited and burned furiously, a number of bombs landed either in the sea or in rural districts. There were comparatively few casualties.

The *Luftwaffe* did not return to the great naval base until 28 December, when 21 aircraft of 'fire-raiser' groups scattered 12,500 incendiaries across the city, with some high explosives. Forty-five casualties resulted and damage was caused to homes, shops and hospitals. The attack was short in duration. These two raids caused little disruption in the city. The real ordeal for people there was yet to come.

Britain's other great naval base on the south coast was bombed by night on 5 December. Portsmouth, only 60 miles from the French coast, had suffered daylight raids from mid-August and was inured to attacks from the air. For that reason Air Raid Precautions in the city were well prepared for defending citizens. The Council learned on 22 October that the authorities 'had provided 24,000 Anderson shelters, 2,200 brick shelters (1,000 in the course of erection), 800 strengthened basements, Communal Shelters for 5,000 people and also public shelters'. They were told nearly three weeks later that 'there were 3,058 full-time paid A.R.P. workers', ten voluntary full-time workers at First Aid Posts 'and 1,445 part-time workers operating regular shifts'.[73]

In spite of all precautions, the raid on 5 December, the twenty-fifth on the city, killed 44 people and injured 139 others. Three of the dead were firemen who had been tackling explosive incendiaries. About 75 bombers of *Luftflotte III* bombed on an evening of gales and cloud, dropping 90 tons of high explosives and 5,300 incendiaries. They caused one serious, nine medium and many small fires, while two major fires burned in the Dockyard. One was on the Southern Railway Jetty and the other at Number 8 Dock, which so badly burned an ex-US Navy destroyer 'that she had to be declared a total loss'.[74] Fire also affected HMS *Vernon*, the naval shore establishment, and the Royal Clarence Yard.

The Council learned that 'a large number of businesses and private properties were demolished and a considerable number of others wrecked and damaged to a varying degree'.[75] A bomb hit the Carlton Cinema in Cosham High Street, causing 43 casualties, and two hospitals suffered from fire. After the raid, although quite a number of people 'trekked' into the surrounding countryside to escape attack, the Germans did not return until the New Year.

'For months we had told each other, "They're bound to come here", and we almost resigned ourselves to the inevitable', wrote a Sheffield man in 1942.[76] At about the same time an official publication remarked that 'ever since Henry Bessemer built his first works at Attercliffe in the eighteen-fifties, Sheffield had been one of the world's great arsenals'.[77] Consequently there was little surprise when over 300 bombers, mainly from *Luftflotte III*, arrived on the evening of 12 December to carry out Operation 'Crucible'.

Heinkel 111s of *II/KG 55* dropped a combination of flares and large high explosives as a prelude to nine hours of attack. Over 350 tons of high explosives and incendiaries fell, starting many fires. 'The air was thick with black specks cascading to earth, as snow descends, and smoke and stench and fumes,' wrote one inhabitant. 'Great landmarks of yesterday smouldered and towered like giant dirty stalactites [*sic*] from brick-encrusted streets.'[78]

The main German aim of halting British industrial production in the 'City of Steel' was never realised. As the Official Historian points out, 'Practically nothing in the great mass of factories engaged in the essential production along the Don Valley was touched.' That, he added, was the key to the situation. 'An industrial city had suffered a devastating raid but its factory buildings and machinery remained undamaged.'[79] What destruction there was came mainly from fire. 'For every ton of steel destroyed in factories by high explosives, ten tons had been destroyed by fire.'[80] Four factories were affected but, as happened in most provincial centres, repair was rapid and production only temporarily disturbed. Transport suffered, nevertheless, with most of the trams destroyed, roads and railways blocked and many vehicles damaged.

Although a number of raiders dropped bombs over nearby places, the centre of the city was badly affected. The greatest number of casualties occurred when the Marples Hotel, at the corner of Fitzalan Square and the High Street, collapsed on to its basement where 75 people were sheltering. In spite of a twelve-day search and rescue operation, only seven escaped alive. Heavy damage was also caused in King Street and the Moor. One reason for the extensive ravages to commercial property was noted at the time. 'These were our stores and shops, destroyed because there were not enough fire-watchers, at that time, to keep them safe.'[81]

Three nights later, following a pattern of *Doppelgänger* (double-attacks), German bombers returned. Eleven aircraft of *KGr. 100*, using *X-Gerät* beams, opened the raid by dropping 11,500 incendiaries, and this was followed by more bombs from another 80 aircraft. Once again, nearby places, including Leeds, Barnsley and Batley, received bombs probably meant for Sheffield, but the city itself was badly affected by fire. Several factories were hit, the railway line to York was blocked, and many houses were damaged, so that over 6,000 people were made homeless.

Another problem was posed by unexploded bombs. A Royal Engineer officer reported that, during the two raids, 394 UXBs fell on Sheffield. Although the greatest number dropped in one raid had been 566 on 19 September, 'these were not concentrated on one target'.[82]

The two raids led to over 750 civilians being listed as killed or missing, with 500 seriously injured—a particularly heavy toll. In addition to homes, about 1,200 business premises were hit, affecting the employment of thousands of people. Nonetheless, the inhabitants reacted vigorously to their troubles, and 'soon after the raids, Sheffield was perhaps never more feverishly active in its life'.[83]

The ARP services reacted well to the demands of fighting fires, rescuing the trapped and clearing streets. Plans for providing accommodation, meals and clothing for the homeless had been well prepared, with 63 rest centres available, and worked thoroughly. 'They have performed their arduous and exacting duties,' wrote the Regional Commissioner for Civil Defence, 'with a zeal and efficiency beyond praise.'[84] As an example, 'the Institution at Fir Vale turned out 60,000 meals in the first twenty-four hours'.[85] When the King and Queen visited Sheffield three weeks later they were able to meet citizens whose spirit was not only unbroken but forged with a determination to hit back. The city's factories were soon restored to full production and expanded their output of war material.

The last of the big industrial centres to be attacked in 1940 was Manchester, which suffered the customary *Luftwaffe* 'double raid' on the successive nights of 22 and 23 December. As a large city, Manchester contained many factories producing war materials of all kinds and these were to be the targets.

In the first raid, 370 aircraft each dropped about one ton of HE, adding to them with the high total of 37,000 fire-bombs. The crews made wide use of *Knickebein*, *X-Gerät* or *Y-Gerät* to locate the city after *KGr. 100*, *II/KG 55* and *III/KG 26* had dropped flares and incendiaries to mark the target zone. Some aircrews were helped by the fires still burning in Liverpool after the previous night's attack. 'The bright white light of the flares lit the sky above the city from end to end,' stated a later account. 'Soon the colour changed from white to red, as the incendiaries took hold and the clouds reflected the crimson of growing fires.'[86] There were 400 of these, especially in the city centre and at Stretford.

Damage to factories and commercial premises was heavy, and one of the most dramatic photographs of the Blitz shows the collapse of the buildings at the corner of Deansgate. Railway stations were also hit, as was the main bus depot. An exceptional number of incendiaries caused great problems. On paper, Manchester had 3,500 full and part-time firemen, but a number were in nearby Liverpool, helping there. The remainder were unable to cope immediately with the scale of attack. In some buildings there were few, or no, fire-watchers, so flames soon took hold across the city. Fires burned in Piccadilly and the Royal Exchange, the Shambles and the Cathedral, Cheetham's Hospital and around Albert Square, Portland Street and Trafford Park.

There were many acts of heroism from wardens and policemen, women ambulance drivers and rescue workers, but the raids exposed some weaknesses in the organisation of civil defence services, especially of fire-fighting. Lessons were learned and new measures implemented. The Emergency Committee reported 'no feeling of helplessness but a general desire to bring every effort to bear to restore normal conditions in the city so far as this was possible'.[87] Nonetheless, there was a feeling among some civilians that the attacks had caught the city somewhat unprepared for an onslaught that was bound eventually to come their way.

BACK TO LONDON

Although the *Luftwaffe* shifted its aim to include industrial cities and ports, it did not neglect to attack London often and regularly. The sequence of unbroken night assaults on the capital had been interrupted in mid-November by the Coventry raid, but London was such a large and accessible target that the German Air Force lost few opportunities to drop further bombs there. On each of the nights of 15, 16 and 29 November London was subjected to major attacks. During the last of these, 335 bombers reached the metropolis, dropping 380 tons of high explosives and almost 30,000 incendiaries, with the main aiming points being the City and Whitehall. Destruction was widespread and included a number of factories, the Civic Centre at Dagenham and several railway lines. The Ministry of Home Security estimated that there were about 300 casualties.

During December the Germans launched three more major raids on the capital, despite the attacks on provincial cities. In these they claimed to have dropped over 600 tons of high explosives and more than 4,000 canisters of incendiaries on London, which was more by far than any other city received during the month. The *Luftwaffe* launched its heaviest raid on the capital for two months on the 8th when, apart from 380 tons of high explosives, over 400 aircraft dropped the incredible total of 115,000 fire bombs. Great damage resulted, especially in areas close to the Thames. Bombs landed in the Surrey Commercial Docks, where the Night Blitz had started. Offices of the Port of London Authority were hit, as was Marylebone Station and many shops and houses. Some factories producing war equipment were also damaged and the devastation was considerable in many boroughs across the capital, from Shoreditch to Tottenham and from Marylebone to Wanstead. One large parachute mine exploded outside Broadcasting House, but wireless transmissions were not stopped.

Most of the damage was caused by incendiaries. By the next morning there had been reported 'nine major, twenty-four serious, 202 medium and 1,489 small fires'—a total of 1,724.[88] The raid was the largest made on London up to that time, and when the bombers left next morning, about 250 people had been killed and over 600 seriously injured. Once again the *Luftwaffe* had demonstrated the ease with which it could reach and cause destruction to London.

Two days later Hitler spoke to factory workers in Berlin and blamed Churchill for 'starting unlimited warfare at night', a form of fighting he claimed to dislike. The British, he went on, had bombed civilian targets, 'so this kind of warfare had to be waged'. He said that 'it is being waged with all the determination, all the material and with all the courage which are at our disposal and when the hour of final reckoning comes, this reckoning will come too'.[89] Insofar as he referred to the bombing campaign for both nations, these were indeed to prove prophetic words for the German people.

On 20 December an American correspondent wrote that 'the big news locally is the sudden cessation of all air activity, which has given London some of the quietest nights since the blitz started'. Although conditions had been perfect, 'the boys just haven't been coming'.[90] The optimism was reinforced a few days later when neither side launched sorties on either Christmas Eve or Christmas Day. 'Everyone in good spirits,' Churchill's daughter Mary recorded. 'No reports of any air, land or sea activity.'[91] Across the Channel, 'From 24 to early 26 December,' wrote Milch in his diary, 'no air attacks on Britain on *Führer*'s orders.' On Christmas Eve Hitler's train arrived at the Air Staff headquarters in northern France and he spent some time with men of the *Luftwaffe*, showing an active interest in his air force that had been singularly lacking since the opening of the daylight Battle of Britain.[92]

The lull in bombing was broken on 27 December by another sharp attack on London. It ended before midnight, but in that time about 100 bombers unloaded 111 tons of high explosives and 11,000 incendiaries, which caused over 600 casualties, 50 of them in an air raid shelter in Southwark which was hit. Much damage was suffered by bus, tram and railway services, and rescue and repair services were hard-pressed. This raid, however, paled beside the next, made two nights later. The Germans chose as the *Schwerpunkt*, or centre, of the attack, the City of London; in just over three hours they concentrated 120 tons of high explosives and 22,000 incendiaries on that small area. The 'fire-raisers' of *KGr. 100* opened the raid, using *X-Gerät*, and claimed that after 30 minutes they could already count 54 fires burning below. As the buildings of the City burned in Newgate Street, Ludgate Hill and Paternoster Row, flames leapt easily across narrow alleys, joining to create giant conflagrations. Into these were showered hundreds more incendiaries to stoke the fires, until the air raid defences were swamped.

The *Luftwaffe* that night were helped by two natural factors. One was a neap tide, so the level of the Thames was very low. Consequently the fire brigades which used the river as a source of supply soon found that water pressure fell. Mains were broken and hydrants in the City dried up, leaving firemen helpless in the face of six conflagrations and sixteen major fires. 'The greatest were the half a square mile of fire in the Moorgate–Aldersgate Street area, and another, half this size, in the Minories.'[93] The second factor was the growth in the strength of the wind. 'At about 7.30 p.m. the south-westerly breeze which, at the beginning of the raid, was only slight, had increased to gale force,' wrote a woman who watched the attack from the West End.[94] Burning embers floated across the narrow streets to start new blazes.

On that Sunday night the great City buildings were empty, with insufficient fire-watchers to guard them. Soon the area was experiencing its most terrible destruction since the ravages of the Great Fire in 1666 as buildings crashed to rubble, blocking access to civil defence workers. 'It seemed impossible,' wrote one watcher from Lambeth, 'that the City, that London, could be saved.'[95] Another spectator wrote that 'St Paul's during this night provided the most inspiring and terrifying sight that Londoners had ever seen', where the dome 'seemed to ride the waves like a galleon, and the golden cross to scintillate above the reach of earthly harm'.[96]

Nevertheless, surrounding buildings, many of great antiquity, suffered in a swathe of devastation across 'The Square Mile'. The fifteenth century Guildhall was badly damaged and eight Wren churches were destroyed. The Central Telegraph Office was hit and patients had to be moved from Guy's Hospital. Around St Paul's, Amen Court and Ave Maria Lane burned, together with several old houses, but the Cathedral itself, although hit by one incendiary, escaped further bombs. The whole City appeared to be enveloped in flames, with temperatures in places reaching 1,000°C.

Nearby areas were also badly affected. Five main-line and sixteen Underground stations were closed, with both rail and road traffic suffering disruption. The Victoria and London Docks received many bombs and the Port of London's trade was interrupted. The intensity of the raid was severe and fires were burning fiercely next morning. 'Some of the fires were still smoking,' a woman wrote several days later, 'and the firemen were hard at work in their tin hats, thigh boots, and dirty uniforms, which they probably hadn't scrambled out of since Sunday.'[97]

Casualties were heavy. Over 160 civilians were killed and 500 badly hurt. Sixteen firemen were killed and 250 were kept in hospital for treatment, particularly from burns. Eight of the firemen who died were near Fleet Street, with their trailer pump. As one observer watched them, 'a wall, which looked as if it was bulging dangerously, crashed down on them. As we looked round all we could see was a heap of debris with a hose leading towards it.'[98] The casualties suffered in London that night brought the month's total to 3,793 killed, and over 5,000 seriously injured.[99]

Churchill and his wife visited the City, picking their way through rubble and over fire hoses to see the destruction. According to one newspaper, he 'looked grim and determined', but before long he was accompanied by 'a crowd of cheering Londoners'.[100] During the evening he wrote, 'They burned a large part of the City of London last night, and the scenes of widespread destruction here and in our provincial centres are shocking', but then added that he found the spirit of Londoners to be 'as high as in the first days of the indiscriminate bombing in September, four months ago'.[101]

Nevertheless, there was some concern over London's air raid precautions. How was it that the incendiaries had been able to cause such catastrophic fires in the City? Why had the defensive measures not worked? Herbert Morrison, the Home Secretary since the end of September, was aware for some time of the weaknesses of civilian defence. On 31 December he broadcast to the nation with new orders and suggestions. 'Some of you lately, in more cities than one, have failed your country,' he said, adding that 'we need a Home Guard—a Civil Defence Home Guard.' People had a duty to guard their homes, businesses and factories from fire bombs so that 'not a single incendiary, wherever it falls, has the chance to get a firm hold'. There would be compulsory fire-watching for men up to the age of 60, but he also wanted volunteer groups everywhere, men and women, to be formed to protect households and businesses. 'See your warden at once,' he concluded. 'Fall in the fire-bomb fighters!' In this way he hoped to protect empty buildings, such as offices and commercial premises in the City of London, which had been the seat of great fires two nights earlier.[102]

The year ended with Britain standing alone but still fighting. The Germans had failed to defeat the RAF in daylight and had turned their attacks to the hours of darkness. The devastation caused across the nation, especially in cities and most particularly in London, had been enormous, yet it had failed to prevent industrial production from growing. As for the spirit of the civilian population, the answer was given by a visitor to several shelters in a London borough. 'How is morale down there? Are the people really taking it?' she wrote. 'Yes. How splendid they are!'[103] Such tenacity enabled Britain to be a beacon, not of burning city fires, but of hope to many nations which had fallen under the might of Nazi Germany. That notwithstanding, all citizens of the United Kingdom recognised that the New Year would bring no remission in the ordeal by bombing.

NOTES

1. Savage, 201.
2. F. Hinsley, *British Intelligence in the Second World War*, vol. i (HMSO 1979), 315.
3. AIR 41/17, 82.
4. N. Longmate, *Air Raid* (1976), 15–16.

5. *Ibid.*, 16.
6. *Ibid.*, 32.
7. *Ibid.*, 58.
8. See Hinsley, 317; also see Gilbert, vi, 912–15.
9. *Secret War*, 199–200.
10. *Ibid.*, 207.
11. See Gilbert, vi, 912.
12. *Blitz*, ii, 257.
13. AIR 41/17, 83.
14. Longmate, 64.
15. *Blitz*, ii, 257.
16. Stahl, 81.
17. AIR 41/17, 82.
18. Stahl, 81.
19. *Ibid.*
20. Price, *Blitz on Britain*, 103.
21. Beardmore, 102.
22. Longmate, 190.
23. *Ibid.*, 216.
24. *Ibid.*, 189–90.
25. *Ibid.*, 182.
26. Provost R. T. Howard, of Coventry Cathedral.
27. Longmate, 142.
28. Stahl, 81.
29. AIR 41/17. Among the fighter pilots over Coventry that night was Squadron Leader D. Bader.
30. Price, *Blitz on Britain*, 103.
31. *Blitz*, ii, 273.
32. AIR 41/17.
33. Longmate, 205.
34. Ministry of Home Security, Key Points Intelligence Survey, 1940.
35. AIR 41/17, 96.
36. Longmate, 212.
37. Sir Arthur Harris, *Bomber Offensive* (1947), 83.
38. B. Pimlott (ed.), *The Second World War Diary of Hugh Dalton* (1986), 102.
39. *Daily Express*, 20 November 1940.
40. Beaverbrook Papers, BBK D/29, 20 November and 22 November 1940.
41. Report of Air Fighting in No 11 Group Area, November 1940, Appendix F.
42. See Gilbert, vi, 929.
43. *The Aeroplane*, 13 December 1940.
44. AIR 41/17, 93.
45. Gilbert, vi, 929.
46. Colville Diaries, 14 June 1940.
47. *Hansard*, cols. 24–7, 21 November 1940.

48. Stahl, 82–3.

49. *Ibid.*

50. *Daily Express*, 2 December 1940.

51. B. Knowles, *Southampton—The English Gateway* (1951), 85–6.

52. Mass Observation Report, 4 December 1940.

53. See A. Rance, *Southampton Blitz: The Unofficial Story* (1991), 8.

54. *Ibid.*, 91–3.

55. *Ibid.*, 99.

56. Ministry of Home Security Appreciation, November 1940, 26.

57. Price, *Instruments of Darkness*, 45.

58. See *Blitz*, ii, 282.

59. A. Douglas, *Birmingham At War* (1982), 12.

60. J. Waller and M. Vaughan Rees, *Blitz: The Civilian War 1940–1945* (1990), 113.

61. AIR 41/17, 96.

62. See *Secret War*, 407–10; also see J. Nissen, *Winning the Radar War* (1987), 82.

63. Ministry of Home Security Appreciation, November 1940.

64. *Ibid.*

65. H. Thomas, *With An Independent Air* (1977), 60.

66. Mass Observation Report, Bristol, December 1940.

67. *Front Line*, 112.

68. *Ibid.*

69. *Ibid.*

70. Stahl, 103–4.

71. Pile, 179.

72. *The Aeroplane*, 6 December 1940.

73. V. Blanchard (ed.), *City of Portsmouth: Records of the Corporation, 1936–1945* (1960), 151. Records of 22 October and 10 November 1940.

74. P. Jenkins, *Battle Over Portsmouth* (1986), 98.

75. *Ibid.*, 155.

76. J. Abrahams, *Sheffield Blitz* (1942), 7.

77. *Front Line*, 101.

78. Abrahams, 15.

79. O'Brien, 637.

80. Ministry of Home Security Weekly Appreciation, December 1940.

81. Abrahams, 15.

82. Hunt, 127.

83. Abrahams, 21.

84. *Ibid.*, 25.

85. *Front Line*, 104.

86. *Ibid.*

87. Manchester Emergency Committee report, December 1940.

88. Ministry of Home Security Weekly Appreciation, December 1940.

89. Hitler speech, Berlin, 10 December 1940.

90. Panter-Downes, 122.

91. M. Soames, *Clementine Churchill* (1979), 300.
92. Irving, *Rise and Fall*, 114.
93. *Front Line*, 22.
94. Henrey, 44.
95. *Front Line*, 32.
96. Henrey, 44.
97. Panter-Downes, 129.
98. *Front Line*, 33.
99. See Gilbert, vi, 963.
100. *Daily Mail*, 31 December 1940.
101. Gilbert, vi, 963, quoting Premier Papers 4/17/1, f. 88.
102. Broadcast, BBC Home Service, Herbert Morrison, 31 December 1940.
103. M. Perham, 'The World of Dockland', *The Spectator*, 10 January 1941.

CHAPTER EIGHT

THE CAMPAIGN IN EARLY 1941

INTRODUCTION

By early 1941 the centre of Germany's immediate attention had shifted from the sole objective of overwhelming Britain. This is shown particularly through Hitler's War Directives. In November 1940 he was planning to attack Gibraltar and the Atlantic islands, as well as contemplating moves in North Africa and the Balkans. Regarding Britain, he suggested that Operation 'Sealion' might be resurrected in the spring of 1941 and asked all three services to 'make every effort to improve in every way the conditions for such an operation'.[1] In December, as relations with the French had worsened, he was scheming to invade Unoccupied France.[2] Plans to attack Russia surfaced five days later, with sweeping demands on the *Luftwaffe*. They were ordered to support the Army, to 'protect from air attack the whole combat and arsenal area we control' and to ensure that raids on Britain, 'especially on her imports' should continue.[3] By the following month, because of Italian reverses in North Africa, he was again having to commit German forces, including aircraft, to action in the Eastern Mediterranean.[4]

However, the thorn of British resistance was still not removed and was a constant irritation in any plans made for action elsewhere. Therefore, in early February he issued directions 'for operations against the English war economy', in which he sought a combined effort against British sea trade by submarines and aircraft. He suggested that the effect of bombing raids on the armament industry 'is difficult to estimate', but then offered the hope, unsupported by evidence, that attacks on factories 'must lead to a considerable fall in production'. Significantly, he added that the least effect had been 'upon the morale and will to resist of the English people'.

In future, aircraft would be withdrawn for operations elsewhere, and those remaining would have to operate against 'targets whose destruction supplements our naval war'. They would therefore attack 'harbours for imports, especially port installations' and homeward-bound shipping. Merchantmen should be targeted in preference to warships, and minefields should be laid. 'No decisive success can be expected from terror attacks on residential areas,' he announced, implicitly acknowledging the strength of British civilian resistance. Until the opening of the forthcoming Russian campaign, sea and air warfare against Britain would be intensified, giving the impression that 'an attack on the British Isles is planned for this year'.[5]

The fear of a new German air offensive was not erased for Britain by the success of Fighter Command in the Battle of Britain. 'I have no doubt at all in my mind that it is going to be a very heavy attack,' Sinclair wrote to Portal in January. He believed that it would be greater 'than it was last Autumn' and that 'the main German effort in the Spring will be made against these Islands'.[6] Consequently, between January and June 1941 the *Luftwaffe* in the West was faced with a double demand. Raids on Britain had to be sustained, while at the same time units were moved to other parts of Europe for supporting new campaigns. Several leaders had distinct reservations over the proposed invasion of Russia, raising the traditional German fear of war on two fronts. Goering, however, believed in the *Führer's* judgements. 'We lesser mortals' should follow him in faith, he said. 'Then we cannot go wrong.'[7]

TARGETS OLD AND NEW: JANUARY AND FEBRUARY

Goering sent a New Year message to *KGr. 100*, which had played a prominent part in the night campaign. 'I express to the CO and to the *Gruppe* my sincere thanks for an achievement unique in history.' He spoke of their effort and added, 'I am convinced, my comrades, that in 1941 as well, you will know only victory.' The *Reichsmarschall* wished each of them 'much luck and continuous success in the coming year. Heil Hitler!'[8]

Although Hitler's Directive ordering attacks on ports was not issued until early February, raids by the *Luftwaffe* had been continuing from the start of the year. A limiting factor for the German Air Force in the first two months was bad weather, which prevented attacks for almost half the nights of January and led to only three big raids during the following month. Snow, sleet, ice and low cloud lay widely across Northern Europe, hampering the *Luftwaffe* by causing a number of accidents to aircraft taking off and landing. However, such conditions did not prevent some sorties, and these opened against western Britain.

On the night of 2 January Cardiff, which had received a few minor raids previously, was heavily assaulted in what became known as 'The *Luftwaffe's*

New Year Gift'. 'The raid on Cardiff,' stated a contemporary magazine, 'was made as a reprisal for the R.A.F.'s raid on Bremen, according to a communiqué.'⁹ Over 100 bombers unloaded high explosives and 14,000 incendiaries, with the main aiming point over the docks and a steel works. Nevertheless, as with so many raids, comparatively little damage was caused to the economic life of the city, but residential and commercial property suffered heavily. A rubber works, paint factory and transport offices were hit, and railways affected, but over 500 houses were destroyed or made uninhabitable. Among districts of destruction at the city's west end were Wembley Road, Ninian Park Road and Blackstone Street, while Llandaff Cathedral was damaged by a parachute mine. About 160 people were killed, with a similar total badly injured. 'The Cardiff raid,' stated an official publication, 'was in almost every aspect an example of effective defence.'¹⁰ The civilian services reacted promptly and efficiently, so that fires were quickly extinguished.

Another western target, Bristol, received three raids during the month. The first, on 3 January, involved 160 bombers each dropping about one ton of high explosives and a combined total of 53,500 fire bombs. In the City Docks about 8,000 tons of grain were destroyed in a granary, as well as further destruction, but the port's working was not stopped. The Royal Exchange and Guildhall were struck, as were a number of schools and hospitals. There were 500 casualties and much damage in the city centre to shops, offices and homes, and to Temple Meads station. The night was bitterly cold. 'Two houses might be seen side by side, one in flames with the firemen at work on it, the other hung with long icicles where the streams of water had splashed and frozen.'¹¹

The following night 124 aircraft of *Luftflotten II* and *III* set their sights mainly on Avonmouth Docks, where thousands of incendiaries fell. Overall, the raid failed because of prompt measures to put out fires. 'The experience of London in the raid of December 29 had given warning to other cities,' stated one report, 'and the enlistment of extra fire-watchers helped to diminish the effects of incendiary attacks.'¹² Although much damage was caused in the city, casualties, fortunately, were light. There was a similar story twelve nights later when over 120 bombers returned amid snow showers to target both Avonmouth and Bristol. Further casualties occurred, and although damage was caused in both the docks and the city the raid was less fierce than some earlier attacks.

Swansea, another important western port, received four particularly heavy raids, the first coming on 17 January from 100 bombers of *Luftflotte III*. Some high explosives burst in the dock area, where the Prince of Wales Dry Dock was hit. Fires were caused by 32,000 incendiaries, but the main results were felt by commercial and domestic premises. The experience gained then by ARP services was certainly beneficial in the following month when Swansea was heavily assaulted on three successive nights starting on the 19th. Then the town centre received a five-hour bombardment. 'From the "blood, sweat and toil" of the triple bombardment,' the ARP Controller reported to the Town Council, 'the devotion and heroism of a people emerged.' Swansea, he said, was 'a community of courage'.[13]

The worst night was the 21st, when a fire covering about one mile square burned in the town centre and the glow was visible from the north Devon coast. By then 'the whole civilian centre of the town was levelled to the ground by bomb and fire',[14] with great destruction in districts including Castle Street and the High Street, College Street and Caer Street. Churches and chapels were smashed, together with fourteen schools. Many water, gas and sewage pipes were fractured and the death toll from all the raids reached 230. Swansea had been deluged with 160 tons of high explosives and nearly 60,000 incendiaries 'dropped simultaneously in an attack which lasted $3^1/_2$ hours'.[15]

Local authorities reacted swiftly to deal with subsequent food shortages and the need to care for 6,500 homeless people. Volunteers worked with little respite in Rest Centres and emergency canteens, offering a magnificent response to disaster. 'All were neighbours,' wrote the ARP Controller. 'There were no strangers within its battered gates.'[16]

The wrath of the *Luftwaffe* fell also on South Coast ports. Portsmouth endured a particularly heavy raid on 10 January when nineteen He 111s of *KG 55* dropped 28 flares, quickly followed by very heavy bombs. About 150 aircraft then unloaded 40,000 incendiaries, as well as high explosives, causing devastation in Portsmouth, Southsea and Gosport. Warehouses and timber yards burned and railway services were broken, but dockyard installations generally received little damage. 'Much damage was done to houses, churches, cinemas and commercial property by incendiary and high explosive bombs,' stated one report, and the Guildhall was gutted after blazing furiously.[17]

That night water supplies failed. 'Here, alas, as in many another fire town, the constant cry was for water, water, and still more water,' a fireman observed.[18] Some supplies had to be pumped over three miles. In Southsea shopping areas were burned, as were schools, churches and two hospitals. The Harbour Central Station was badly damaged, as was HMS *Vernon*. About 250 people were killed or injured.

Sixty-two aircraft of *Luftflotte III* raided Southampton on 19 January, led by six pathfinders of *KG 26* using *X-Gerät* beams for navigation. By then, three-quarters of the town centre had been destroyed in earlier attacks, although more damage was done to houses, shops and offices when fourteen fires burned. The Southern Railway Locomotive Works at Eastleigh were hit, but little damage was caused to docks or factories. Casualties were light.

In spite of the widening of the *Luftwaffe*'s Blitz to include provincial towns and cities, the German High Command could not forbear to make at least a few raids on London. The flight to the capital for bombers operating from Northern France and the Low Countries was comparatively short and straight-forward, and the city still contained many prime targets.

Throughout January there were four main attacks. The first, on the 11th, was a major assault concentrated into three hours and made during bad weather. It was described as a 'short but intense raid' at the time.[19] Over 130 tons of bombs fell as 137 bombers cruised over the capital, also dropping 21,000 incendiaries. Much damage occurred in the City and south London. Liverpool Street Station was hit, killing 43 people, including eighteen on a bus which was struck. 'The worst single incident occurred at the Bank Station in the City,' reported the Ministry of Home Security, 'a direct hit with an H.E. bomb causing booking hall and circular gallery to cave in.'[20] Probably about 50 people died there and an enormous crater in the road, which was not finally repaired until May, caused dislocation of traffic. Altogether in the raid over 100 civilians were killed, some at Lambeth Hospital which was hit.

On the following night a slightly greater tonnage was dropped by 141 bombers. They aimed particularly at dock installations along the banks of the Thames, starting fires in, among other places, the Victoria and Albert Docks and Woolwich Arsenal. Industrial premises at Crayford and oil tanks at Purfleet were also hit. In south-east London alone there were some 150 civilian casualties.

Exactly one week later, during a raid by about 50 bombers, the *Luftwaffe* employed two Stukas to open the attack, each carrying an SC 1000 bomb. Although 50 tons of high explosives were dropped, with nearly 12,000 incendiaries, little industrial damage was caused. The Beckton Gas Works were struck, but supplies were barely affected, and various commercial buildings along the riverside were also hit.

The night of 29 January was marked by low cloud and rain, when 37 bombers attacked several boroughs in the south-east of the capital. The Port of London was the main target, yet little destruction resulted there and casualties were comparatively light.

SUMMARY

Despite the use of beams, the weather during the first two months of 1941 was a restraining factor on *Luftwaffe* activity over Britain. The dangers of flying at night in bad conditions were a threat to German bombers not only in British skies but also over Occupied Europe. 'Meteorological records last week had a picturesque variety,' noted a writer at the end of January. 'On one day the wind went round the compass' but 'could not rid the sky of its opaque veneer, which day after day brought snow, sleet, rain and gloom alternately'. This had defeated 'both friendly and hostile aeroplanes' and proved that 'weather can be a country's most effective form of defence against air attack'.[21] In Portsmouth, 'the coldest day was January 21st when there were 18 degrees of frost'.[22]

In *Luftwaffe* raids during January and February wide use was made of incendiaries, which had greater potential than high explosives for doing damage. In the opinion of one observer, this was caused either by the Germans viewing their effects on British cities 'or by the results of similar R.A.F. bombing on German targets'. Raids on London had shown that when incendiaries were 'strewn with sufficient liberality', they could defeat fire-watchers, 'even in daytime'.[23]

The diminishing scale of raids brought the blessing of lower civilian casualties than suffered in previous months. During January 922 people were killed and 1,927 seriously injured. Figures in February were even lower, with 789 dead and 1,068 badly hurt from a total of 1,644 sorties flown over Britain by night. These were, nonetheless, terrible losses for people still vulnerable to attacks in darkness. A further worry came with the destruction or shattering of homes across the country. Up to mid-February, during raids on the United Kingdom, about 94,000 houses had been either destroyed or damaged beyond repair and almost 1.4 million damaged to a greater or lesser degree. A great burden was thereby thrown especially on to local authorities to care for and rehouse their occupants.

The British Government carried wider burdens, related to the nation's ability to stay in the war. They were reassured when, in November 1940, President Roosevelt was re-elected to office in the United States. Over the following weeks, however, differences grew between the two nations over the extent of war supplies needed by Britain and her ability to pay for them.

Therefore, in early January Roosevelt sent an emissary to London to discuss and resolve problems. The man chosen was Harry Hopkins, who arrived on 8 January and stayed for almost four weeks.

On 31 January he accompanied Churchill on a visit inspecting bomb damage at Southampton and Portsmouth. 'It is a dismal sight,' wrote one of Churchill's secretaries, 'particularly at Portsmouth', and was comparable 'only to the damage I saw in France in the last war'. Of destruction in Southampton he commented, 'They say that it is even worse there in places.'[24] Hopkins was able to report at first hand on the ordeal undergone by the British people and on their reaction to the presence of the Prime Minister. 'He had indeed become the symbol of his country's hope and courage,' wrote Churchill's daughter Mary, 'and under the flail of war the usual reserve of the British character had melted away.' Wherever he went, 'crowds appeared, cheering and clapping', even from the ruins of their homes.[25]

Three nights later Churchill spoke to the British people in his first broadcast for five months. 'In order to win the war Hitler must destroy Great Britain,' he announced, after applauding civilians and defence workers who had faced a 'formidable ordeal'. He appealed for the confidence, faith and blessing of the USA. 'Neither the sudden shock of battle, nor the long drawn trials of vigilance and exertion, will wear us down,' he promised. A direct plea followed: 'Give us the tools and we will finish the job.'[26] A BBC clerk wrote in his diary after the broadcast. 'His genius is that while he puts into magnificent words what we ourselves are thinking, he manages at the same time to inspire.' The closing passage was so intense 'that it kept a roomful of us silent for three minutes after he had gone'.[27]

DEFENCES UNTIL THE END OF FEBRUARY

'Night fighting is the most intense and important battle of those on which we are now engaged,' Sinclair wrote to his CAS early in January 1941. In this, he showed the responsibility borne particularly by Fighter Command. 'It would be a great mistake to under-estimate the effect which repeated night attacks on the scale of the recent attacks on Coventry, London and other cities will have upon civilian morale.' He believed that 'the fairly stout-hearted civilian' wanted retaliation, but also 'wants us to shoot down the attackers'.[28] Here was the goal which Fighter Command was not attaining.

'They realized that the only hope lay in the application of radar techniques,' wrote Wykeham of the burdens facing the planners of night air defence, 'but at the same time they could not gamble the country's safety solely on the production of apparatus not yet existing.' Consequently, 'all weapons to hand' had to be deployed, although some were unsatisfactory.[29] This dilemma had faced Dowding and remained as an even greater threat for his successor, Douglas. In his memoirs, the latter remarked that in late 1940 it was unknown whether fighters 'not equipped with radar would be able to make interceptions at night', but experience showed it to be 'well-nigh hopeless' unless the moon was well above the horizon.[30] These 'cat's-eye' fighters were fortunate, then, to spot, let alone engage, enemy aircraft.

The three months following Douglas's assumption of the leadership of Fighter Command were a time of great experiment and frustration for the RAF. Not only did the Command begin offensive operations over Northern France in daylight, but also night defence squadrons increased in number. On 14 November 1940 the Order of Battle showed nine squadrons available, spread across three Group areas, but only No 219 at Kenley was equipped with Beaufighters. By 16 February 1941 the total had grown to twelve squadrons, plus one section of Defiants, spread over five Groups; four squadrons were composed completely or partially of Beaufighters.

Douglas's brisk and businesslike approach to problems was manifested on his taking over. On 8 December, at a conference, he laid down requirements for a good night defensive system, although appreciating that his needs would not be fulfilled for some time to come. First, he believed that at least 20 squadrons equipped with AI should be dispersed in a semi-circle from Devon to Newcastle, with a squadron each to cover Birmingham and Coventry; later, a squadron could be stationed in the Glasgow area. Secondly, specialised night flying airfields should be established, having Lorenz blind landing facilities and AI homing beacons. Next, he hoped for at least one large Regional Control airfield in different areas, with control staff to ensure safety for night-flying airmen. He also asked for special training for night flyers, whose vision should be carefully tested.[31]

Some steps had already been taken. Scientific and meteorological officers had been posted to night squadrons to assist with maintaining apparatus and assessing weather on hard winter nights. Furthermore, No 54 Night Operational Training Unit was shortly set up at Church Fenton. Dowding's experiments with GL radar at Kenley were discontinued by August as 'uneconomical in the use of sets'; instead, he decided to create a 60-mile GL 'carpet', extending from Kent towards Bristol.

However, all plans depended on two factors which the RAF was unable to alter speedily. One was the rate of production of night fighters, especially the Beaufighter, together with the new AI Mk IV radar. The other was the number of trained pilots available to fly effectively in action. In the case of aircraft production, there was some disappointment. Douglas had wanted six additional twin-engine squadrons to be formed, yet even by February 1941 'only one of these had in fact come into being, and it was being supplied with Blenheim Is thrown up by the re-equipment of other squadrons'. The output of Beaufighters and of the Douglas Havoc night fighter 'had not come up to expectations'. As for having trained crews, expansion was held back so that by early February the C-in-C estimated that there was a shortage of 74 pilots. His nine squadrons had a total of 84 pilots, of whom 75 were operational. This was a slender resource to combat the scores of *Luftwaffe* bombers which nightly invaded Britain's air space.[32] Some veteran pilots with civilian experience were drafted in, together with some from Bomber Command who were experienced in night flying. One was Guy Gibson, of future Dambuster fame, who in November was posted to No 29 Squadron and became a night fighter pilot on Blenheims. Later the squadron was equipped with Beaufighters at West Malling, and Gibson did not revert to Bomber Command until late 1941.[33]

The weaknesses of Britain's night fighters were reflected in the figures of successes. From November 1940 until February 1941, the *Luftwaffe* lost more aircraft from accidents over Occupied Europe than from British fire. For example, during November and December 1940, while German bombers flew over 9,000 night sorties across Britain, fighters claimed only six victories. In January 1941 Fighter Command flew 486 sorties against 1,965 made by enemy bombers, of which they claimed to have destroyed three, together with twelve reckoned by AA defences. In reality the *Luftwaffe* lost, generally at night, 28 aircraft destroyed, with 37 damaged. Most were involved in crashes on take-off or landing, or in faulty navigation over France during bad weather.

Thus the RAF made experiments with different forms of weapon, attempting urgently to frustrate the enemy. 'No opportunity of discovering a means of defeating the night bombing menace was neglected', even though some appeared bizarre.[34]

One of these, code-named 'Mutton', a plan favoured by both Lindemann and Churchill, was the dropping by parachute of aerial mines in the path of raiders. The idea had been put to Dowding in September and was inherited by Douglas, who thought it 'a complete waste of time and effort' which troubled

Fighter Command.[35] The task was to be carried out by obsolescent Harrow bombers of No 420 Flight, which laid several 'aerial minefields'. They had little or no effect. On 7 December 1940 the Flight became No 93 Squadron, with twelve DB-7s (Havocs) allocated for dropping Long Aerial Mines and six Wellingtons for towing mines. Yet the Progress Report in February 1941 showed that the idea 'never truly bore fruit', and it was later abandoned.[36]

Neither was the 'free balloon barrage' successful, which Douglas considered was foisted on him after originating from 'some fertile brain in the Royal Navy'.[37] In this operation, code-named 'Pegasus', balloons containing lethal charges were released into the bomber stream, but they could only be successful if employed in huge density and with favourable wind conditions. Although twice used over London, the balloons destroyed no bombers and some drifted across the Channel to France. Similar ineffective results came from dropped or towed flares intended to illuminate enemy aircraft. During the bad weather of February, Fighter Command put up 568 sorties to counter the *Luftwaffe*'s 1,644 night sorties over Britain but could claim only four successes. Four RAF aircraft were lost.[38]

Another plan was to use 'cat's-eye' aircraft, often Hurricanes or Defiants, on 'Fighter Nights', or 'Layers Operations', which had been attempted to defend Scapa Flow in April 1940. During bright moonlight, AA guns over certain areas would not fire, or would shoot no higher than 2,000 feet below the level of patrolling fighters. Then aircraft were given free rein to operate in conjunction with searchlights. Unsuccessful attempts were made with 'Hampden Patrols' over Birmingham on 11 December 1940. During a heavy attack, twenty Hampden bombers, flying in layers, sighted 26 enemy aircraft, but were too slow and undergunned either to catch or destroy them. These patrols were soon abandoned and replaced by fighters. On 10 January 1941 fourteen Hurricanes flew over Portsmouth on a mission, while the same city had a 'Fighter Night' on 5 February 1941, but neither occasion brought success.

Douglas's priority to have GCI sets installed at all fighter sector stations, especially near London, was soon recognised as 'by far the most important development in the Command'.[39] Although difficulties of production had to be overcome, in January six sets were erected, enabling a standardised procedure to be followed. This was particularly necessary for 'cat's-eye' fighters, whose pilots relied on visual contact and thus had to be led to the enemy by Controllers. 'In Hurricanes we still lacked the missing link, A.I.,' wrote one pilot. On the night of 8 December he flew from Gravesend to defend London, patrolling in his Hurricane at 16,000 feet. Below, from 'all that immensity of black sky', he could see the city being 'consumed by fire'. However, 'for two hours, while the enemy was killing hundreds of our people', he searched vainly for the bombers, 'desperate and ashamed at our impotence to defend the defenceless'.[40] And yet there were remarkable successes for individual pilots. On the night of 15 January, Flight Lieutenant Stevens, in a Hurricane, shot down both a Dornier 17 and a Heinkel 111.

Greater success came gradually to aircrews equipped with AI Mk IV radar, who were guided by the Controller, then used their own set to draw close enough for visual contact. 'The GCI Controller's function was to place his fighter in A.I. contact with the incoming enemy aircraft',[41] and this was done for Flight Lieutenant J. Cunningham in a Beaufighter. With his navigator he had scored the first success on 19 November, and a second on 12 January. Then, on 15 February, he brought down a Heinkel 111 to which the Controller had led him.

'This was a secret war,' Churchill believed, 'whose battles were lost or won unknown to the public.'[42] The description certainly applied to GCI radar, which resulted particularly from experimental work carried out by the TRE at Swanage. In early 1940, 'G. W. A. Dummer had demonstrated a new type of display called the Plan Position Indicator or "PPI", which presented targets as bright areas on a screen.' Of the greatest importance to the Controller, 'the map and relative positions of a bomber were shown at the same time' by apparatus that could traverse through 360°.[43] 'When the fighter had been put on the tail of the bomber by directions from the GCI station,' the scientist A. P. Rowe explained, 'the latter would give the signal "Flash weapon".' Then the fighter crew would switch on their AI set and complete the interception.[44] At Sopley, where GCI apparatus was set up in December 1940, the Controller, Squadron Leader Brown, 'evolved effective techniques for controlling fighter–bomber interception directly from the P.P.I. display', methodically bringing the two together.[45] The seeds of success were sown, although results were still poor by the end of February 1941.

During this period both sides employed patrols over enemy aerodromes during darkness. The *Luftwaffe* hoped to catch British bombers returning from raids over Germany, or night fighters as they landed after sorties. The *Fernnachtjäger* (night intruder force) flew Junkers 88s and Dornier 17s to some effect, bringing worries to returning RAF crews. During the first two months of 1941 they destroyed eight RAF aircraft and damaged nine others over

Britain.[46] In the case of the RAF, sorties over enemy territory at night to 'hinder the smooth running of enemy operations' were known as 'Security Patrols'. Before December 1940 they had been flown by No 2 Group Bomber Command but were then taken over by No 23 Squadron's Blenheims as 'Intruder' operations. They attempted to hit German bombers taking off from, or landing at, their French bases. There were a few successes but, overall, the Intruders were unable to reduce the scale of raids on British cities.[47]

Consequently, by the end of February 1941 the main burden of defence still rested with AA Command, using guns, searchlights and balloons. One of Pile's difficulties arose from the positioning of his limited number of guns. From the previous November the enemy had moved the assault to industrial centres and ports, yet he occasionally launched heavy raids on the capital. Eighty-nine guns were moved from the London region in November to protect cities such as Bristol and Liverpool, but at the end of the year the *Luftwaffe* carried out the intensive fire Blitz on the metropolis.

Pile's reports during the period showed the increasing accuracy of gunfire and searchlights, both using radar control, over several months. Whereas, in the previous September, 20,000 rounds had been expended for each night raider brought down, the figure had reduced to 4,087 in January 1941 and 2,963 a month later. However, in those two months only eight bombers were brought down over Britain by AA fire, a small fraction of those employed. Steps were taken to improve accuracy as wild 'unseen' barrages were abandoned and more careful plots issued from Gun Operations Rooms. Although some German pilots gained a healthy respect for the power of gunfire, others showed less concern. 'The flak batteries?' wrote one. 'They may impress the folk on the ground, but not us up here.'[48] Nonetheless, the sight and sound of gunfire were reassuring in cities suffering devastating raids.

To assist ground defences, 'dummy' fires, known as 'Starfish' sites, were sometimes lit close to important targets. 'These were carefully constructed so as to simulate the lights of a town being dimmed on the approach of raiders,' Armitage notes, adding that 'even the effects of blast furnaces and the sparks from tramlines' could occasionally be reproduced.[49] From the early days of the war, Colonel J. Turner organised the building of dummy airfields, later adding decoy factories, which were 'K Sites' (daytime) or 'Q Sites' (night). After the Coventry raid of 14 November, the control of decoys passed to No 80 Wing, and by the end of December eighteen sites had been built close to industrial centres. Near London, the largest 'Starfish' was at Richmond Park. Through the winter months, about thirty sites were ignited, attracting a number of bombs. Bristol benefited on 2 December.[50] 'When our aircraft had approached the city,' admitted a gunner in a Dornier 17, 'a special detail of soldiers, trained for such actions, had lit several fires on the outskirts, imitating a city on the ground, to mislead our navigators'. The defences were successful. '*II/KG 3* neatly dropped its bombs into a swamp and Bristol itself was spared.'[51] During February three were lit at Swansea and one at Cardiff during raids, twice drawing bombs. Nevertheless, most *Luftwaffe* crews, relying on beams, dead reckoning or moonlight, were not fooled and continued to locate the intended city.

During the early months of 1941 the 'Wizard War' continued, with No 80 Wing taking every opportunity to jam or distort German navigation signals. 'Aspirin' transmitters were used against *Knickebein* beams, while 'Bromide' attempted to counter *X-Gerät*. By mid-January a 'Bromide' was positioned to cover each large city in the southern half of Britain. The individual *X-Gerät* beam stations, formerly known to the RAF as 'Rivers', had been codenamed 'Ruffians', with the titles of 'Hess', 'Schirach', 'Hitler', 'Ribbentrop', 'Goering' and 'Himmler'.

From December 1940 it became apparent that the *Luftwaffe* were employing a new guidance system, the *Y-Gerät*, in which a single beam was used to carry bombers directly to, and over, their targets, without the need for any cross-beams. The Germans called the device *'Wotan II'*, after the Teutonic god who had only one eye. In Britain the system had the code-name 'Benito' because, according to Jones, 'we reckoned that Mussolini was the one-eyed end of the Axis'.[52] The signals came from near Poix, where *III/KG 26* was stationed, and that unit was its pioneer. To counter the threat, No 80 Wing introduced the 'Domino' system, employing the BBC's powerful transmitter at Alexandra Palace to re-radiate and distort the signal from the aircraft to the ground station. Consequently, doubt of the aircraft's exact position was sown on the German side.

The work of No 80 Wing's 'Meacons' certainly led to a degree of confusion for bomber pilots, who sometimes came to mistrust beam systems. 'By February 1941 the Battle of the Beams was as good as won,' Jones wrote.[53] However, not all *Luftwaffe* aircrews would have agreed. When attacking London, or ports, as opposed to inland industrial cities, they were less affected by countermeasures. During January and February 1941 bad weather caused them greater problems.

THE BATTLE OF THE ATLANTIC

When planning their strategies, neither the British nor the German Government had disregarded the importance of sea power a quarter of a century earlier. In 1917 U-boats had sunk 6.6 million tons of shipping in a campaign which threatened to alter the outcome of the conflict. By the following year the Royal Navy's blockade was making a crucial contribution to German collapse. One of Hitler's beliefs, 'which came to the fore again and again', was 'that Britain could be defeated by cutting her overseas supply line'.[54] On the British side, Liddell Hart observed that 'the value of the sea-moat was diminished by the development of air power. The industrialisation of the island had made it dependent on imports and thus multiplied the menace of submarine power.'[55]

After the success of German forces by June 1940, Britain's position was precarious, with access only on the western seaboard for vital trade. In Porten's belief, 'The French armistice completely transformed the naval war.'[56] A campaign was launched against these routes, the bases stretching from the North Cape to the Spanish frontier but sited particularly on the western coast of France. 'The blockade of these islands,' suggested an official narrative, 'had become the paramount principle of the enemy's Grand Strategy.' To achieve it, 'both the naval and the air arm had been in the broad sense integrated'.[57] The *Führer*'s Directive of 6 February 1941 was therefore no more than a decision to intensify an existing campaign. Through the employment of warships and armed merchant raiders, together with U-boats and bombers, a full-scale assault was launched against trade and commerce. For the *Luftwaffe* this implemented a pre-war strategic aim which had been interrupted by the daylight Battle of Britain.

Air activity against shipping had been used from the start of the war, first in attacks on maritime traffic and warships in the North Sea and Scottish naval bases. 'On the east coast route, minelaying by aircraft had caused more damage than U-boats in the later months of 1939.'[58] By the end of November 46 British merchant ships, displacing 180,000 tons, had been destroyed by magnetic mines, and this figure rose to 79 vessels by the end of the year. This was expanded during the Norwegian Campaign, when *Fliegerkorps X* led the *Luftwaffe* effort, making particular use of *KG 26* and *KG 30* for anti-shipping work. One of the pioneers of strikes against merchant vessels was Major Harlinghausen, a veteran of the Spanish Civil War. His method of approaching a ship from just above sea level, so that the silhouette stood out clearly, especially at dusk or on moonlit nights, was nicknamed the 'Swedish turnip' system. It brought him successes over the North Sea.[59]

The daylight Battle of Britain saw the main thrust of German action launched against Fighter Command airfields and aircraft factories on the British mainland, yet, during the Contact Phase of the battle in July, many raids were made on Channel convoys. At the same time the *Luftwaffe* expanded its cooperation with the German Navy. Units of both services were established on the west coast of France, with the tempting targets of Atlantic shipping set out before them.

From early August, '15 Heinkel 111s and 6 to 8 Focke-Wulf 200 Condors were being employed for this purpose by *Marine Gruppe West* at Lorient'.[60] On 7 September *I/KG 40*, with a strength of seven Condors under the leadership of *Major* Peterson, were stationed near Bordeaux especially for reconnaissance work. In the next month Admiral Dönitz moved his headquarters from Paris to Kernevel, near Lorient, to be close to his naval forces, and the Battle of the Atlantic began in earnest.[61] Dönitz, who had had reservations over the practicability or wisdom of Operation 'Sealion', was about to implement the policy in which he placed his faith—the overwhelming of Britain by the strangulation of her sea trade. By then, large modern airfields were being constructed in France at Bordeaux, Cognac, Dinard, Evreux, Rennes and Vannes, and at Banak, Bardufoss, Gardemoen, Kirkenes, Stavanger and Trondheim in Norway.[62] By the end of the year the North-Western Approaches to Britain were patrolled regularly by German aircraft. Soon a reconnaissance 'shuttle service' was operating with two planes a day, 'one of which flew from Bordeaux to the Western Approaches and landed at Stavanger, Norway, while the other returned by the same route'.[63]

The aircraft mainly employed was the Focke-Wulf 200 Condor, developed from a pre-war design by Kurt Tank for a commercial transport. With a span of almost 108 feet and a length of 77 feet, the Condor was powered by four Bramo 323R-2 engines, each of 1,200hp, giving a speed of 224mph at 16,000 feet and a range of 2,100 miles. The crew of seven were protected by six machine guns. The maximum bomb load of 4,620lb consisted of twelve 50kg bombs in the ventral gondola, one 500kg below each outboard engine and one 250kg on each of two underwing racks. This formidable armament, combined with the aircraft's long range, threatened great danger to British shipping. On many occasions, however, the Condor carried only a fraction of that bomb load, not having been designed as a bomber. Little imagination is required to appreciate what could have been achieved in these conditions had the *Luftwaffe* pressed ahead with the production of the Heinkel 177.

The Condors suffered casualties. One crashed near Sunderland on 19 July, struck by AA fire while minelaying. Five days later another, on a similar expedition near Belfast Lough, had engine failure, coming down in the sea. On 20 August a Condor was hit by gunfire from a cargo steamer over the Irish Sea and crashed. Yet the aircraft had successes. Its greatest *coup* came on 22 October when a Focke-Wulf 200C sighted the Canadian Pacific Company's flagship *Empress of Britain*, bound from Cape Town to Liverpool. The vessel, of 42,000 tons, was 150 miles from Ireland, carrying 643 people. The pilot attacked immediately from a height of 500 feet. 'There was loud cheering when the tail gunner reported a hit on the forward part of the ship,' he reported, adding that 'the ship had already started to burn and the fire was spreading rapidly'.[64] Most of the passengers and crew were rescued from the vessel, which was sunk by a U-boat two days later. The aircraft's captain, *Oberleutnant* Jope, had another success on 22 January 1941, when he sank the *Kapetan Straits*.

Attacks on shipping were partly governed by the weather. Thus although in November 1940 the German Air Force launched 2,350 daylight sorties, this figure was halved in the following month. In January 1941 twelve vessels were sunk or damaged within 40 miles of the British coast in night and day attacks.[65] The figure grew sharply over the subsequent three months, to 25, 68 and 78 respectively. Of these, seventeen were sunk at night, and in March, at a Fighter Command conference, a naval officer admitted that 'moonlight attacks on shipping are now becoming a menace from Southwold to the North'.[66]

In the spring of 1941 the *Luftwaffe*'s effort expanded. Two vessels totalling 10,857 tons were sunk by Captain Verlohr of *I/KG 40* west of Ireland on 16 January. Almost four weeks later five Focke-Wulf 200s, including Jope's, struck at convoy HG.43, bound for Britain from Gibraltar. They sent five ships to the bottom. The experienced Harlinghausen was appointed to the new command of *Fliegerführer Atlantik* in mid-March. 'Imagine our situation as a land problem,' Dönitz told him in stressing the imperative need for aerial reconnaissance, 'with the enemy convoy at Hamburg, and my nearest U-boats at Oslo, Paris, Vienna and Prague—each with a maximum circle of vision of twenty miles.'[67]

The German Navy 'had long been sure that the Air Force alone could sink 300,000 tons of shipping per month', a figure almost achieved between March and May.[68] The peak was reached in April, with a total of 296,000 tons. In the view of the Naval High Command, a total of 750,000 tons sunk monthly 'would force Britain out of the war if maintained for a year'.[69] An official British Admiralty booklet admitted that 'the intensification of the Focke-Wulf attacks led to heavy losses of ships, particularly during the early months of the year'.[70] To provide even greater problems, in March 1941 *II/KG 40* was re-equipped with the new Dornier 217E-2 for anti-shipping work and the unit often shadowed convoys, reporting their positions to naval headquarters for action by U-boats.

Submarines posed greater threats than aerial bombing to ships.[71] Between June 1940 and February 1941 U-boats sank over two million tons of shipping and this was a 'happy time' for German crews. By March three submarine 'ace' commanders were at sea, gaining great success. Otto Kretschmer (*U99*) sank two auxiliary cruisers in one night, Günther Prien (*U47*), who had earlier sunk the battleship *Royal Oak* at Scapa Flow, added many merchant vessels to his score, as did Joachim Schepke (*U100*). However, vigorous countermeasures from the Royal Navy led to the destruction of all three submarines early in March, only Kretschmer, of the commanders, surviving as a prisoner. By then he had sunk one destroyer and 44 merchantmen—a stark reminder of the peril facing Britain's sea trade, and thus her ability to fight on.[72]

The role of the *Luftwaffe* in guiding and supporting submarines brought grave worries to the British Government. The Germans' 'Atlantic Command' increased from 44 aircraft in March 1941 to 83 in April, thence to 155 by July. In a sense, the effort was belated. According to an RAF estimate, 'had the German Air Force General Staff taken the decision to concentrate large air forces against merchant convoys in the Atlantic and Western Approaches in the autumn of 1940, the situation for the supply of Great Britain must surely have reached a more critical situation than it did'. This fact serves to accentuate the effect of the burden of the Night Blitz carried by civilians on the British homeland at that time.[73]

Understanding the severity of the problem, Churchill at a meeting of the Chiefs of Staff Committee on 27 February 1941 decided to give 'absolute priority' to the defence of shipping in the North-Western Approaches. Ten days later the Air Staff wrote to Douglas, telling him that his prime task was no longer to defend the aircraft industry but to guard the area of the Bristol Channel, the Mersey and the Clyde. At the same time, the problems of dealing with Condor raids were exercising the mind of Portal, the CAS. In his lucid way he wrote to the Chiefs of Staff, suggesting that the RAF lacked sufficient aircraft to 'secure our shipping in the Atlantic against the scale and type of long-range air attack that we must now expect'. The only effective method of defence would be 'the ship-borne high performance fighter operating from specially converted ships which must accompany every convoy in the danger area'. Here was the germ of an idea which developed into the 'Hurricat'—a catapult-launched Hurricane fighter—for use at sea.[74]

As ever, Churchill's response to impending danger was to call for aggression. 'The next four months should enable us to defeat the attempt to strangle our food supplies,' he wrote in a Directive; he added, 'and our connection with the United States'. This was a point of the highest importance, with his appreciation of the need to expand the American link for both diplomatic and economic reasons. 'For this purpose we must take the offensive against the U-boat and the Focke-Wulf wherever we can and whenever we can.'[75]

The task was formidable. Apart from Condor attacks over the North-Western Approaches, many German units launched strikes at night against coastal shipping. From February, '*I/KG 26*, a crack unit, had moved from Beauvais to Aalborg, [and] *II/KG 76* returned from Germany re-equipped with Junkers 88s and began anti-shipping operations in our eastern coastal area'. Among units flying from Northern France, Holland and Belgium were '*I/KG 27*, *I/KG 1* and elements of *KG 2*, *3*, *30*, *53* and *Gr. 122*'.[76] Figures for ships either sunk or damaged in night attacks rose from five in February to 15 in March, then to 40 in the two following months. There were estimates that during April 1941 a total of 614 minelaying sorties had been made round Britain's coastline. At the time, because of the limitations of AI in locating aircraft below an altitude of 5,000 feet, 'there was no effective fighter defence against low-flying minelayers'.[77] Although the Condors continued to have success, they also suffered further losses. On 10 January one was shot down while attacking the *Seaman*, an ocean-going tug, about 200 miles north-west of Ireland. On 5 February another was brought down by gunfire from the SS *Major C*, falling in Eire. Three others crashed in the sea.

What finally reduced the *Luftwaffe*'s involvement in the Battle of the Atlantic by mid-1941 was the approach of the Russian Campaign. At that stage, many bomber units were moved to Eastern Europe, providing the British with a small, though welcome, easing of pressure. By then the Blitz on western ports, with which the assault on shipping was so closely linked, was also easing.

Nonetheless, Britain's maritime fleet had suffered heavily. Losses from U-boats in the period between 31 March and 31 May totalled 142 ships, grossing over 800,000 tons. Of these, 99 vessels were British. 'In the same three months enemy aircraft, surface vessels and mines had accounted respectively for another 179, 44 and 33 merchant ships.' During that period 412 ships, British, Allied and neutral, were lost, displacing 1,691,499 tons—'up to date the worst three months of the war'.[78] Both sides had victories and defeats. The battle was still unresolved.

NOTES

1. Trevor Roper, Hitler Directive No 18, 12 November 1940.
2. *Ibid.*, Directive No 19, 10 December 1940.
3. *Ibid.*, Directive No 21, 18 December 1940.
4. *Ibid.*, Directive No 22, 11 January 1941.
5. *Ibid.*, Directive No 23, 6 February 1941.
6. AIR 19/230, 21 January 1941.
7. Irving, *Rise and Fall*, 117.
8. Goering note, 1 January 1941.
9. *The Aeroplane*, 10 January 1941.
10. *Front Line*, 110.
11. *Ibid.*, 100.
12. *The Aeroplane*, 10 January 1941.
13. E. Webb and J. Duncan, *Blitz Over Britain* (1990), 91.
14. *Front Line*, 111.
15. *The Aeroplane*, 28 February 1941.
16. Webb and Duncan, 91.
17. *The Aeroplane*, 17 January 1941.
18. *Front Line*, 107.
19. *The Aeroplane*, 17 January 1941.
20. Ministry of Home Security Appreciation, No 223, 12 January 1941.
21. *The Aeroplane*, 31 January 1941.
22. *City of Portsmouth Records 1941*, 167.
23. *The Aeroplane*, 7 February 1941.
24. See Gilbert, vi, 999.
25. *Clementine Churchill*, 302.
26. Gilbert, vi, 1008.
27. Beardmore, 109–10.
28. AIR 19/230, Sinclair to Portal, 12 January 1941.
29. Wykeham, 156.
30. *Years of Command*, 104.
31. F.C./S 22104, 8 December 1940.
32. AIR 41/17, 93.

33. A. Cooper, *Born Leader* (1993), 44–60.
34. AIR 41/17, 93.
35. *Years of Command*, 106–7.
36. AIR 41/17, 92.
37. *Years of Command*, 107.
38. DCAS note on Night Air Defence (41), 3, 18 February 1941.
39. AIR 41/17, 90.
40. See Townsend, *Duel in the Dark*, 134–51.
41. The importance of the Controller's role in the defence systems, both by day and night, has never been sufficiently acknowledged.
42. Churchill, ii, 337.
43. W. Penley and R. Batt, *Dorset's Radar Days* (1994), 8.
44. W. Gunston, *Night Fighters* (1976), 61.
45. Penley and Batt, 8.
46. S. Parry, *Intruders over Britain* (1987), Appendix 12, 173–5.
47. AIR 41/17, 92.
48. *Eagle's Wings*, 69.
49. Sir Michael Armitage, *The Royal Air Force* (1993), 110.
50. See *Blitz*, i, 223–9.
51. Von Ishoven, 88.
52. *Secret War*, 238.
53. *Ibid.*, 239.
54. Dr Karl Klee in H. Jaconsen and J. Rohwer, *Decisive Battles of World War Two* (1965), 75.
55. B. Liddell Hart, *History of the Second World War* (1970), 109.
56. E. Porten, *The German Navy in World War Two* (1970), 109.
57. AIR 41/17, 99.
58. Liddell Hart, *Second World War*, 371.
59. Bekker, 325–7.
60. Air Ministry, *Rise and Fall*, 104.
61. See Porten, 188.
62. Air Ministry, *Rise and Fall*, 104.
63. Porten, 189.
64. Ishoven, 105.
65. AIR 41/17, Appendix 15.
66. F. C. ORB, Appendix D, 9 March 1941.
67. Bekker, 327–31.
68. Ishoven, 161.
69. *Ibid.*, 190.
70. The Admiralty, *The Battle of the Atlantic* (HMSO, 1946), 25.
71. See Hinsley, i, 334.
72. Porten, 190–2.
73. Air Ministry, *Rise and Fall*, 106–7.
74. See AIR 41/18, paras 52–64.

75. AIR 41/12, 6 March 1941, 151–2.
76. F. C. ORB, Appendix D, 9 March 1941.
77. *Ibid.*, Intelligence Summary, April 1941.
78. *Battle of the Atlantic*, 31.

CHAPTER NINE

THE FINAL ONSLAUGHT

THE BALKAN CAMPAIGN

The period from March to May 1941 marked the culmination of the Night Blitz against Britain. At the same time as the *Luftwaffe* were continuing (yet running down) their attacks on cities, they were opening, or preparing for, campaigns elsewhere in Europe. Events demonstrated Hitler's dilemma. On the one hand, as Britain continued stubbornly to resist, he was compelled to sustain pressure against the United Kingdom. On the other, Mussolini's blunders against Albania and Greece, together with the British victories over the Italians in North Africa, called for a response. Hitler therefore decided to send land and air support via the Balkans and thus became embroiled in south-eastern Europe. In addition, he hoped that the intervention would guard his flank during the major forthcoming campaign. That was to be the rapid overthrow within a period of months of Bolshevik Russia, which was Britain's only possible, though unlikely, European ally. Then he would be able to return to a final settlement with the United Kingdom.

A German Air Force mission to Romania had been dispatched in September 1940, followed by one to Bulgaria in December. Throughout the following January and February *Luftwaffe* units were moved in. During March 400 aircraft were posted south from Romania into Bulgaria with the intention of attacking Greece. The Germans believed that the Yugoslavs would agree to their plans, but on 27 March an anti-government *coup* in Belgrade altered that nation's policy. For Hitler, this spelled danger and he immediately ordered *Luftwaffe* reinforcements to the region.

'The *Führer* is determined, without waiting for possible loyalty declarations of the new government,' announced a Directive on the same day as the *coup*, 'to make all preparations to destroy Yugoslavia militarily and as a national unit.' The blow was to be carried out with 'pitiless harshness'.[1] The forces available were quickly gathered, under the overall control of General Loehr, C-in-C of *Luftflotte IV*. In immediate charge was General von Richthofen, who had seen previous service during the Western Campaign and the early stages of the Battle of Britain. Aircraft units were posted to the Balkans from France, Germany and the Mediterranean. From France came three *Gruppen* of long-range bombers, two *Gruppen* of Stukas and six *Gruppen* of Bf 109s. 'The main task of the *Luftwaffe*', a meeting at the German Chancellery decided, 'is to start as early as possible with the destruction of the Yugoslav Air Force ground installations and to destroy the capital city, Belgrade, in waves of attack.'[2]

The assault on both Yugoslavia and Greece opened on 6 April. 'Yugoslavia was overrun within a week, and her capital devastated by the opening air attack,' Liddell Hart wrote, adding that the Greek Campaign lasted for three weeks.[3] 'In Belgrade,' Irving notes, 'seventeen thousand people were killed and the government quarters paralysed.'[4] The bombardment extended over two days and the city on Palm Sunday was packed with people from surrounding areas.[5] There was little opposition to the onslaught from either air or ground. Civilian defence services were virtually non-existent. Such an attack was straightforward for units like *Stukagruppe* 77, which had not enjoyed such unopposed activity since the French Campaign. The *Luftwaffe* was able to gain the kind of success that it sought, yet failed to gain, against Britain.[6] (After the war, Loehr was executed for launching the attack.)

The Balkan Campaign brought succour to the Italians and, after the occupation of Greece and Crete, removed the British from south-eastern Europe. At the same time it brought the Germans new allies and widened options for the forthcoming war against Russia. In that context the *Luftwaffe* showed its ability to launch ruthless and successful assaults on ground defences and gain the results for which it was renowned. That notwithstanding, the campaign did nothing to bring the defeat of Britain one step nearer. Without that, Germany would never achieve total victory.

RAIDS ON SEAPORTS: MARCH TO MAY

For the Germans, the corollary of attempting to strangle Britain's sea trade was to sink merchant ships in harbour and destroy shore-based facilities. As the weather improved over northern and western Europe in the spring of 1941 the Germans intensified their campaign, particularly against seaports on the western side of the United Kingdom. Conditions were generally good in the first half of March, although bad weather during the last week, stretching into early April, curtailed raids. Nonetheless, the *Luftwaffe* flew about 4,400 night sorties over Britain, a figure rising to 5,500 during April and to 4,500 in May, even at a time when the Night Blitz was ending. Considering the number of machines that had been transferred for campaigns further east, that was a remarkable achievement by the *Luftwaffe*'s bomber force.

With the German occupation of western France and the intensification of submarine attacks in the Atlantic, Merseyside grew in importance as a centre of trade. For many vessels this was the terminus of the route from North America, via the Western Approaches. Vital supplies of food and, from early 1941, a growing volume of war materials poured into the area, then were distributed over the United Kingdom by road and rail.

A major raid on Merseyside was launched on the night of 12 March in good visibility and with a full moon. For four hours 340 bombers of *Luftflotten II* and *III* dropped 300 tons of explosives and 64,000 incendiaries; a smaller yet still heavy follow-up attack occurred on the next night. The first raid was opened by pathfinders of *KGr. 100*, who were too high at 12,000 feet and too distant from their stations for *X-Gerät* to work efficiently but who bombed visually. Another pathfinder squadron, *III/KG 26*, used *Y-Gerät* and marked targets clearly with incendiaries from heights ranging between 12,000 and 19,000 feet. Following at lower levels were such experienced units as the Heinkel 111s of *KG 27*, *KG 51* and *KG 55*, together with Junkers 88s of *KGr. 806* and *II/ KG 76*. To confuse the defences they ran in from different directions, and they had little difficulty, particularly at Birkenhead, in locating their bombing points.

The main aiming places were the area of docks and Cammell Laird's shipyard, the latter being allocated to *II/KG 76*, who could see the site clearly. 'With the shining water to help them, the German bombers could not fail to drop many of their missiles on the docks themselves,' reported an official publication. It added that if the Germans incidentally damaged 'densely packed houses away from, as well as close to, the waterfront', their intention was to strike at 'the nerve and courage of civilians' as well as disrupting everyday life.[7] There was considerable destruction in the docks, where crews claimed to have hit cold stores and granaries, machines and equipment. Two ships were sunk and others received hits at their moorings. Flour mills were damaged and gas holders struck at Wallasey. In Liverpool, the Cotton Exchange, General Post Office, Municipal Annex and White Star Building were all set ablaze.

To the west of the Mersey, Birkenhead suffered the heaviest casualties, with 264 people killed. Three hospitals were hit and many civilians rendered homeless. At Wallasey 198 died, with a further 49 in Liverpool. The casualties across the area over the two nights totalled about 1,300 killed or injured. However, by now the civil defence system, helped by small service units, had gained good experience in dealing with the effects of bombing and 'went about their work with full mastery'.[8] Fire crews and rescue teams, medical staff, police and wardens all acted magnificently in saving people and property. Then, problems resulting from widespread homelessness had to be faced under the most trying circumstances, especially as one-third of the Rest Centres were damaged.

In spite of heavy fire from ground defences, the bombers, as Baldwin had predicted nine years earlier, got through. Over 3,000 rounds were fired from AA batteries, and although a contemporary magazine claimed that four aircraft had been brought down 'by anti-aircraft gunfire', in reality the artillery hit none.[9] Over the whole country, nevertheless, there was increased night fighter activity: altogether Fighter Command flew 261 sorties, destroying five bombers over Britain, four of which had attacked Merseyside. Compared with earlier results this was a cheering score, but, considering the size of the bomber force, nothing was achieved to deflect the *Luftwaffe*'s intentions.

The importance of north-western England to Britain's position was underlined at the end of April. The Prime Minister toured the areas of Merseyside, Liverpool and Manchester, accompanied by two Americans, James Forrestal and Averell Harriman. On 24 April he sent a message to President Roosevelt explaining that he wanted at first hand 'to study the position in the Mersey area, so important to the North-Western Approaches'. As ever, he was cheered as he passed through streets by civilians who had suffered severely—and recognised that further tribulations lay ahead.[10]

After his return Churchill broadcast on the evening of 27 April, telling listeners that he had been at 'the front', which he listed as the streets of several cities, including Liverpool. This was, he said, 'like going out of a hothouse on to the bridge of a fighting ship', then he paid tribute to ordinary people in the 'battered cities' he had visited. 'What a vindication of the civilized and decent way of living we have been trying to work towards in our island.'[11]

After further lesser raids on 7 and 26 April, Merseyside bore the brunt of a sustained onslaught on the first seven nights of May. 'The occurrences point to the probability of heavy attacks on this area,' the Ministry of Home Security predicted after 1 May, 'which must be made within the next three weeks if the enemy is to take advantage of the hours of darkness.' Further comments referred to 'the vital importance of the western ports', asking that 'all possible steps should be taken to minimise the dislocation' on Merseyside.[12] In that period, remembered as 'The May Week', over 860 tons of high explosives and 106,000 incendiaries had rained down. 'Only two of those raids were extremely heavy, but none was negligible.'[13] The first two bombardments caused destruction not only to industry, utilities and transport services but also to private and commercial property. Several public shelters were struck on the second night, causing many casualties.

The heaviest bombing occurred during the third raid. In the words of one historian, 'The night of 3/4 May was, without the slightest doubt, the worst in the city's entire history',[14] as almost 300 aircraft concentrated on Liverpool. Considerable destruction resulted in the dock area, where some large ships, barges and tugs were sunk and other vessels and landing facilities damaged. The most spectacular disaster happened at the Huskisson No 2, or Branch, Dock, where the SS *Malakand*, carrying one thousand tons of ammunition, was moored. The ship was set ablaze and valiant attempts were made to overcome the flames, then to scuttle the vessel. They failed. She blew up in an explosion so vast that *Luftwaffe* crews reported flames rising to 1,600 feet. The ship's anchor was thrown a hundred yards, some steel plates were discovered over two miles away, and the dock area was devastated.

Many acts of considerable bravery were shown in rescuing and caring for people. Others responded stoutly to danger as, for example, when a munitions train received a direct hit. For several hours ten Liverpool men 'led by Goods Guard George Roberts, worked at the risk of their lives. Regardless of danger from continuous explosions in the munitions train and from h.e. bombs which continued to fall in the vicinity', the men fought to overcome damage and danger.[15] Their example could be multiplied many times in various forms.

By dawn on 8 May wide districts of Merseyside were desolated. Soon it became clear that of 144 shipping berths, about half were unusable and, for a time, the handling of cargoes was reduced by three-quarters. Altogether, 57 vessels of various sizes, displacing 80,000 tons, had been sunk or destroyed and other shipping could neither enter nor leave the docks. On land, railways had been shattered and roads blocked.

Casualties were heavy during the week, especially on the third raid. Altogether about 1,900 people were killed and 1,450 seriously injured, with thousands of others slightly hurt. An enormous burden fell on the police, medical and mortuary services, a problem compounded by the destruction of 66,000 houses. About 70,000 people were left homeless.

In Liverpool, the Corn Exchange and several hospitals received hits, with fire damage also to shops, schools and houses. Fire crews, as in other cities, were sometimes thwarted when water pressure fell after hydrants and pipes were fractured by further bombing. The position was sometimes exacerbated by outside brigades, sent in to help, lacking equipment of standard size. The fire problem was particularly great on the night of 3 May.

What of the effects of the week's raids? It was 'the longest unbroken series of serious attacks on any provincial area of the whole war'.[16] Churchill later suggested that if the *Luftwaffe* had persisted with these raids, 'the Battle of the Atlantic would have been even more closely run than it was'. However, as soon as the onslaught finished, work began at pace to repair and restore. Before long even the heaviest damage to docks, railways, roads and factories was at least patched up and work recommenced. As for public morale, there was an obvious immediate feeling of despair for some people whose homes had been destroyed and who had lost family or friends, whose workplaces lay shattered and whose problems appeared to overwhelm local officials. In some places rumours spread of defeatism and, as ever in war, stories were magnified. The people of Merseyside naturally were stunned by the severity of the continuity of attack, a point reinforced by some Mass Observation reports.[17] Such writings, however, often overlooked the resilience of 'Scousers' under pressure. One Liverpudlian, quoted by Whiting, later spoke of the fantastic spirit which made him proud of his fellows. The people of Merseyside did not crack and went on to play a part in the maritime war so far insufficiently acknowledged, and unmatched by that of any other British seaport.

A point to lift their morale, although not immediately apparent to those suffering deprivation by bombing, was that night fighters were gaining greater success. During the first seven nights of May, when Merseyside was a prime, yet not sole, target, 38 bombers were brought down over Britain, the great majority by Beaufighters and Defiants. At last they were locating the enemy.

Writing of Clydeside in September 1940, Sir Patrick Dollan believed it 'unlikely that Glasgow will be attacked from the air in the same way of London'. German planes, he suggested, lacked fighter escorts in raiding so far north. He also claimed that 'Glasgow houses are more solidly built than those collapsed from concussion in London'.[18] The Lord Provost of Glasgow was wrong on two counts. First, *Luftwaffe* bombers at night needed no fighter escorts. Second, German bombs ensured that architecture north of the border 'collapsed from concussion' as readily as it did further south.

Clydeside was a prime target on the *Luftwaffe*'s calling-list when the Night Blitz turned particularly against seaports. As Britain's second city, with a population of well over a million, Glasgow was 'of world-wide repute as a hive of industry and a metropolis of commerce' and contained 'shipbuilding yards on the Clyde and the iron, steel and chemical works in the city and neighbourhood'.[19] In the 1930s, local yards had built over 750,000 tons of shipping in a single year, more than one-third of the United Kingdom's total. Businesses included such renowned names as John Brown's, Beardmores, A & J Inglis, and Harland & Wolff. The Fairfield Engineering Company was 'one of the largest establishments of the kind in the world, employing at a busy season as many as ten thousand men'.[20] Great dock areas serviced cargoes from across the globe, while in the war thousands of service personnel and their equipment left for overseas from the waters of the Clyde. Queen's Dock covered 34 acres and the Prince's Dock was larger, with a quay face of 3,737 yards. A writer referred to the main road from Glasgow, running through Clydebank: 'Between the highway and the river is the kingdom of ships; north of the road are tenements and houses.[21]

On this area, in bright moonlight during the consecutive nights of 13 and 14 March, fell two heavy raids. The first was led by *KGr. 100*, followed by over 200 aircraft dropping 272 tons of high explosives and almost 60,000 fire bombs. In particular they aimed for the Bowling Shipyards, the oil tanks at Old Kilpatrick and an ammunition depot at Dalmuir. Widespread destruction resulted at Clydebank, the home of about 60,000 people, especially in districts close to the river. Large fires were started in Singer's timber yard and at Rothesay Dock, while a distillery was hit at Yoker. At Yarrow's shipyard one bomb hit a shelter, killing 80 workers, and the Radnor Park area was badly affected. Troubles increased when the Communications Centre at Clydebank was put out of action, greatly hampering civilian defence services. 'The building shook and the dust of ages came down on us. The lights went out, and we did not know whether we were going into Kingdom Come.'[22] In Glasgow itself less damage was caused, yet a hospital, a school and the University were hit.

When an equal number of bombers returned on the following night, fires were still burning along Clydeside and could be seen by airmen one hundred miles away. 'Like raindrops in a storm or locusts settling upon ripe grain',[23] 230 tons of explosives and 28,000 incendiaries came down on the previous night's targets, to which was added the Rolls-Royce aero-engine factory at Hillington.

Oil tanks were hit at Dalmottar, as was a power station at Yoker. A large fire raged in Prince's Dock, Govan, and there was generally extensive industrial damage. However, the *Luftwaffe* failed in its basic strategy because the shipyards, docks and factories of Clydeside were not totally disabled and continued to operate.

Greater destruction, nevertheless, occurred in residential and commercial areas. Radnor Park was devastated in Clydebank, where, of the town's 12,000 houses, only eight escaped damage. Fires raged fiercely. 'From Knightswood we could see glorious colours in the sky,' one lady recollected. 'It was horrific to think that this was a town burning.'[24] As a result, thousands of people were evacuated from Clydebank to Rest Centres, but in some cases civilian defence services were overwhelmed by the scale of the attacks. Earlier, plans had been laid by ARP authorities, although insufficient shelter accommodation was provided, but no one could foresee the severity of concentrated bombing on a limited district. And yet the tenacity of the Scots was soon displayed. For a few days production was reduced, particularly because of a lack of sources of power, but the workforce soon returned, many journeying in from outside the devastated area.

On the second raid there was greater havoc in Glasgow, where Drumchapel, Maryhill, Partick and Govan were particularly heavily bombed. In the worst incident a parachute mine landed on a four-storey tenement in Kilmuir Street, causing 83 deaths and rendering one thousand people homeless. Altogether across the Clydeside region, 55,000 people lost their homes.

Considerable argument arose over the number of casualties suffered altogether in both raids. At first, the wireless announced that they had been light, when it was patently obvious locally that a considerable number of civilians had been killed. A few days after the second raid the Ministry of Home Security suggested a casualty total of 500, a far from accurate figure and hurtful to those who had suffered. According to O'Brien, 'Rumour then took the upper hand, and some lack of confidence in the official communiqués developed.'[25]

In reality, it appears that there were 1,085 deaths, with 1,603 people badly hurt. As some small consolation for the civilian victims of aerial terror, during the two raids RAF night fighters destroyed five Heinkel 111s, three Junkers 88s and one Dornier 17 over Britain. For the *Luftwaffe*, however, this was a small price to pay. In a letter to Roosevelt, Winant, the American Ambassador, referred to the raid and its heavy casualties. 'I was told by competent witnesses that while the families waited to be taken to what shelters were available,' he wrote appreciatively, 'they rested on what little they had been able to save of their belongings, silent and grim, "without a fear in the lot".'[26]

The weather at the end of March and into early April was poor, temporarily curtailing the *Luftwaffe*'s operations. 'German aerodromes in France are still waterlogged,' reported a magazine, 'and are more suitable for the operation of seaplanes than landplanes.' The same writer next displayed alarming fears over future aerial warfare. He was convinced that invasion would come, although not in the near future and then 'the use of gas seems certain'. The German adversary 'will not refrain from its use on mere humanitarian grounds'—an assessment offering little solace to those on Clydeside who had suffered so heavily from what were euphemistically called 'conventional weapons'.[27]

They, however, were faced with more immediate problems when *Luftwaffe* bombers returned on 7 April. That night 172 aircraft jettisoned 200 tons of high explosives and 26,000 incendiaries, with Hillington, Dumbarton and Greenock as particular aiming points. Inevitably, pathfinders of *KGr. 100* were involved in the early stages of the raids, followed by other bomber crews who were by now highly experienced in navigation. Several thousand Glaswegians lost their homes, but casualties were comparatively light and fire services reacted magnificently to extinguish blazes. Many bombs fell at Clydebank on the sorely stricken sites of three weeks earlier, but, although shipyards were struck, only slight damage resulted. Greater destruction was caused to utility and transport services.

A final onslaught fell on Clydeside in early May, near the end of the *Luftwaffe*'s campaign. Just before midnight on the 5th, the first of 280 aircraft began to arrive, especially over Dumbarton, Gouroch and Greenock but also other places from Dalmuir to Rutherglen. Throughout the following three and a half hours they cruised across their targets, dropping 350 tons of explosives and about 47,000 incendiaries. Damage resulted at Yoker, in Rothesay Docks and at Clydebank in the famous John Brown's shipyard. Work was held up there not so much by the effects in the yards themselves as by the interruptions to railway transport and utility services. In addition, tenement blocks inhabited by many families were demolished, leading to widespread homelessness.

During the following night the *Luftwaffe* returned as part of a large-scale offensive across various parts of Britain. Of 400 bombers in total, 232 raided Clydeside. Severe damage was caused at Greenock, whose ordeal, 'though not as heavy as that of Clydebank, was met in the same spirit'.[28] Many fires were started there, followed by a large explosion when the gasworks was hit. Once again houses and commercial property suffered badly and a casualty count over both nights showed that some 300 people had been killed, with a greater total injured.

By then Clydeside had suffered grievously, especially from the bombing of residential districts. In his diary, the local Director of Education believed that Clydebank had received 'a bad knock, probably severer than Coventry or any English town, since the whole town "got it" and no single area or district escaped'. It is difficult to discover another place of similar size in Britain that was virtually obliterated. Nevertheless, the diary added that work in factories was not halted and people were 'beginning to trickle back'. No praise, he added, 'is too great for the people'.[29] For the rest of the war Clydeside played an inestimable role, especially in the Battle of the Atlantic.

Another area of Britain which had considered itself reasonably safe from air attack was Northern Ireland. 'Its people might be forgiven for making up their minds that their remoteness from enemy bases was a permanent safeguard,'[30] commented a writer in 1942. Because of its distance from the main centres of action, the region was less prepared for attack than other parts of the United Kingdom. There were no more than two dozen anti-aircraft guns, of No 12 Group AA Command, in Northern Ireland, a small balloon barrage and no searchlights. No night fighters were stationed there. In addition, civilian defence services were less developed and prepared than elsewhere, and few air raid shelters had been built. And yet Belfast held some prize targets for the *Luftwaffe*. The Harland & Wolff shipyards covered many acres. The same company had a large aircraft factory, while the Short & Harland Works also was important to the aircraft industry. The vital position of Belfast, not only to war production but also as a haven at the end of the Western Approaches, was made all the stronger by Eire's neutrality in the war. The Treaty Ports had been denied to Britain, increasing the difficulty of defending Atlantic sea routes. It was an unsatisfactory situation, Churchill told Roosevelt in December 1940, that British merchant seamen should have to transport goods not only to their own country, but also 'that we should have to carry Irish supplies through air and U-boat attacks and subsidise them handsomely when De Valera is quite content to sit happy and see us strangled'.[31]

The first attack on Belfast arrived as a small raid 'of no great severity'.[32] A few fires were started by incendiaries dropped from aircraft of *Luftflotte III*. Some landed in Harland & Wolff's shipyard and others ignited a timber yard. The bombing had shown the province that it was not beyond the *Luftwaffe*'s reach. Thoughts were concentrated rapidly on necessary countermeasures.

On 15 April came a far heavier raid, when 200 *Luftwaffe* aircraft unloaded 200 tons of high explosives and 29,000 fire bombs on three main areas of the city. The assault started soon after midnight and continued for seven hours into the following morning. Damage was done to industrial targets, including shipyards and factories, which had been special aiming points. In addition, as happened commonly in the Blitz, widespread destruction was wrought in the city itself to domestic and commercial property. 'Streets of houses and shopping centres blazed into walls of flame in which bombs exploded with a continuous rumbling crash.'[33]

Soon many fires burned almost out of control and the fire services were hard-pressed. Reinforcements were sent over from the British mainland and also came to the north from Eire, where volunteer firemen 'came racing through the night with their peace-time headlamps blazing',[34] driving thirteen fire engines. The initial figures given for casualties were too low and possibly 800 to 900 people were killed, with a further 1,500 injured. About 1,600 houses were destroyed, 28,000 were damaged and some 20,000 civilians were rendered homeless. Soon, 40,000 people were in Rest Centres and 70,000 were being fed in emergency centres as defence services struggled to deal with the unexpected and brutal assault. The intensity of the attack drove some people out of the city as 'ditchers', equivalent to the 'trekkers' of the mainland. They 'took to the fields each evening and could be seen making their way up the Cave Hill or the lower slopes of Divis Mountain,' an observer recollected. Some went to live in other places, away from vulnerable areas. With shades of Douhet and pre-war predictions of collapsing morale, he added that 'people were bewildered and did not know what to do'. However, before long essential services were re-established and people returned to work.[35]

The *Luftwaffe*, in the last throes of the Night Blitz, returned on 4 May with a major raid. Over 200 bombers during the hours of darkness jettisoned 235 tons of explosives and 96,000 incendiaries on to the docks and shipyards of Belfast, as well as on the city centre. Many separate fires were started and soon these appeared to join into one. Flying over Belfast, one German spoke of 'just one enormous conflagration which spread over the entire harbour and industrial area'.[36]

At ground level, the Shorts factory was badly hit, as was the harbour area, where the power station received damage. Bombs struck the York Street railway station and, among other areas, the High Street, Crumlin Road, Carlisle Circus and St Patrick's Street. Water mains were broken, hindering the work of fire brigades who were, once again, helped by crews from Eire. ARP services, by now experienced and improved, worked courageously to rescue and care for civilians. Casualties were lower than in the previous raid, yet about 150 people were killed, with a similar number seriously injured.

The devastation affected industry and work in the docks for a period of time, but production was restored before long. The social effects on civilians, however, threatened to be of greater duration. 'In one district 20,000 people were sleeping out at night,' reported a newspaper, referring to a debate on the issue held by the Northern Ireland Parliament. It was believed that 'if 40,000 family huts were not provided around the city before the winter, there might be an unspeakable calamity'.[37] Such a disaster did not occur, as the people of Belfast, in company with those of other British cities, learned to cope with the catastrophic effects of blast and fire. In the following months the civilian defence services in Northern Ireland grew and 'became as strong in numbers as the raids of April and May proved it to be in fortitude and resolution'.[38]

During the period from March to May 1941 many sorties were flown against other British ports. Such places as Cardiff and Southampton were bombed several times, extending the destruction of earlier raids. Portsmouth, on the south coast, was, because of its proximity to *Luftwaffe* bases, a vulnerable target and received a major raid. This, added to a number of other sharp attacks, made the city a particular victim of the Blitz. 'The Second Blitz and the thirty-seventh raid reached the City,' noted the local records, 'on the night of 10–11th March.'[39] There was little cloud and visibility was good for 240 bombers from both *Luftflotten* as they made the easy flight northwards across the Channel. Navigation was straightforward, although units of *KG 26* employed *Y-Gerät*, and crews generally had little difficulty in reaching the target.

They aimed to attack dock basins, shipyards and factories, and dropped 193 tons of explosive bombs, added to 46,000 incendiaries. Many bombs weighed 250kg according to the City Records and included 49 unexploded or delayed-action bombs. 'The attack was concentrated on the southern half of the City, including naval and military establishments', where many fires were started among fuel storage depots and at the Royal Naval Barracks. 'Five naval oil tanks were fired, two magazines exploded and the town's electricity system was badly damaged.'[40] Casualties were not heavy, with fewer than 50 people killed in Portsmouth and Gosport, but houses, shops, offices and public buildings suffered. For a time, electricity supplies were affected but ARP workers reacted well to the ordeal.

A further major attack came on 17 April when 346 tons of high explosive and 46,000 incendiaries fell from 250 aircraft over five hours. Units of *KG 53* opened the raid for *Luftflotte II* and many following units were armed with large parachute mines. When *Luftflotte III* arrived they were led by Heinkels of *KG 26*, followed by 94 aircraft of other units. Bombs landed in the area of the dockyard, causing fires; again, electricity supplies failed temporarily. Buildings in the city were hit and many houses destroyed, especially from the blast effects of the 200 mines dropped. Fortunately, civilian casualties were light. A heavy barrage of over 2,000 anti-aircraft shells was fired and managed to bring down two Junkers 88s, but the gunners could do nothing to lessen the scale of the attack.

A sharp raid followed ten nights later, when 70 tons of HE and 7,000 incendiaries were dropped by 38 aircraft. Damage was severe. 'The main line was blocked at the rear of the Prison', it was stated. 'Major fires occurred at H.M. Dockyard and Messrs McIlroys Ltd., Commercial Road.' About two-thirds of the city was affected by widespread damage to homes and business property. Parachute mines, with their great fields of blast, struck several buildings. They 'registered hits on the Casualty Ward of the Royal Portsmouth Hospital', which had been bombed in earlier raids. They hit Madden's Hotel, where 28 people were killed in an explosion which also damaged the Town Station and General Post Office. Mines caused the destruction of 'private and residential property in all parts of Portsea Island'.

Casualties were later assessed as 102 killed, 140 seriously injured and 130 slightly hurt. By April the treatment and reception of those whose homes had been bombed had greatly improved in Portsmouth, as in other cities. Writing of the Emergency Centres, the City archive reported that all were 'fitted with gas and electric stoves, and electric water heaters. Should these fail, it was possible to use coal.' In addition, every Centre had a store of food.[41]

The night of 16 March was foggy across much of Britain, but this failed to prevent 184 bombers of *Luftflotte III* from launching an attack 'of some weight' on Bristol. This was the heaviest raid suffered there since 3 January. The raid 'did not appear particularly unusual',[42] but, as with so many blitzed towns and cities, it left behind a catalogue of misery and devastation. Four hundred civilians were killed or injured, many from the increasing use of high explosives and parachute mines included among the 55 tons dropped. About 11,000 incendiaries caused over 150 fires, and most destruction occurred in 'the centre of the city which had been lucky enough to escape damage in the previous raids'.[43] The districts worst hit were Eastville, Fishponds and Whitehall. Churches were damaged, fifteen people being killed when the crypt of St Barnabas's received a direct hit. Water and electricity supplies were cut and a hundred gas mains broken. Destruction or damage occurred to 6,000 houses; two public shelters were also struck, causing heavy casualties.

The *Luftwaffe* returned on the consecutive nights of 3 and 4 April, attacking both the city and Avonmouth Docks. They were led by *KGr.100*, using *X-Gerät*. In the first, heavy damage was brought to both places by 76 aircraft, especially at Avonmouth, and, once again, residential property was badly affected. On the second night 85 bombers aimed particularly for the Avonmouth Docks, which were showered with 20,000 incendiaries and 80 tons of explosives. There was widespread havoc, yet once again the workings of the port were not halted—an important factor when assessing the impact of night bombing.

Fire was a problem in both places, but it was dealt with rapidly. 'The Civil Defence and the people were among the quickest in all the country to tackle it at its root—the fire bomb.'[44] Other ARP workers also responded well, a contemporary writer recorded. In one raid, rescue parties were called to 266 incidents from which 'they rescued 135 persons alive and recovered many bodies'. At another time they worked at 35 recorded incidents.[45]

On 11 April a further major attack, often known locally as 'The Good Friday Raid' arrived, in which 150 bombers of *Luftflotte III* took part. They discharged nearly 200 tons of HE and 35,000 incendiaries, bringing wide destruction to both Bristol and Avonmouth. Docks and industrial buildings were blasted, especially in Bristol, and rail and road transport suffered. One bomb aimed at a power station hit the nearby St Philip's Bridge, breaking communications. Among buildings devastated in the south of the city were a girls' school and a public library. A diary entry noted that the raid grew intense just after midnight: 'Flares floating, a series of whistles, threw ourselves down at least four times, alternating with visits to the shelter.' There, at 2 a.m. 'the pavement trap-door was blown in and the flame-lit sky became visible from inside'.[46] Casualties were estimated at 150 killed and 146 badly injured.

That night Winston Churchill was on his way by train to Bristol, together with the Australian Prime Minister, Robert Menzies, and the American Ambassador, J. G. Winant. Churchill, as Chancellor of the University of

Bristol, was due to present honorary degrees to his companions the next day. The train was kept in a nearby siding overnight, from which all could see and hear the raid. On Saturday morning they entered the city, where fires still burned and civilians were being rescued as Churchill toured the streets. His presence boosted morale. The people 'were brave and were thrilled,' wrote his secretary, 'at the sight of Winston who drove about sitting on the hood of an open car and waving his hat'.[47] At the University the ceremony went ahead, with the Prime Minister congratulating the city on its fortitude. 'Many of those here today have been all night at their posts,' he said, 'and all have been under the fire of the enemy, under heavy and protracted bombardment.'[48]

By the end of the Night Blitz, Bristol's position in British defence was still high. The devastation to docks and factories was soon repaired and morale recovered. However, the destruction was a legacy of the city's sacrifice. 'A great part of the centre of the city was burnt out,' remarked an official publication 'and stands dumb witness to the meaning of total war as the Nazis taught it to the world.'[49]

One of the most intense series of aerial attacks to fall on a built-up area anywhere in the world struck Plymouth in 1941. The importance of the city, with the naval base of Devonport, to Britain's defensive system, covering seas to both the south and the west, was considerable, as it had been for centuries. Its proximity to *Luftwaffe* bases in north-western France, together with the ease of uninterrupted access for aerial attack, made it a prime target in the spring of 1941, when German raids were aimed at ports.

On 20 March the King and Queen visited Plymouth for a morale-boosting occasion. Local people then 'enjoyed a gala day with bands and dancing on the Hoe'.[50] Shortly after their departure came the first of the now customary raids on successive nights. Led by sixteen Heinkel 111s of *KGr.100*, 125 bombers delivered 32,000 incendiaries and 160 tons of high explosives, aiming primarily for the dock and harbour areas. During the next night the scale was intensified, with 170 bombers dropping larger weights and numbers. On both occasions damage was caused to the stated targets, but many bombs also fell in the city itself.

By the end of the two raids the centre of Plymouth had been almost destroyed and an area of 600 yards' radius from the skeleton of the Guildhall was described as 'a brick-pitted desert'. The City Hospital, the General Post Office and the Library, together with the Old Guildhall and the City Court, were among dozens of buildings wrecked. A number of department stores, such as Spooner's and Coster's, were hit, as were the Promenade Pier, the Guinness Clock and Derry's Clock. Six schools and eight churches were badly damaged and a BBC news bulletin announced that Plymouth had been 'Coventrated'.

'Of the raids on the ports, that on Plymouth on March 21 was particularly severe,' wrote one commentator. 'Twenty thousand incendiary bombs were dropped and many serious fires were started.'[51] This underlined the troubles caused during the raid by a shortage of water, because the authorities had neither anticipated nor prepared for such a heavy assault by fire. 'A large part of the shopping centre was destroyed by fire as a result of a complete failure of water supplies', which resulted in some cases in fires being left to burn themselves out.[52]

Over the two nights 336 people were killed, 283 seriously hurt and 5,000 made homeless when 18,000 houses were damaged or destroyed. The city, smaller than many others which were blitzed, suffered severely. Adding to the public worries, Plymouth lacked sufficient post-raid services for feeding, clothing and housing the victims of raids, 'for which the provision made beforehand proved quite inadequate'. For this, over the years, the city authorities have sometimes been censured by those writing with the benefit of hindsight. At least one relevant geographical handicap is often overlooked, namely that 'the hinterland was rural and sparsely populated'.[53]

Plymouth's predicament was compounded in the following month when the Germans launched an all-out assault on the city, with major raids on five nights out of seven. The intensity of attack presented enormous problems. First, sustained bombing led to the complete obliteration of some targets, showing what might have been achieved by the *Luftwaffe* if a similar strategy had been followed against other cities earlier in the campaign. Secondly, the work of defence services such as fire brigades and rescue parties was at times overwhelmed through the sheer volume of devastation. Thirdly, a weighty burden was laid on civilian morale, which was under almost unrelieved pressure for a whole week, with virtually no time to recover.

Over the five nights—21, 22, 23, 28 and 29 April—641 bomber sorties crossed Plymouth and Devonport. They rained down 772 tons of high explosives and UXBs, accompanied by parachute mines, and scattered 139,000 incendiaries on the city and nearby naval base. 'There was not a single part of the city, industrial, business or residential, which was not touched to a greater or lesser degree.'[54]

In stark terms, the centres of both Plymouth and Devonport were eradicated, with a few shells of buildings left standing. According to a Mass Observation report, 'The civic and domestic devastation exceeds anything we have seen.'[55] The American journalist Quentin Reynolds, who had visited several blitzed cities, wrote, 'Nothing I had seen prepared me for the sight of Plymouth.'[56] A woman who drove a mobile canteen into the stricken city spoke of passing 'through frightful rubble and desolation . . . I couldn't have imagined such scenes, whole streets nothing but twisted girders and rubble'.[57]

In Plymouth, streets were wiped out completely and thousands of homes added to the total of those lost in April. Residential properties, including most in Union Street, Bedford Street, Courtenay Street and Westwell Street, were demolished. Property in the Hoe and North Road areas was destroyed. At Millbay, businesses were burned out and buildings such as the Drill Hall, Stonehouse Town Hall, the Ballard Institute and the Royal Western Yacht Club were devastated, Across the area some 50 churches and chapels were destroyed, including St Peter's, St James-the-Less, the Salvation Army Congress Hall and Treville Street Unitarian. Among the many schools hit were Notre Dame Girls' and the Hoe Grammar School.

Devonport suffered no less severely and was 'practically wiped out'.[58] The shopping districts of Queen Street, Catherine Street and Fore Street were smashed. As had happened in the first London Blitz on Dockland, whole streets of small houses close to dockyard targets were blown down. This happened particularly in the Ford and Keyham residential districts. Among public and famous buildings blasted were The Royal Sailors' Rest (Aggie Weston's), the Post Office and the Alhambra Theatre. More than ten churches and chapels were shattered. A local trader wrote that he could 'stand in the central shopping area of Plymouth and Devonport without being able to see an inhabited building and practically without seeing any walls standing'.[59]

A Ministry of Home Security Report on 30 April believed that the *Luftwaffe* intended 'by these heavy attacks to further Germany's success in the battle of the Atlantic'. What, then, had happened to the stated targets? In the Millbay district, docks were badly battered and at one time Devonport Dockyard appeared to be a sea of flames. The Regional Information Officer was sure that 'there must have been extensive damage', although the Admiralty and military authorities were, not unnaturally, reluctant to disclose any details.[60] Among sites hit were the Royal Naval Barracks, the Army Gun Wharf, the South Raglan Barracks and the Royal William Yard. Returning German aircrews on all nights reported enormous blazes and blast at the dockyards and oil installations, in shipyards and on vessels. Many service personnel were killed or injured in the area.

That notwithstanding, the dockyards were not brought to a halt: their work, and production in shipyards, was affected only temporarily. At Devonport Dockyard the damage was less severe than many had anticipated and 'within five months the establishment was back to 90 per cent of its efficiency'.[61] On 2 May, when Churchill visited the dockyard, he 'walked four miles, along quays, through workshops, over ships'—which would have been impossible had they been totally out of action.[62] Thus the Germans failed to achieve their stated objective. On that day the Prime Minister was accompanied by his wife, Clementine. Her appearance, she wearing 'a coloured handkerchief over her head with phrases of her husband's speeches printed on it', drew appreciative comment.[63] According to his daughter, some were surprised that 'Winnie had such a fine, fresh-looking wife'.[64]

And yet great travail was caused by the stress laid on the local population, and on civilian services set up to cater for their needs. During the five nights nearly 600 people were killed and another 450 seriously hurt. In addition, the destruction of thousands of homes, when added to those destroyed during the March raids, provided problems of unforeseen complexity for local authorities. The provision of Rest Centres, finding accommodation for 40,000 homeless and supplying food 'when only 10 per cent of the city's food distribution facilities remained' became acute problems.[65] 'Whole affair rather a muddle—no organisation yet,' wrote the driver of a Queen's Messenger van on 4 May, summarising the conditions which inevitably followed such intensive raids.[66]

The troubles were generally threefold. First, many local inhabitants were incensed when, after the raid on the 21st, the Ministry of Information issued a BBC communiqué playing down its effects. The offending message claimed that 'the raid did not last long' and that 'neither damage nor casualties were as serious as in previous attacks'.[67] Those in the city who had suffered so tragically believed that Plymouth's Blitz was exceptional and should be so recognised. Their MP, Lady Astor, complained bitterly, referring to the 'Ministry of Inflammation' and, as a result, the Regional Information Officer was asked to produce a report on the events of 2 May. By then he had written to the *Western Evening Herald* complaining that her criticism was 'misdirected'. The argument continued to run for some time.

Secondly, there were official fears that the concentrated bombardment had affected local morale. Rumours spread that police and soldiers had been called in to keep order and that thousands of terrified people fled the city every night. Herbert Morrison's fears over public spirit were mentioned in Harold Nicolson's diary for 7 May. 'He keeps on underlining the fact that people cannot stand this intensive bombing indefinitely', and that they would lose their morale, 'even as Plymouth's has gone'.[68] That people were shaken is unquestioned. They suffered immediate fear and the depression of loss. Nevertheless, as the Regional Officer predicted, 'given a few weeks, all will recover their poise' and the city would 'resume its shaken life'.[69] Both the community and individual citizens did that. This was not achieved, however, without concern and effort. Senior officials 'established headquarters at Tavistock to try to restore the life of the community'.[70] Some writers have exaggerated the drop in morale. The best summary was offered by the Inspector-General of the Home Office Intelligence Branch after a three-day visit in May. 'The morale of the people as a whole appeared to be good,' he reported, adding that there was still some way to go. They were recovering from their 'harassing experience and were showing a high degree of courage and individual adaptability'.[71]

The third area of complaint concerned the frailties of organisation at both national and local levels. Lord Astor commented on confusions in a letter to a friend:[72] 'If the public only knew, there would be a major scandal,' he thundered. There had been difficulties with the Ministry of Home Security and the Ministry of Health. In addition, 'the inertia, jealousy and lack of imagination among Local Authorities is even worse than in Whitehall'. Astor went on to complain of the Mayor of a nearby town, holding refugees from Plymouth who with 'his voluntary workers had all thrown in their hands'. The Mayor did not know who was paying for their welfare, cooking equipment, etc., or which authority was responsible for hundreds of people 'who were living like pigs'.[73]

Undoubtedly there was sometimes a poor response to the desperate needs of victims of the bombing. However, Wasley offered a balanced assessment. 'Even those who are good and honourable make mistakes,' he wrote, 'and these mistakes are part of the history of the Plymouth Blitz.'[74] Civilians returned to help their city play a vital part in the rest of the war, especially in the Battle of the Atlantic and in the Normandy landings.

Ports and industrial areas on the east coast of England were considered vulnerable to air attack at an early stage of the war. With the assumption that

German raids would approach Britain from a generally eastern direction, across the North Sea, it appeared likely that raids would be made on Tyneside, Wearside and Humberside. In those regions lay coalfields and factories, docks and shipyards, offering prime targets to an enemy seeking to wage a campaign against Britain's economy.

From the start of the war until the end of 1940, however, the area suffered far less than had been expected. Sorties were flown against shipping in the North Sea and there was extensive minelaying, but few raids ventured inland. During the daylight Battle of Britain the main weight of the German assault fell on southern England and only on 15 August was there any sizeable raid against targets in the north. That day the Germans were singularly unsuccessful and did not repeat the attempt.

In fact, between September 1940 and May 1941 there were only four major raids in the area, two on Hull and one each on Newcastle and Sunderland. German sights were then set more on London, on the Midlands and on western ports. In matters of civil defence the region seemed 'to have planned air raid precautions more thoroughly than the *Luftwaffe* planned to attack the area'.[75] Heavier raids with greater destruction and casualties were launched against the north-east after the end of the main Night Blitz.

Lesser raids occurred. For example, on the night of 15 February 1941, 130 bombers, many of them minelayers, operated against the stretch of coast between St Abbs Head and Flamborough Head. 'That night,' wrote an observer, 'will be long-remembered in South Shields.' Seven people were killed and 24 injured there. 'Many houses were severely damaged and widespread breakage of windows was suffered in many parts of the town.'[76]

The first major raid on Hull fell on the night of 18 March, when 378 aircraft of *Luftflotten II* and *III* bombed the port. One of the Ju 88s from *Luftflotte II* was flown by Stahl; his task was to open the assault with mines and flares. 'Turning away for home,' he noted afterwards, 'we can clearly see the fires starting below, the result of our mines and those of the other crews. Our task is finished.' Then over 300 tons of explosives and 77,000 incendiaries followed.[77]

The main aiming points were docks and industrial buildings, but fog and mist made identification difficult for the crews. Therefore, although bombs landed in the port area, causing some fierce fires, many shops, homes and commercial premises were also demolished. The utility services of gas, water and electricity were affected, although most of the fires were soon under control. 'Heavy attack on Hull,' a local resident remarked. 'H.A.A. [heavy anti-aircraft] fired 2,600 rounds. 62 civilians killed. Factories hit and private houses.'[78] On the other side of the North Sea, Stahl read German High Command reports of fires in Hull and these gave him satisfaction. 'We are quite proud of ourselves,' he claimed. 'After all, we were the ones to do all the hard and necessary preliminary work.'

After a further sharp attack on Hull on 31 March, when buildings were hit right across the city and 200 casualties suffered, the next major raids came on 7 and 8 May. During clear moonlight on the 7th, about 110 tons of HE and nearly 10,000 incendiaries rained down in a two-hour attack. A further 167 tons and 20,000 fire bombs followed on the next night, when 120 aircraft, some of which were diverted from other targets, flew over the port.

Great devastation resulted, especially to riverside buildings. 'Alexandra Docks chiefly damaged but land-mines in many parts of the town,' a diarist recorded. 'Fires whole length of both sides of Heddon Road to Saltend from blazing stacks of timber.'[79] Some of the great grain warehouses were shattered, their contents spilled and left smouldering for days. A Mass Observation reporter listed that among premises completely destroyed were those of Ingleby & Gilboys, Spillers, and Lofthouse, Rishworth & Ranks, the largest of them. Many buildings were shattered in the city centre, often as a result of fire which also damaged houses. There was considerable interruption to utility services and heavy pressure followed on the civilian defences. Four hundred of the city's wardens were women, and others worked in fire stations. Of the latter, one fire officer reported that they 'braved the blitz and turned out and did wonderful work. The coolness of the younger ones was an inspiration, even when the stations had direct hits.'[80]

From both raids about 450 civilians were killed, with at least an equal number injured. As over 30,000 houses were destroyed or battered, thousands of homeless people soon required care and attention. Among local services, 1,200 women of the WVS were prominent, helping and feeding 10,000 people on the first night and 6,000 on the second. The total of homeless rose to 40,000, and excellent arrangements were made to re-house them. The burden of feeding was also tackled efficiently. 'In the eighteen days after the May raids 460,000 communal meals were provided, averaging more than 25,000 a day.'[81] By then the city authorities had learned much from the experience of bombing and had laid plans accordingly.

In the matter of food, the suffering citizens of Hull would have been horrified to hear that when Stahl's bomber returned to its base at Mariahof in

Holland, 'our good Dutch ladies' received his crew with food. They were 'touchingly concerned' and would 'cry for joy' when *Luftwaffe* airmen were safe. They would grieve over a missing crew 'as if they were their own sons'. The ladies would always be in the kitchen 'ready to read our every wish in our eyes'. War certainly produces strange friendships, enmities and bedfellows.[82]

Raids on other parts of the north-east—that is, Tyneside and Wearside—had gone on regularly, yet in a comparatively small way, for some time. The first major assault came on the night of 9 April 1941, when 120 bombers of *Luftflotte II* chose Newcastle as their destination. In a five-hour attack, 150 tons of explosives and 50,000 incendiaries fell widely across the region, hitting Jarrow, North and South Shields, Hebburn, Gateshead, Wallsend, Tynemouth and Newcastle itself. 'It soon became clear that a large-scale attack was developing and directed mainly on the ship-building, ship-repairing and timber yards on the riverside,' the authorities reported.[83] Large fires were started in several of the Tyne docks, timber stores, sheds and warehouses, but many bombs hit domestic and commercial premises. In South Shields the Queen's Theatre was set ablaze, as was Sunderland's Town Hall. In several areas gas mains, telephone and electric cables and sewers were broken, while bombs also fell on railway lines, 'where passenger coaches were flying about like toys'. People in one surface shelter were amazingly unharmed when a bomb exploded within twenty feet, moving the whole structure nine inches at its base. The scattered nature of the raid brought fewer casualties than feared, with about 40 killed and 100 injured.

A short but savage raid was carried out on the night of 25 April, when the Germans claimed that about 60 aircraft of *Luftflotte II* dropped 80 tons of high explosives and 9,000 incendiaries on Sunderland. In reality, many of the bombs landed in Newcastle. Also affected were South Shields, Hebburn, Tynemouth, Wallsend and Jarrow. The raid 'was notable for the number of Parachute Mines dropped and the consequent large areas of damage from blast'. In one incident in Newcastle several houses were destroyed and 35 people killed, six of them from one family. Although a number of small fires were started, they were quickly dealt with. Unexploded bombs and mines landed and many inhabitants were evacuated for a time while these UXBs were tackled by service teams, including 'the Naval Bomb Disposal Squad under the direction of Lt. Apps, R.N.'[84]

There were further small raids on the north-east before the end of the main Night Blitz. However, they, like earlier assaults, certainly did not achieve the

German aim of crippling the region's industry, halting naval and maritime movements, or breaking civilian morale.

RAIDS ON INDUSTRIAL CITIES: MARCH TO MAY

Although the main night offensive from March to May was sustained against ports, the *Luftwaffe* continued to raid industrial cities. The first of these, Birmingham, was attacked on 11 March when 135 aircraft unleashed 120 tons of HE and 30,000 incendiaries. Some bombs landed on industrial sites but far more fell on built-up districts of civilian development. Defence services, particularly the fire brigades, reacted quickly to quench blazes and thereby prevent extensive damage. Casualties also were comparatively light.

A two-night assault followed on 9 and 10 April, with successive major raids. In the first, 235 bombers of *Luftflotte III* dropped 40,000 incendiaries and 280 tons of explosives on chosen targets. Within a short time the centre of Birmingham was suffering severely, with huge fires burning in the Bull Ring, the High Street, New Street and Dale End. The Midland Arcade blazed furiously. Firemen were impeded by low water pressure, which resulted partly from damage to mains, yet they bravely struggled on. One recollected his fear while at the top of a ladder, hearing bombs exploding and having no protection—a common experience for those who could not hit back.[85] Among other districts affected were Small Heath, Aston and Nechells, and many houses, churches and public buildings were smashed.

During the following night, 43,000 incendiaries and 245 tons of high explosives were carried to the city by a combined force of 245 aircraft from both *Luftflotten*. Once again many fires broke out, with considerable destruction in Solihull, Halls Green and Erdington. The ARP services faced great demands that night, but the city coped well, with 11,000 wardens on duty. In the two raids about 350 people were killed and hundreds more injured, but neither casualties nor damage were sufficient to interrupt the general life and production of the nation's vital industrial centre.

What may be considered the *Luftwaffe*'s last throw in the Night Blitz was launched against Birmingham. On the night of 16 May, as German aircraft were already in the throes of moving from their bases in France for action further east, over 100 bombers from both *Luftflotten* raided the city. About 150 tons of bombs fell, including 27 parachute mines. However, navigation that night was difficult and most of the bombs fell at Nuneaton, away from the intended targets. There, 83 people were killed. In Birmingham, Wolseley

Motors and ICI Chemicals were among industrial targets hit and moderate damage was done, although insufficient to bring production to a complete halt. Many houses and shops were struck, with more than 30 people dead. High above the city, night fighters flew on patrol, yet in the darkness they destroyed none of the intruders. For Birmingham the worst had passed. But the burden had been great: 'Throughout the war Birmingham received 1,800 tons of high explosives. Only Liverpool/Birkenhead and London were more heavily bombed.'[86]

On the night before Birmingham's double attack in April, the *Luftwaffe* turned its attention once again to Coventry, in what was to be the city's final raid in this period of the Blitz. Over 230 bombers jettisoned 315 tons of HE and 25,000 incendiaries across the target that had suffered so severely five months earlier. Much of everyday life there had been patched up and restored, with industrial production rising, and the raid was a sharp reminder to local citizens of the power of the *Luftwaffe*. Wide destruction was caused in several factories and to public and commercial buildings. The Coventry and Warwickshire Hospital was hit, bringing casualties. Taken together with those from a minor raid two nights later, the casualty list totalled 451 killed and 720 seriously hurt—a heavy price. However, by then many lessons had been learned, especially from the previous November's devastating assault. Civilian defence services, from fire brigades and police to wardens and rescue parties, worked hard to limit the effects. This was the close of an ordeal for a city whose name had become known round the world.

On 8 May another Midlands city was hit, although mainly through errors of navigation. This was Nottingham, previously untouched by heavy raids in the catalogue of locations for the Night Blitz. Air Raid Precautions were well advanced in the city, particularly as a result of lessons learned generally from what had occurred across Britain. Medical and fire services were prepared and ample shelter accommodation had been provided. For example, nearly 5,000 surface shelters had been built and 24,000 Andersons installed.

That night the *Luftwaffe* planned a minor raid on Nottingham, aiming at an arms factory and a railway works. They also selected Derby for a major raid, targeting the Rolls-Royce works and other factories. Leading the Derby raid were two Heinkels of *KGr.100*, relying on the usual *X-Gerät*, but their beams were successfully jammed. Further confusion for the raiders ensued when a 'Starfish' site was lit near Cropwell Butler, a small village lying in the Vale of Belvoir to the south-east of Nottingham. The result was that aircraft bombed

Nottingham heavily, over 200 explosives and hundreds of fire bombs landing around the 'Starfish' site, and Derby was mainly spared.

In Nottingham considerable devastation occurred at Leenside and in the city centre. Nearly 100 fires burned, half of which ranged between 'major' and 'serious', resulting from 135 tons of high explosives and 7,000 incendiaries. More than 430 civilians were killed or injured, either in the city or in nearby areas such as West Bridgeford. About 50 people died when bombs struck two air raid shelters situated below the Co-operative Society's bakery in Meadow Lane. Hundreds of others became homeless as 350 houses were wrecked, as were shops, but ARP services responded well to their needs.

The Moot Hall and Lace Market were struck, and two churches, including St Christopher's, were destroyed. University College was hit and great damage was caused by fire to rolling stock at the Central Railway Station, which was one of the *Luftwaffe*'s intended aiming points. In a city renowned for sporting traditions, bombs landed on Notts County's football pitch and on the cricket ground at Trent Bridge.

This late bombing campaign against industrial centres failed. Although much misery was spread, neither morale nor production was affected enough to change Britain's war aims or her ability to carry them out.

LONDON: MARCH TO MAY

Because of the importance of London to the British as a bastion against Nazism, and to the Germans as a symbol of their enemy's stubborn resistance, the *Luftwaffe* sustained attacks on the capital right up to the end of the Night Blitz. In the period from March to May 1941 London was subjected to six major attacks and a number of lesser raids. Two of the former led to the heaviest casualties suffered on any individual night of the campaign.

The opening major assault fell on the city on 8 March, the first for about two months. Explosives weighing 130 tons and 30,000 incendiaries were scattered widely across fifty of the capital's boroughs. They were dropped by 125 aircraft of both *Luftflotten* in a period of just over three hours. Many fires were started, although they were quickly tackled by civilian defences. Railways were affected, with three large stations hit and rolling stock damaged. Elsewhere, a bomb struck Buckingham Palace, a number of public buildings were wrecked and St Bartholomew's Hospital received damage.

Although the raid came as something of a surprise after a break of eight weeks, casualties were not generally heavy. One incident, however, caught the general interest. Two bombs penetrated a cinema by Leicester Square and crashed through to the Café de Paris, which was situated in the basement. Ironically, because of its position it had been known as 'London's safest restaurant'. The dining tables and dance floor were packed with many officers on leave, accompanied by ladies in evening gowns, all listening or dancing to a jazz band. A bomb exploded among them, killing 34 and injuring a further 80. The band leader, 'Snakehips' Johnson, was killed; among those injured was Betty, the daughter of the former Prime Minister Stanley Baldwin.

On the following night almost 100 tons of bombs and 16,000 incendiaries were dropped by aircraft of *Luftflotte III*, led, inevitably as it seems, by *KGr. 100* using *X-Gerät*. Much of the bombing hit north-eastern districts of the capital and at St Pancras both a church and a hospital were struck.

Six nights later came another major raid, when over 100 tons of explosives and 14,000 fire bombs were unloaded, particularly over areas in the south and east. As well as damage to docks, three hospitals were hit and many houses, shops and offices destroyed across thirty boroughs. Heavy casualties resulted, especially in Southgate where 42 civilians died. As a small consolation, Londoners learned that for several nights Bomber Command had been hitting back at targets in German cities.

A huge assault arrived on the 19th, a night usually referred to as 'The Wednesday' . The Germans had planned a massive attack, allocating 500 Heinkel 111s and Junkers 88s which, over a period of six hours, scattered 122,000 incendiaries and 470 tons of HE, ostensibly across the dock areas beside the Thames. Churchill, dining with some Americans in Downing Street, went to the roof of the Air Ministry with his guests to view the raid. 'No bombs fell while we were up,' wrote one of his secretaries, 'although fire engines were continually passing, and guns were firing all the time, with planes droning overhead.'[87]

Damage and destruction were widespread among the docks, although the Royal Docks escaped practically unscathed.[88] Many parachute mines floated down to detonate with enormous explosions, devastating rows of houses in West Ham, Poplar and Stepney. The destruction was not surprising because several of the mines were of the SC 2500 type—the 'Max' . At least eight hospitals were hit, as were public buildings as far apart as Leyton and Bromley. Some public shelters were demolished, 44 civilians dying in one at Poplar. In addition, almost 2,000 fires were started, three of which were 'conflagrations', with more than 60 others being classified as at least 'serious'. Great disruption to public services followed and railway travel was interrupted in a number of places. That night the fabric of London took a huge battering.

Casualties were heavy. First reports set the figure too low, but on the 24th the War Cabinet learned that the total had climbed to 504 killed and 1,511 injured.[89] The Official History reports that 'some 750 people were killed and nearly 1,200 badly injured'.[90] Whatever the true figure, it was the highest yet recorded.

Nearly a month passed before another major raid struck the capital. It came on 16 April and turned out to be the biggest assault thus far mounted against Britain during the Night Blitz. For eight and a half hours the *Luftwaffe* flew 685 sorties over London, some bombers making two or even three flights in a shuttle service of punishment. With such numbers involved, the total of bombs dropped was enormous—150,000 incendiaries and high explosives weighing 890 tons. The aiming points were laid down as docks, warehouses and factories beside the Thames, and the Germans were satisfied that the raid had been most effective.

People at ground level felt its intensity. 'We had tried to sleep at the Rectory to fire-watch in our turns,' a vicar's wife wrote, 'but before we had even settled we heard the bombs falling, ghastly shrieking noises followed by sickening thuds. That night in south London she counted sixty of them.[91] Another woman, in the West End, considered the raid 'the most vicious to date'. Fires near her 'appeared to burn white first of all. Then sharp tongues of red flame spat out which painted a scarlet blob in the sky.' High explosives hurled bricks and mortar 'skywards like waterspouts', then left 'minute particles of dust and rubbish which, together with the stench of cordite, burned nostrils'.[92]

The destruction of buildings of all types was widespread. More than 60 public buildings were hit, among them the Admiralty, the Law Courts, the Houses of Parliament and St Paul's Cathedral. Large shops in Leicester Square and Oxford Street were left in ruins. In addition, nineteen churches were either destroyed or damaged and eighteen hospitals affected. Transport was disrupted, particularly on the Southern Railway, where termini were closed, and several stretches of the Underground were brought to a halt. Altogether, the desolation spread across 66 boroughs, covering most of the capital. In his diary the next day, Colville noted that 'London looks bleary-eyed and disfigured. There is a great gash in the Admiralty'. He went on to list places affected, including Chelsea Old Church, St Peter's, Eaton Square, Jermyn Street and Mayfair.[93]

Fire was a testing problem because of the number of incendiaries used. Over 2,250 fires burned, particularly in Central and South London, 50 of them being classified as either 'serious' or 'major'. Crews tackling the blazes laboured under daunting difficulties as bombs and mines fell regularly on to their stations, their equipment and over the sites they were trying to save.

Casualties were heavy, with more civilians killed or hurt than ever before. The figures given were 1,180 and 2,230 respectively and these included many ARP workers who were caught while carrying out their duties. In places, people in shelters on the surface became casualties when parachute mines, with their wide fields of blast, landed close by. The intensity of attack and proximity of death led to a female warden confessing that she 'experienced the only premonition that I have ever felt. I became suddenly convinced that I should not be there for breakfast.' Nevertheless, with others in the defence services, she was too busy to think further on the matter.[94]

The physical damage caused by the raid was heavy, but not disastrous for the nation, and by now the phlegmatic reaction of most Londoners served to withstand the destruction. Although a keen eye was kept by the Ministry of Home Security on their morale, few cases appeared of the breaking of spirit which the *Luftwaffe* hoped to achieve. At ground level, the majority of those who lived or worked in the capital wanted to see greater success from the defences. They also looked forward to the days—or nights—when German cities would be put under similar stress.

Three nights later *Luftwaffe* bombers presented the heaviest assault of the Night Blitz. The crews of 712 aircraft flew over London, some on two or three missions. 'Interrupted for an hour or so by drizzling rain, they nevertheless achieved another attack, more concentrated in area, just as grievous in its casualty results, but with rather less material damage.'[95] For the first time they claimed to have dropped over 1,000 tons of high explosives, accompanied by the daunting total of 153,000 incendiaries. On this occasion, Heinkels of *III/KG 26* opened the raid and the redoubtable *KGr. 100* did not appear until fifteen minutes later. Bombers converged on the area of the Thames, hitting warehouses and docks and, once again, bringing devastation to the East End. 'It was a concentrated attack mainly to the east of us, Walthamstow and East Ham way,' wrote a warden, 'but we had a handsome share of fires, a few HEs and several UXBs nearby.'[96]

Among notable points struck were the Royal Naval College at Greenwich and St Peter's Hospital in Stepney. Museums, churches and other hospitals were included in the list of smashed buildings. Inevitably, many houses, flats, shops and offices were demolished in cataracts of bricks and masonry. Fire brigades responded well when having to contain over 1,400 fires, and by then it was recognised that in large urban areas incendiary bombs presented a greater threat than any other weapon. Rescue services, too, made great and often sacrificial efforts to bring help to civilians. More than 1,200 people were killed and over 1,000 badly hurt. The growing total of casualties was a disturbing feature of the Blitz, and by the end of April the total of civilian deaths for the month had risen to 6,065.[97]

The last great raid came on 10 May and was the *Luftwaffe*'s final throw against the capital in a campaign that had run for eight months. 'The siren was followed immediately by the drone of many bombers,' a woman recollected, 'and there was no doubt in any of our minds that this was going to be a heavy night.'[98] Another woman, living in Mayfair, wrote, 'Never before did so many explosions fall round us.'[99] The rain of bombs caused widespread damage, affecting some famous buildings. These included the War Office, the Royal Naval College again, Westminster School, the British Museum and the London Museum. Bombs also hit the Houses of Parliament, destroying the Commons debating chamber and starting fires in Westminster Hall. The Royal Mint, the Law Courts, the Public Records Office and Mansion House also were struck, as were St James's Palace and the Tower of London. In the City, the Halls of several companies, including Butchers' and Cordwainers', Mercers' and Salters', were destroyed.

Most prominent among the churches hit was Westminster Abbey. Others included St Margaret's, Westminster; St Stephen's, Walbrook; St Clement Danes; and St Mary-le-Bow. The night's bombing was another step in altering the face of London's ecclesiastical architecture. Fourteen hospitals were bombed, including St Thomas's.

This was a night 'that must have graven on many a fire-fighter's heart the words "No water"'.[100] The combination of a concentrated attack with fire-bombs and a low tide on the Thames brought disaster. In addition, explosives soon fractured several important water mains, so that men at the pumps and hoses discovered weak pressure. Altogether, 2,154 fires were reported, with areas of Westminster, Southwark, Whitechapel and Shadwell suffering particularly. Before long, in many parts, fire brigades were fighting a losing battle as the ferocity of the flames overcame the weak power of the jets. At the Elephant and Castle 'a medium-sized fire grew into a great conflagration because every water main was dry'.[101] A curate's wife in the district wrote that 'the Church burnt with white hot flames' and, before long, 'the Great Bells fell from the top of the tower with a mighty rush of sparks and flames'.[102] Houses, shops and offices were smashed. Twelve thousand civilians became homeless when 5,000 houses were destroyed. Casualties were heavy and in a number of places shelters were struck, especially by parachute mines. The total of dead was finally assessed as 1,436, with 1,792 badly injured and hundreds of others slightly hurt. Many of these casualties were wardens, firemen and other ARP workers.

The effects of the raid for Britain, however, hard though they were in general, had some benefits. The American reporter Quentin Reynolds, on viewing both the destruction and the reaction of civilians, believed that this was the time when 'Britain won the war'—a message which impressed his readers in the United States. And one MP wrote to Churchill, 'Don't be distressed at the ruins.' He added that such ruins could be 'good assets—all round the globe, and especially in America'.[103] By next morning, as German bombers droned back to their bases, the people were not to know that they would suffer no more devastating attacks from the main Night Blitz.

NOTES

1. Trevor Roper, Hitler Directive No 25, 27 March 1941.
2. A. Palmer, 'The Balkan Campaign', *Purnell's History of the Second World War*, 4, 64 (1969), 1766–70.
3. Liddell Hart, *Second World War*, 52.
4. Irving, *Rise and Fall*, 118.
5. Gilbert, vi, 1054.
6. P. Smith, *Stuka Squadron* (1990), 84–5: see also A. Palmer, 'Operation Punishment', *Purnell's History of the Second World War*, 2, 1 (1967), 458–75.
7. *Front Line*, 112.
8. *Ibid.*
9. *The Aeroplane*, 12 March 1941.
10. Gilbert, vi, 1069.
11. Churchill broadcast, BBC Home Service, 27 April 19412.
12. See *Blitz*, ii, 580.
13. *Front Line*, 112.
14. B. Perrett, *Liverpool: A City at War* (1990), 97.
15. *Ibid.*, 99.

16. O'Brien, 418, note 1.

17. See *Blitz*, ii, 581.

18. Webb and Duncan, 110.

19. Ward Lock Guide, *Glasgow*, 9th Edition, 9.

20. *Ibid.*, 69.

21. *Front Line*, 116.

22. *Ibid.*, 118.

23. *Ibid.*, 116.

24. Notes from Mrs Marjorie Stewart.

25. O'Brien, 412–13.

26. Winant, 44.

27. *The Aeroplane*, 11 April 1941.

28. *Front Line*, 119.

29. Diary of J. P. McHutchinson, quoted in Webb and Duncan, 117.

30. *Front Line*, 119.

31. Gilbert, vi, 938.

32. *Front Line*, 122.

33. *Ibid.*, 122–3.

34. *Ibid.*, 123.

35. Webb and Duncan, 157.

36. *Blitz*, ii, 586.

37. *Irish Times*, 14 May 1941.

38. *Front Line*, 125.

39. *Portsmouth City Records 1941*, 186.

40. O'Brien, 411.

41. *Portsmouth City Records 1941*, 189–90.

42. O'Brien, 414.

43. *Western Daily Press*, 26 June 1946.

44. *Front Line*, 100.

45. T. Underdown, *Bristol Under Blitz* (1942), 12.

46. R. Winstone, *Bristol in the 1940s* (1970), 26.

47. Colville Diaries, 12 April 1941.

48. Gilbert, vi, 1059.

49. *Front Line*, 101.

50. O'Brien, 414.

51. *The Aeroplane*, 28 March 1941.

52. O'Brien, 414.

53. See *ibid.*, 415–17.

54. H. Twyford, *It Came to Our Door* (1945), 16.

55. Webb and Duncan, 143.

56. Q. Reynolds, *Only The Stars Are Neutral* (1942).

57. Anne Lee-Mitchell, in Webb and Duncan, 154.

58. *Ibid.*, 145.

59. R. J. Hammond, *Food*, vol. ii (1951), 342, note 2.

60. Ministry of Information report, 2 May 1941.

61. Twyford, 16.

62. Colville Diaries, 2 May 1941.

63. T. Harrison, *Living Through The Blitz* (1976).

64. *Clementine Churchill*, 302.

65. O'Brien, 417.

66. Lee-Mitchell, Webb and Duncan, 154.

67. Ministry of Information communiqué, 22 April 1941.

68. H. Nicolson, *Diaries and Letters 1939–45* (1967), diary, 7 May 1941.

69. Regional Officer's report, 2 May 1941.

70. O'Brien, 417.

71. Head of Home Office Intelligence Branch; see G. Wasley, *Blitz* (1991), 188–9.

72. Lord Astor to Lord Camrose, 19 May 1941.

73. See Wasley, 196–7.

74. *Ibid.*

75. Webb and Duncan, 160.

76. Notes from Mr Roy Ripley, 18.

77. Stahl, 148.

78. B. Reckitt, *Diary of Anti-Aircraft Defences 1938–1944* (1990), 30.

79. *Ibid.*, 31.

80. *Front Line*, 125.

81. *Ibid.*, 126.

82. Stahl, 182.

83. Ripley notes, 20.

84. *Ibid.*, 21–2.

85. Webb and Duncan, 81.

86. Several cities lay claim to having suffered most from the Night Blitz, although various factors make an absolute judgement difficult. These include the geographical location and size of the city, the population, the frequency of raids and the total weight of bombs dropped. See Appendix B.

87. See Gilbert, vi, 1039, quoting Eric Seal.

88. C. Demarne, *The London Blitz* (1991), 68.

89. Gilbert, vi, 1038.

90. O'Brien, 414.

91. M. Moynihan (ed), *People At War 1939–1945* (1989), 147.

92. Henrey, 53–5.

93. See Gilbert, vi, 1062.

94. Nixon, 116.

95. All of these effects were achieved in spite of the capital being covered by cloud during most of the raid.

96. Nixon, 123.

97. See Gilbert, vi, 1062.

98. Nixon, 128.

99. Henrey, 60.

100. *Front Line*, 33.
101. *Ibid.*, 36.
102. Moynihan, 148.
103. See Gilbert, vi, 1086.

CHAPTER TEN

HITTING BACK

THE DEFENCES

Reading the calendar of heavy German night bombing, which took the lives of thousands of British civilians and left swathes of destruction through many towns and cities, the impression could be gained of a helpless victim, unable to fight back. This, however, overlooks the supreme effort made by the defences, both service and civilian, to counter the effects of the Blitz. By May 1941, when, after some eight months of bombardment, the *Luftwaffe*'s effort eased, increasingly successful steps had been taken to locate, intercept and shoot down raiders. In particular, the period from March to May 1941 witnessed an alteration in the balance between the invisible night bomber and the defences.

The improvement came to defences of all kinds. AA Command made advances in systems of firing at intruders, with success. For Fighter Command, benefits accrued from the introduction of improved equipment and training of personnel. Across the nation civilian defences against fire and blast damage, then for dealing with victims, were revised.

In addition, the RAF in two ways demonstrated the power of the offensive in showing their long-held belief that attack was the best method of dealing with an enemy. First, during the spring of 1941 Fighter Command increased the level of daylight raids across northern France, attempting to draw German formations into air battle. At night, the Command expanded the number of Intruder operations, trying to hit *Luftwaffe* bombers over Occupied territory. Secondly, Bomber Command went increasingly on to the offensive in the same period, starting to implement the policy of striking in force at the enemy's economy and morale.

Throughout the Night Blitz the sight and sound of anti-aircraft fire was reassuring to the public, and after March 1941 ground defences had growing success. There were more guns and searchlights. On 1 July 1940 the Command's numbers were 1,200 heavy guns, 599 light guns and 3,932 searchlights, figures which, eleven months later, had grown to 1,691, 940 and 4,532 respectively. The output of artillery had improved, so that, in January 1941, 54 3.7 in. guns were produced, with 90 in February and 102 during March. Most of the heavy guns were controlled by GL radar, adding greatly to their accuracy. By May 1941 twelve AA Divisions were operating, arranged in three AA Corps, corresponding to the Groups of Fighter Command. Personnel at their disposal had increased over the same eleven months from 157,319 to approximately 300,000.[1]

As the German attack moved primarily towards the ports, guns were moved from industrial areas such as Birmingham, Coventry and Sheffield to the coast. Thus from March 1941 Clydeside's total increased from 112 to 144, while Merseyside's grew by sixteen.[2] In addition, by the end of March the first rocket-powered Unrotating Projectiles (UPs) were available. The defences had received 7,500 launchers, but only 840 of these could be used because of a shortage of ammunition. As only 8,400 rounds had been supplied to AA Command, each projector was limited to a mere ten rounds. Pile complained on 23 April, but two months later he was still dissatisfied with the shortage of ammunition. The 'Z–Batteries' which were formed were arranged in groups of 64 and provided, at the least, a spectacular addition to the defences. Their first success was claimed near Cardiff on the night of 7 April.

Expansion in numbers of the Command was vital and here General Pile showed foresight. At the end of 1940 he was short of 19,000 men. 'Something dramatic had to be done. I suggested once more that women should be employed in large numbers in an operational role.' This was part of the wider movement to encourage women into skilled work, for example engineering, and into the services. In March 1941 the Registration of Employment Act was passed, directing women aged 20 and 21 into essential war work, and over the following year their conscription was extended. Pile was in favour of mixed batteries, and on 19 May 1941 a document announced their formation, 'in which the instrument numbers and a large proportion of the administrative personnel will be Auxiliary Territorial Service personnel'. However, it was not until 21 August that the first mixed battery, situated in Richmond Park, began to operate.[3]

The guns had better results, part of which came from improved radar but some from the increasing experience and efficiency of gun crews. Successes claimed at night rose from seventeen in March to $39^1/_2$ in April, then $31^1/_2$ during the shortened period of Blitz in May. The greatest success came on 11 May, when AA fire was responsible for all six aircraft shot down over Britain.[4]

Also at ground level, increasing use was made of 'Starfish' sites to draw bombs away from cities. In March seventeen were lit, of which sixteen attracted bombs, the best results being obtained at Cardiff on the 4th and twelve days later at Bristol. The same number were lit the following month, with eleven being hit. The most successful occasion was at Portsmouth on 17 April when over 200 HEs and parachute mines, with 5,000 incendiaries, hit the site at Sinach Common. By May, with better weather, 'Starfish' enjoyed less success. Nevertheless, seventeen were lit, drawing 52 high-explosive bombs and several hundred incendiaries.[5]

Throughout the same period Fighter Command's night efforts brought greater reward. For this, much credit must be accorded to its senior officers under the leadership of Douglas, who had been faced with formidable problems since taking over. In the first place, at Headquarters Fighter Command a number of officers were appointed specifically to deal with night operations. These were an Air Commodore, a Group Captain, two Wing Commanders and a Flight Lieutenant who, together, covered all aspects of fighter work in darkness, from experimental tests to the provision of instruments and from aerodromes to meteorological requirements.

In addition, there was an expansion in numbers both of fighter Groups and also of squadrons specialising in night operations. By May 1941 No 9 Group had three squadrons, No 10 Group four, No 11 Group four, No 12 Group three and No 13 Group one. Of these fifteen squadrons, six were equipped either wholly or partly with Beaufighters, with their remarkably heavy armament.[6]

Improvement in the techniques of interception was shown at all levels, from scientists planning and building apparatus, to Ground Controllers and to aircrews, all of whom benefited from experience and training. 'Night interception was proved in last week's actions,' wrote a correspondent on 21 March, 'to have advanced to a stage at which success is no longer a flash in the pan.' He added that the RAF was starting to show 'a consistent record of success at night'.[7]

Of improvements to GCI apparatus in this period, one commentator described it as 'soplified', in tribute to the work done at Sopley. He believed it to be the closest cooperation ever seen between scientists and servicemen. 'We all worked together—seventeen hours a day, seven days a week—until the job was finished.'[8] In March one new GCI installation was built and another re-sited. The total increased by four the next month and two more in

May. 'The effect of G.C.I. was as revolutionary and decisive to night fighters as G.L. was to the gunners,' Dowding believed.[9] A few disadvantages intruded, however, because in very heavy raids only a few fighters could be operated at one time. For example, during the London raid of 10 May 'cat's-eye' fighters claimed more success than aircraft guided by GCI and carrying their own radar.

Over three months, Fighter Command increased the number of night sorties. The figure for March was 1,005, resulting in 149 sightings of enemy aircraft and leading to 56 attacks. During April there were 94 combats resulting from 1,184 sorties. In May, compressed mainly into the opening fortnight, almost 2,000 sorties were flown, leading to the greatest number of interceptions and attacks on bombers, together with the highest claims for success yet registered.

These claims of *Luftwaffe* aircraft destroyed, by both single-engine and twin-engine fighters, rose from 22 in March to $48^1/2$ in April and 96 in May, a total of $166^1/2$. To them must be added those claimed by AA and by 'other causes', which amount to $104^1/2$. This gives an overall total of 271. It is of interest to set the figures beside those given in an authoritative post-war work, compiled after extensive research. Here they are listed under two headings: first are those bombers shot down over, or very close to, the shores of Britain, and second are those registered as lost over or close to their European bases. These totals include those destroyed by both air and ground defences. They are, respectively, 23 and 19 for March, 45 and 32 for April and 63 and 18 for May—a grand total of 200.[10]

Although Douglas disapproved of the effort and resources put into 'Mutton' and 'Albino' operations, both were still occasionally used in the early months of 1941. On 13 March a Harrow bomber sowed aerial mines and claimed one of the enemy, but generally this was a wasteful method of defence. Experiments continued in April, with Harrows of No 93 Squadron attempting to sow further minefields, but without success. 'Albino' operations, the scattering of explosive balloons into the bomber stream, also failed. Wind conditions were often unfavourable and the balloons ended many miles from their intended victims. Although no 'Albino' flights were made during April, the idea was retained that it could have future use, and an Instruction was issued on 3 May.[11]

More acceptable to pilots were Fighter Nights, previously known as 'Layers Operations'. An Instruction from Douglas showed how conditions for combat were set by airmen. 'The Fighter Group concerned will in agreement with the appropriate AA formation order the maximum height to which guns may be permitted to fire.'[12] This led to some criticism from gunners, whose heights of fire were restricted and who 'found that the presence of one aircraft overhead led to some confusions in the workings of their G.L.'[13] Nevertheless, the system was the most effective in defence for single-seat fighters, and from March to May 40 enemy aircraft were claimed during sixteen operations. In April, Fighter Nights were flown over Birmingham, Bristol, Coventry and London.

Another experiment came with 'Turbinlite', 'the combined use of radar and an airborne searchlight', of 2,700 million candlepower, fitted into the nose of a Havoc, accompanied by two Hurricanes. The optimistic plan was for the Havoc to locate and illuminate a bomber, then for the Hurricanes to shoot the enemy down. 'But the weight of all its equipment and the obstruction in its nose slowed up the Havoc too much when it came to chasing the enemy bombers'. The accompanying Hurricanes had no success.[14]

Fighter Command also increased the number of 'Intruder' operations. These were flown by No 23 Squadron, stationed at Tangmere, first using Blenheims before changing to the faster and more powerful Havocs. In three months from March 1941, 40 night operations took place, with 83 attacks on enemy airfields.

'Intruders' claimed sixteen *Luftwaffe* aircraft, for the loss of three of their own. They induced enemy aircrews to be wary, even near the safety of their own bases, from which some had to be diverted. They also 'caused discomfiture among German ground crews' as they bombed and machine-gunned flarepaths, hangars and runways.[15]

The 'Wizard War', with beams and navigation systems, continued until the end of the Night Blitz. In March the *Luftwaffe* was still using *X-Gerät* widely, even though No 80 Wing's counter-measures were increased. To counteract them, German operators used various methods of their own, for example, switching on beams only shortly before a raid, or changing frequencies once it had started. By the end of April there was evidence from prisoners-of-war that British interference was recognised, but as more of an irritating drawback than a threat. In the view of No 80 Wing, 'the failure to make use of this system in its present state on $33^{1}/_{3}$ per cent of operations' could not be ignored and was proof of their success.[16] However, it did not prevent *KGr. 100* from ranging far and wide and leading destructive attacks on British cities.

By then, *Knickebein* had largely been bypassed. According to Hinsley, at the start of the year 'it was apparent that the GAF was beginning to believe pilots' reports of unreliability'.[17] The more sophisticated *Y-Gerät* was still used, but No 80 Wing's interference caused increasing problems for *Luftwaffe* aircrews. The apparatus, carried by *III/KG 26*, was jammed in March and false beams were laid for its pilots. Bomb release signals were interfered with and in the first fortnight of the month only eighteen out of 89 sorties over Britain received dropping instructions. In April and May 'it was noted that on only two occasions did more than 25% of aircraft get the dropping signal'.[18] The worst night for *III/KG 26* was 3 May, when three of its Heinkels were shot down over Britain and the *Y-Gerät* equipment was removed for investigation.

A further measure causing trouble to the raiders was the use of 'Meacons'. During March they confused some pilots seeking directions and afterwards the four stations were increasingly successful in confusing the enemy by issuing false instructions. The greatest success came after the main period of the Night Blitz. In July 1941, then in October, two German pilots were 'persuaded' to land their aircraft in England after being totally bewildered about their true position.

It is interesting to note here an attempt to counteract the effect of *KGr. 100*, the best-known of the *Luftwaffe*'s 'fire-raisers'. The Special Operations Executive devised a plan to attack its pilots not in the air but at their base near Vannes in Brittany. The German airmen travelled to their aerodrome in buses and it was intended that parachute troops should ambush them during the journey. On hearing of the scheme, Portal, the CAS, objected and wished to withdraw the RAF's involvement in what he termed an unethical plan. It was an 'entirely new scheme of dropping what one can only call assassins'.[19]

However, Operation 'Savanna' went ahead and on 15 March five Free French soldiers were parachuted nearby from a Whitley bomber. The mission was abandoned when they learned that German crews travelled not by bus, but in several cars. The Frenchmen were brought back to Britain later by submarine. Whether the attempt was morally justifiable or ethically wrong is a matter for debate—in which it would have been interesting to hear the opinions of some of the civilian victims of *KGr. 100*'s activities. The episode reinforces the concern felt at the time over the very successful activities of the 'fire-raisers'.

LEANING INTO FRANCE

One aspect of Fighter Command's response to night attacks on Britain was to employ fighters in an aggressive role, in strong formations, across the Channel in daylight. The RAF's motive was to 'lean forward into France', thereby seeking to destroy enemy aircraft over their own territory. This was to be a kind of Battle of Britain in reverse—with attendant drawbacks for the intruders. The pilots of Fighter Command, according to Bowyer, were 'in precisely the same circumstances as their former opponents: detailed as relatively close escort to much slower bomber formations, unable to engage in the individual freedom of choice open to the pure fighter'.[20]

For Fighter Command there were two particular disadvantages. One was that they no longer had the benefit of RDF stations locating the whereabouts of enemy formations, which had been of such benefit to them in contests over Britain. The other was that they could not be guided by the civilian 'eyes' of the Observer Corps, whose invaluable work was recognised in April 1941 by the award of the prefix 'Royal' to their title.

Douglas epitomised this new, aggressive role of the Command. Bowyer describes him as having 'an unconscious aura of aggression'.[21] Wykeham also referred to him as 'burly, immensely strong and of a commanding presence' yet called him 'most friendly and approachable'.[22] Douglas himself recollected that in November 1940 Portal spoke to him of Trenchard's suggestion that 'we should now "lean towards France"', advocating a system of fighter sweeps. These were to be on the same lines as those employed over the Western Front in the First World War.[23]

A factor strengthening their case was the growing power of Fighter Command. The immense efforts made by the Ministry of Aircraft Production, first emanating from the pioneering work of Sir Wilfrid Freeman, then through the energy of Beaverbrook, led to a large increase in the numbers of Hurricanes and Spitfires. By the end of the Night Blitz on Britain the Command had at its disposal 79 squadrons, far more than had been available during the daylight battle. Now Wing formations were organised, each led into action by a Wing Commander. Spitfire Wings were formed at Hornchurch and Biggin Hill, Hurricane Wings at North Weald and Kenley and mixed Wings at Wittering, Duxford and Middle Wallop. Their opening sorties, known as 'Rhubarbs', were fighter sweeps, while 'Circus' operations contained bombers escorted by fighters.

'Circus 1' was flown on 10 January 1941, when six Blenheims bombed enemy emplacements in the Pas de Calais and were covered by no fewer than nine fighter squadrons. Hardly any resistance was encountered and the operation was considered a reasonable success. On 5 February 'Circus 2' followed, with an attack on St Omer airfield by twelve Blenheims escorted by nine squadrons in all. However, several errors of timing led to an uncoordinated raid in which two Bf 109s were destroyed at the cost of seven RAF pilots, with two others wounded. Being tied tightly to their bombers, British fighters repeated the mistakes of the Germans in the previous year. Consequently, Fighter Command was using its aircraft defensively, not offensively as was intended. For pilots, such actions were most demanding. 'The brain is working fast, and if the enemy is met it seems to work like a clockwork motor,' reported one. Any nerves suffered came 'not from fear, but from excitement and the intensity of mental effort'.[24]

There was some confusion over the respective aims of Bomber and Fighter Commands, leading to disagreements which affected the organisation and running of some early sweeps. Bomber Command wanted to raid enemy ports and shipping, with the secondary aim of drawing his fighters into battle. On the other hand, Fighter Command intended 'to destroy enemy fighters enticed up into the air'.[25] Later they agreed on a common purpose, in which bombers would cause so much damage that enemy fighters would be forced to intervene under conditions favourable to the RAF.

Although these operations continued, they proved costly to Fighter Command. Their figures of success against German machines were overestimated. In the first six months of 1941, 'Circus' and 'Rhubarb' operations together consisted of 2,700 fighter and 190 bomber sorties. During these there were claims of 44 enemy aircraft shot down in return for the loss of 51 pilots, although the numbers were exaggerated. What the RAF did not appreciate at the time was that by June the Germans had moved many fighters to the East, leaving the defence of the West to a small number of German pilots.[26]

Criticism of the policy of 'leaning into France' includes the suggestion that more RAF aircraft could have been sent, for example, to the Middle East. Nevertheless, judgement must be tempered with the opinion, held by many pilots, that they thereby received invaluable experience in air fighting which was put to good purpose later in the war. In addition, there was still a widely held view that the Germans would try to invade Britain in the summer of 1941: therefore pilots needed to be battle-hardened.

BOMBER COMMAND, OCTOBER 1940–JUNE 1941
Until well into 1942 the efforts of Bomber Command in raiding Germany were smaller than those of the *Luftwaffe* over Britain. Protestations by Nazi

leaders that the Night Blitz was a form of retaliation for RAF attacks on German towns and cities disguised the imbalance. Between October 1940 and June 1941 Bomber Command was unable to match the *Luftwaffe*'s assaults in numbers of aircraft, weight of bombs dropped or accuracy of locating and hitting targets. And yet the bomber was still the linchpin of RAF planning for war and Trenchard's 'Bomber Doctrine' held. As early as July 1940 Churchill stated that Britain had only one means of winning the war. This was 'an absolutely devastating, exterminating attack by very heavy bombers from this country upon the Nazi homeland', to destroy both Germany's economy and civilian morale. Without that, he added, 'I do not see a way through'.[27]

Therefore, from the opening of the Night Blitz against Britain, Bomber Command were required to hit back at Germany. At first it was hoped that their assaults would destroy oil supplies, always believed to be a weak link in the Nazi economy. The raids were also intended to affect civilian morale, which would be taken beyond breaking point.

There was, in addition, the tacitly understood aim of retaliation for *Luftwaffe* depredations against British cities. In 1940 the British people generally 'called for nothing less than revenge and the complete obliteration of the scourge by every possible means', according to one bomber pilot. When on leave, RAF aircrews 'used to be urged to "Drop one for me"—"Write my name on one next time"—"Give the bastards Hell", etc.'.[28] Some strategists believed that indiscriminate bombing would not achieve the aim of affecting the enemy's economy. An aviation writer in April 1941 agreed, explaining that '100 dead civilians count for less than one hit on a factory or communications line'.[29] These thoughts, however, did not allow for the inability of bomber crews to select only legitimate targets. Once the *Luftwaffe* embarked on the wholesale slaughter of civilians, retaliation was inevitable.

Until late September 1940, when the fear of seaborne invasion began to recede, the Continental Channel ports, with their concentration of barges and shipping, were still a prime objective for Bomber Command. Throughout this period, the anticipation of invasion was strong. During an interview with Crozier, editor of the *Manchester Guardian* at the end of January 1941, Sinclair believed 'that Hitler would come to invading us. By no other means could he hope to win the war in 1941.'[30] Therefore the Command was compelled to keep a watchful eye on those areas.

Other potential targets lay in northern Italy, especially the industrial complexes of Milan and Turin. On 6 October, renewed attacks on the region were permitted, although little was subsequently attempted in that direction. The length and difficulties of the flight, combined with demands nearer home, ensured that bombers concentrated on Germany.

In late October Peirse, Commander-in-Chief Bomber Command, received Directives laying down his force's aims. First came the bombing of oil targets in western Germany, as well as the bombing of towns. Detailed instructions were added on the methods of attacking built-up areas, showing how much had been learned from *Luftwaffe* techniques over Britain. Raids should be opened with incendiaries to start large fires. 'Successive sorties should then focus their attacks to a large extent on the fires with a view to preventing the fire-fighting services from dealing with them and giving the fires every opportunity to spread.'[31] The destinations were, according to Richards, 'profitable targets in profitable areas'. He noted that 'from this to "area bombing" was a short and natural progression'.[32]

One of the particular difficulties facing Bomber Command was the distance of targets from British bomber bases, leading to flights over hundreds of miles, lasting for many hours, across a country far larger than the United Kingdom. The flights for *Luftwaffe* aircrews raiding London were only one-fifth of the distance and duration of those for RAF aircrews flying to Berlin. There was also the difficulty, without the aid of navigation beams, of locating individual German cities, let alone the targets within them. Consequently, oil refineries and storage tanks were not heavily bombed, and cities and towns became more convenient targets. Here were the seeds of area bombing, a practice well taught by the *Luftwaffe*. At that stage 'it was the custom for a considerable number of small targets to be attacked during the same night', each by small groups of aircraft. A change came on the night of 7 December when a large force bombed 'not a single factory, but an industrial area in Düsseldorf where both factories and railway targets were concentrated'.[33]

Compared with those of their adversaries, Bomber Command's raids were small. In November and December 1940 Cologne was attacked on six occasions, Berlin on five and Hamburg three; other centres, including Bremen, Essen, Kiel and Munich, each received one assault. When Mannheim was raided on 16 December in retaliation for Coventry, in an operation code-named 'Abigail Rachel', only 134 bombers were sent. Their bomb-load of 90 tons of high explosives and 14,000 incendiaries was smaller than those aimed at many British cities. It was reported as a seven-hour operation against 'the chief industrial centre of the upper Rhine. Targets in surrounding districts, included a large aniline dye factory at Ludwigshafen, aircraft factory buildings at Speyer'[34] and other economic targets. However, aerial photographs taken a week later showed that damage was spread across the city and not limited to industrial sites. This certainly met the War Cabinet's aim that there should be 'the maximum possible effect in a German town'. Yet even here, by the standards of what happened in Coventry, casualties were light, with 34 killed and 81 injured.

Photographs supported the opinion expressed at a Group Navigation Officers' conference on 12 November that only three or four out of every ten bombs were finding their actual target.[35] Through the early months of 1941, while the *Luftwaffe* were confidently reaching cities across Britain through employing beams, aircraft of Bomber Command, using visual methods, were struggling to locate places in Germany. Bombs were missing their targets by miles. 'The crews had conscientiously been doing their best,' wrote a former pilot, 'but it was worrying us who had the job to do as well as those in higher places.'[36] What became obvious to all involved in Britain's bomber offensive, from men flying over enemy territory to those politicians and members of the Air Staff who created policy, was the need for scientific navigational aids. These would enable skilled crews to mark the bombing points with flares or incendiaries, thereby easing the task of the following main force.

With the benefit of hindsight, it is apparent that the aim of the Oil Plan to destroy Germany's war economy was over-ambitious. That nation's economic strength expanded, particularly through conquests. In addition, photographs taken after raids on these targets at Gelsenkirchen showed conclusively that many bombs had missed.[37] Furthermore, Peirse's bomber force was smaller than his opponent's. With the development of night bombing, his Battles and Blenheims no longer had a role to play and his realistic maximum strength for these operations amounted to about 150 aircraft.

Bomber Command's attentions were then turned in early 1941 to the more immediate problem of the Battle of the Atlantic, a policy laid down in Churchill's Directive of 6 March. Day and night attacks were demanded, with both bombing and minelaying, to meet the maritime threat. By then, Focke-Wulf Condors were an increasing danger to shipping, so both their bases in north-west France and the factories at Bremen which built them were added to Bomber Command's list. So, too, were U-boat bases at St Nazaire, Bordeaux and Lorient, and German submarine factories. From March to May, Kiel and Hamburg were frequently raided, suffering damage to industrial sites.

In mid-April, on successive nights, 288, then 159, bombers struck at these targets, showing the Command's commitment. The battlecruisers *Gneisenau* and *Scharnhorst*, both holed up at Brest, also were bombed. However, many small, specific targets were difficult to hit. Peirse wrote on 15 April, 'We are not designed for this purpose and we are not particularly effective in its execution.'[38] He wanted his aircraft to return to a general assault on Germany. That notwithstanding, the raiding of naval targets 'had a greater effect upon the German war effort than the continuation of the oil campaign would have done'. In Middlebrook's view, there was not 'the slightest chance' that RAF bombing at the time could have halted supplies of synthetic oil.[39]

Over the following months various questions were raised over Bomber Command's role. Here was Britain's only immediate offensive weapon to be employed against an enemy who had enjoyed an almost unbroken run of successes. At night the Command was not suffering crippling losses, as the German night fighter force was not yet organised with its later efficiency. Bearing in mind the proven limitations of accuracy, which targets should be selected? Would an extension of strikes against oil plants be effective, or would attacks on communications systems of rail, canal and road cause more disruption to industry? Such raids, being aimed generally in built-up areas, were bound to cause increased civilian casualties. Would that lead to a rapid breakdown in their morale? Therefore, would it be best to concentrate on area bombing, striking immediately at the German people and repaying some of the wanton destruction which the *Luftwaffe* had spread across Britain? Until the end of the Night Blitz German civilians escaped with far fewer casualties than those exacted from Britain by the *Luftwaffe*. For example, between March and July 1941 'Hamburg would suffer 331 deaths in eighteen raids compared with 125 deaths in its first seventy-two raids of the war'. The comparable figures for Kiel were 254, 17, 25 and 16, numbers that places like Liverpool, Bristol or Plymouth would gladly have exchanged for their own.[40] Discussion at Bomber Command was long, detailed and controversial. Eventually the experiences of late 1940 and early 1941 were sufficient, in the words of the Official History, 'to convert Bomber Command from a force which had previously been mainly devoted to the aim of precision attack to one which was now predominantly concerned with area bombing'.[41]

New policies required larger bombers. The *Luftwaffe* was still generally employing the Heinkel 111 as its largest strike machine, carrying a bomb load of some two tons. The Whitleys, Hampdens and Wellingtons flown by

Bomber Command were, however, insufficient for a concentrated strategic air offensive. Therefore, in the early months of 1941 the new generation of heavy bombers, planned from the later 1930s, came into operational use. On the night of 10 February the Short Stirling first saw action. This giant four-engine aircraft, 'an Empire boat on wheels',[42] had entered service the previous August and now three of the machines from No 7 Squadron dropped fifty-six 500lb bombs on oil storage tanks at Rotterdam. The bombers could each carry a bomb load of 14,000lb over a distance of 600 miles and, in spite of weaknesses, were a formidable addition to Bomber Command's armoury. One month later the first Handley Page Halifaxes flew on a raid when No 35 Squadron employed them to attack Le Havre. Two nights after this they raided Hamburg, being the first four-engine bombers to fly over Germany. Initially less successful, twin-engine Avro Manchesters entered the battle on 24 February. They flew with No 207 Squadron to raid Brest but from the start had trouble with their Vulture engines. Problems of engine and design were solved when the designer turned the aircraft into a four-engine bomber, powered by Rolls-Royce Merlins, and thereby produced the Lancaster.

The second of Bomber Command's difficulties, that of navigating accurately to targets, was addressed in detail later in the year. Discussion took place at one of the 'Sunday Soviets' held in Swanage by the TRE, and before long the scientist R. J. Dippy, who had suggested methods of doing this before the war, provided solutions.[43] It involved sending pulses from three stations in Britain: 'From the differences in the times of arrival of the three pulses at the aircraft, the navigator could determine his position'[44] For aircrews later in 1941, this was a giant advance in navigation.

By the close of the *Luftwaffe*'s Night Blitz on Britain and its subsequent turning to the invasion of Russia, Bomber Command was already preparing for the great offensive over Germany. It was about to implement the theories of aerial power held by the Air Staff since the 1920s. 'There are people who say that bombing can never win a war,' stated Harris, their future leader. 'My answer to this is that it's never been tried. We shall see.'[45]

CIVILIANS AND THEIR DEFENCES

The last phase of the Night Blitz was in many ways the most intense and violent. It appeared that the *Luftwaffe*, in raids which had started with the daylight attacks of August 1940, was determined to administer a few final kicks of frustration before turning to the new campaign in Russia. For example, the onslaught against Plymouth at the end of April, and particularly on Clydeside, Belfast and then London in early May, caused very heavy casualties and cut vast deserts of destruction across those cities. These were savage reminders of what aerial bombing could achieve at night, in spite of improved defences. The lessons were not lost on Bomber Command.

One of the benefits for civilians during the Blitz was the slow build-up towards action. Fears poured into the public mind during the 1920s and 1930s failed to materialise at the outbreak of war. There was no massive 'knock-out blow' attempted by the *Luftwaffe* from the first hour of hostilities. No formations of up to 1,000 bombers a day crossed the North Sea to attack British targets. No rain of gas bombs fell on cities, bringing death to thousands, mass panic and consequent revolution.

Air attack came gradually to the British people, so they became inured to the threat before the worst effects arrived. From the start of the war raids were desultory, not building in intensity until the daylight Battle of Britain. Those attacks, in the main, were not aimed at civilians, and the night onslaught did not open until the war had been in progress for a year. By then ARP services had used opportunities to organise, train and, in a few cases, see minor action.

As the Night Blitz arrived, casualties rose sharply among civilians, but to nothing like the figures predicted: numbers suggested by the Air Staff in the later 1930s were shown, fortunately, to have been greatly exaggerated. Predictions that the Germans would drop 3,500 tons of bombs during the first twenty-four hours of war, or that each ton would produce 50 casualties, were wide of the mark. Even when 300 to 400 Londoners were killed and over a thousand injured on some nights in September, the numbers were far smaller than had been feared. This resulted in fewer demands being made on hospital and mortuary services, which had been prepared for an avalanche.

What of morale and 'the tangled undergrowth of this topic'?[46] It had not shattered, although on some occasions it had bent under the storm of attack. 'It was thought that civilians, not disciplined to war, untrained in defence, helpless targets for enemy bombers, must crack up on a wholesale scale,' wrote a medical correspondent in September 1941. 'Even mass-hysteria was feared. But nothing of the sort happened—anywhere.' The writer offered other findings. Women suffered less than men from bomb shock. Men were less inclined to discuss their experiences in war. Activity in civil defence services was 'the most efficient antidote' to fear in air raids.[47] The general reaction of British people showed how wide of the mark were the prognostications of writers such as Fuller, Huxley and Haldane. Two particular features impressed Winant, the American Ambassador: 'The first, the effort made to maintain the appearance of normal life in the face of danger, and the second, the patient acceptance of hardships and hazards by ordinary people.'[48]

An investigation of the effects of bombing on civilians was made by the scientist Solly Zuckermann, and it brought some interesting results. 'The most potent casualty producer', for its weight, was the 50kg bomb. 'Ton for ton it was every bit as dangerous as the V2 rocket bomb.' Most injuries resulted from what he described as 'the tertiary effects of an explosion—injuries due to falling and flying debris and other secondary missiles'. After investigating raids made on Hull and Birmingham, he came up with further conclusions. The 'trekking' from Hull was 'much publicised as a sign of breaking morale', but should instead be 'fairly recognised as a considered response to the situation'. There was no anti-social behaviour and no effect on general health. Zuckermann was critical of the findings of Tom Harrison, whose book, *Living Through the Blitz*, has become a bible for writers wishing to reconsider the fortitude of civilian resistance to bombing. Harrison was asked to provide useful material from Mass Observation reports to the Ministry of Home Security and the Ministry of Information but, according to Zuckermann, the latter Ministry 'found all but none in the work which he carried out on its behalf'. Zuckermann 'was fully aware of Tom's propensity to generalise in a sweeping way from selected material'. Extending the criticism, he added that most reports to the Ministry of Home Security were 'so slanted that the book fails totally to reflect the atmosphere of the times and the environment of urgency within which the Ministry had to work'.[49]

In spite of many criticisms of civilian defences, they worked. O'Brien quotes Walter Bagehot's comment on 'the natural impulse of the English people to resist authority'[50] and therefore there were loud voices occasionally raised in protest. In general, the bravery of men and women immediately involved, such as wardens and firemen, police and rescue parties, was not called into question. Blame for shortcomings was more often laid at the door of local government and organisers, those regarded as part of a hidden, heartless bureaucracy. On them fell the wrath of those who believed that there had been negligence in providing shelters and food supplies, housing and clothing.

A heavy responsibility devolved on Regional Commissioners, especially when the threat of invasion loomed after Dunkirk. Had central government broken down then, their role in controlling areas of Britain would have been crucial. The emergency never arose. Nevertheless, their overall duties were widespread, including 'manpower, shelters, fire prevention, and training, welfare and organisation of civil defence services and, to some extent, fire fighting'.[51] They were a vital link between Government Ministries and officials in their own areas who had the immediate task of providing services.

Help was given to civilians by the armed services. 'Recent heavy bombing has considerably strained civilian resources in some areas,' explained an Order from GHQ Home Forces in October 1940. Therefore, 'the Commander-in-Chief wishes military forces to give as much help as possible where damage has been caused to civilian property by bombs'. The help was speedily forthcoming, and in London alone during October 13,500 troops were sent in, some remaining for several months. By the same token, aid was offered from the other two services in areas close to their bases.[52] For example, the cities of Portsmouth and Plymouth received help from the Royal Navy, as did Southampton from the Royal Engineers.

Service personnel not only cleared and repaired bomb damage, an extensive task in some districts, but also restrained people who visited the sites of bombing purely to gaze, sometimes in a ghoulish way. Such actions may have led to the occasional rumours that service units had 'taken over' a city, or that 'military law' had been established. This feeling was supported also by the appearance of posters threatening dire penalties against looters. Looting did occur, with an amount of petty pilfering, but fear of retribution, combined with a widespread feeling of mutual support in communities, ensured that wholesale pillaging seldom happened.

Air raid services learned quickly from war and their response improved radically after September 1940. One of their greatest problems was presented by incendiary bombs which, in spite of their almost innocuous appearance, caused huge fires in every city that was attacked. What were never in doubt were the courage, tenacity and ingenuity of the men and women in the fire service. For the fireman at the pump came, according to the Chief of the Fire Staff, 'tension as the first bomb fell—exhilaration as he left cover to attend the first fire call—exaltation as the raid proceeded and all hell was let loose around him'. He recorded that exhaustion, and satisfaction at a job well done, followed.[53]

However, the bravery of staff was not always matched by an efficient organisation. The 1,600 regular fire brigades, augmented by crews from the AFS, were under-staffed, lacking equipment and suffering from 'the division of control among more than a thousand local government units'.[54] A need existed for a centralised service to tackle the dire emergencies which arose in certain places. Then staff and equipment, communications and water supplies could be employed to overcome some of the petty jealousies and inefficiencies that were obstacles to dealing with the most savage *Luftwaffe* attacks. Matters came to a head during the final heavy raids of April and May, when complaints were registered against the fire-fighting services by, for example, Lady Astor at Plymouth. Therefore, after consultations, changes were proposed to unify fire brigades. By August 1941 a National Fire Service had been formed to tackle future raids; but, in reality, these proved to be far fewer and less ferocious than those experienced during the Night Blitz.

Other changes to air raid precautions came during early 1941 in the provision of shelters. Planners believed that the night bombing offensive could last for several years and steps were taken to improve underground accommodation. By the end of April over 600,000 wooden bunks had been provided in the London Region alone. The Ministry of Health, fearing an outbreak of epidemics, took steps to improve heating, lighting, ventilation and catering for thousands who spent nights underground. At surface level, older shelters were pulled down from March and replaced with stronger structures, built from concrete and steel rods.

An indoor shelter was introduced for people's homes. The 'Anderson', which had generally been positioned in gardens or yards, was augmented by the 'Morrison'. With a length of 6 feet 6 inches, a width of 4 feet and a height of 2 feet 9 inches, this could, in a living room, be a table during the day and a sleeping space at night. The price was £7 12s 6d but they were issued free to families whose income was less than £350 per annum.

Among the prime German aims of launching the Night Blitz against civilians was the destruction of stocks of food and fuel, together with industrial workplaces, so that morale would break. Herein lay the earlier beliefs of Douhet and Mitchell, that if aerial devastation made everyday life unbearable, a government would find its position untenable. It is therefore illuminating, in view of the thousands of tons of German bombs aimed at those targets, to explore their effect by the early summer of 1941. Accurate assessments were made by the Intelligence Branch of the Ministry of Home Security, when summaries were given of damage caused to Key Points.[55]

First, major public utilities were temporarily affected by raids, but there was no long-term threatening damage to public supplies. In the case of electricity, 'the Grid system has stood up to enemy action very well', and few cases of interruption had lasted more than a few hours.[56] In January 1941 Bristol lost power for 16½ hours, Plymouth for a day and Portsmouth for two and a half days, but supplies were then restored. Thus both homes and workplaces were not long without power. Water systems were sometimes temporarily out of action, but, apart from one case in London, 'the main Reservoirs and Pumping Stations have not been hit'. Supplies of drinking water were readily available. Gas supplies were more affected, though not catastrophically. Of the gas producing plants, only five were seriously hit, leading in one case 'to considerable inconvenience for a period of three weeks'. Elsewhere alternative sources were used. In the case of London, the Beckton Gas Works, an aiming point for the first great raid on 7 September, was hit but the Germans failed to sustain attacks through which 'the London gas supply would inevitably have been cut off for a considerable period'.

Although a number of grain stores, warehouses and storage centres were hit, particularly in seaports, food supplies to the nation were never seriously threatened. The policy was to spread storage capacity across Britain, which 'lessened the importance of a successful attack on any one Installation'. The heavy and continued bombing of London's Dockland 'had no appreciable effect on the Food Supply of the Capital'. The raids on Merseyside led to losses which were 'not appreciable'.[57]

The greatest food losses were suffered in early 1941, with nine-tenths during the first four months. Yet here there was a subtle difference between stocks 'affected' and those which were a 'complete loss'. Of the former category, only about one quarter finished up as the latter. Altogether some 70,000 tons were totally lost, about 44 per cent of which were in Liverpool. Of commodities, animal feeding stuffs suffered most, followed by wheat, flour and sugar. However, the Salvage Branch, set up in January 1941, was able to recover large quantities for consumption.

It is often difficult for people over half a century on to comprehend how the British nation managed on a spartan diet of rationed food. The average adult was required during the Night Blitz to exist weekly on 1lb of meat, 4oz of bacon, 2oz of butter, 6oz of fat, 8oz of sugar and 2oz of tea. At that stage eggs, cheese and preserves were not rationed, though they were in short supply, and the 'points' system was not introduced until November 1941.

The system of feeding a nation whose supplies had not been totally cut off by German action was assisted in several ways. American Lease-Lend brought variety to food, although supplies did not arrive in Britain until May 1941. The Ministry of Food, led by the redoubtable Lord Woolton, poured out advice via wireless and the printed word, encouraging housewives to make the best of resources. Bread and potatoes were eaten in large quantities and people started to 'Dig for Victory'. The starchy diet led to a few weight problems, which brought the advice to 'Grow fit not fat on your war diet! Make full use of the fruit and vegetables in season.'[58]

Far more people ate out, often at their workplaces, or in the newly opened British restaurants which 'were born in the Blitz; their parent was the Londoners' Meal Service'.[59] From March 1941 towns with a population of over 50,000 were required to provide emergency meal centres. Thus the nation's diet was sustained, often with Government subsidy. For those working people who had suffered during the Slump of the early 1930s, the standard of feeding rose and with it the quality of health. Neither malnutrition nor obesity was a common condition for the British population during the Second World War.

Civilians' workplaces were affected far less by the Night Blitz than either the Germans had hoped or many 'experts' had predicted. Various key industries had been 'splitting up their shops and locating them in isolated positions in various outlying districts'. Also, new factories were constructed outside cities and towns, making concentrated bombing of single industries almost impossible. For example, in the production of aircraft and aero-engines, where factories had been targeted since August 1940, there had been no damage 'which could be interpreted as a catastrophe'. Any stoppages, although serious, were temporary set-backs.[60]

Even where 'key points' could be neither moved nor dispersed, distress was far less than had been feared. Oil storage tanks in the United Kingdom, which held about two million gallons of fuel, were bombed, in a few cases leading to spectacular fires. Nevertheless, only some 3 per cent of supplies were lost. Docks and harbours also received thousands of bombs, yet, in the case of London, 'at no time have Docks and their Outer Basins been rendered unserviceable'. Civilians were still able to work there.[61]

Consequently, in May 1941 the beleaguered British public, who had endured the lash of assault for eight months, and thousands of whom had lost friends, relatives and homes, were still in the fight. They were not to know that the worst had passed. They still had food supplies and utility services, their workplaces and an improving system of civil defence. These, together with expanding armed services and, over the following seven months, the addition of the world's two most powerful nations as allies, would carry them to a distant victory.

NOTES

1. AIR 41/17, 118.
2. *Ibid.*, 105.
3. See Pile, 186–90.
4. AIR 41/17, Appendix 8.
5. *Ibid.*, Appendix 12.
6. *Ibid.*, Appendix 17.
7. *The Aeroplane*, 21 March 1941.
8. Historical Radar Archive, *Radar Bulletin, 60 Group* (1991), 22–3.
9. AIR 8/863, para. 255.
10. Figures extrapolated from *Blitz*, ii.
11. AIR 41/17, Appendix 20.
12. *Ibid.*
13. *Ibid.*, G.O.C-in-C's Progress Report, 17 April 1941, 104.
14. See *Years of Command*, 107–8.
15. AIR 41/17, 104.
16. Price, *Instruments of Darkness*, 46.
17. Hinsley, i, Appendix 11.
18. *Ibid.*, 863.
19. *Instruments of Darkness*, 120.
20. C. Bowyer, *Fighter Command* (1980), 95.
21. *Ibid.*, 88.
22. Wykeham, 179.
23. *Years of Command*, 113–14.
24. A Flight Lieutenant, *We Speak From the Air* (HMSO, 1942), 24.
25. Fighter Command Operational Instruction No 7, 16 February 1941.
26. See Terraine, 284.
27. Beaverbrook Papers, BBK D/414, vol. i, 8 July 1940.
28. Sawyer, 54.
29. *The Aeroplane*, 25 April 1941.
30. W. Crozier, *Off The Record: Political Interviews 1933–1943* (1973), 203.
31. Directive, DCAS to Peirse, 30 October 1940, Appendix 8(x).
32. D. Richards and H. Saunders, *Royal Air Force 1939–1945*, vol. i (HMSO, 1961), 234.
33. W. Lawrence, *No 5 Bomber Group RAF* (1951), 4.
34. *The Aeroplane*, 27 December 1940.
35. *SOAG*, i, 205.
36. Sawyer, 57.

37. *SOAG*, i, 163–4.
38. *Ibid.*, 168.
39. See M. Middlebrook and C. Everitt, *The Bomber Command War Diaries* (1985), 133.
40. *Ibid.*, 168.
41. *SOAG*, i, 245.
42. Penrose, *Ominous Skies*, 255.
43. Penley and Batt, 10.
44. *Secret War*, 284.
45. Air Chief Marshal Harris, TV interview.
46. O'Brien, 294.
47. A Medical Correspondent, 'The Civilian's Nerves', *The Spectator*, 5 September 1941.
48. Winant, 44.
49. S. Zuckermann, *From Apes to Warlords* (1978), 137–46.
50. O'Brien, 352.
51. *Ibid.*, 612.
52. See *ibid.*, 638–42.
53. Sir Aylmer Firebrace, *Fire Service Memories* (1949), 183.
54. O'Brien, 467.
55. AIR 41/17, Appendix 1.
56. *Ibid.*, 2.
57. See *ibid.*
58. In spite of the limitations of wartime food supplies, many people who had suffered through widespread unemployment during the early 1930s enjoyed a better diet under rationing in 1940–41.
59. A. Calder, *The People's War* (1969), 386.
60. AIR 41/17, 1–2.
61. *Ibid.*, 3.

EPILOGUE

The last phase of the Night Blitz produced one single episode which, at the time, British people found intriguing, bizarre and not without amusement. Its reporting added to a mystery that soon drew newspaper headlines around the world. For months, these had reported raids by hundreds of bombers, opening particularly with the great afternoon onslaught of 7 September when almost a thousand *Luftwaffe* aircraft had moved on London. Yet this new event concerned no more than one pilot flying on a single mission from which he neither could nor intended to return. On the night of 10 May, while *Luftwaffe* bombers were killing or badly injuring over 3,000 Londoners and starting more than 2,000 fires, a lone Bf 110 twin-engine fighter was located over the North Sea by RDF operators in the north-east of England. Its subsequent course, over the coast of Northumberland and the Scottish Borders, raised disbelief in some quarters because that type of aircraft lacked the range to fly so far north and then return to its base. The puzzle deepened when, over southern Scotland, the pilot baled out, allowing his plane to crash. When captured, he claimed to be *Hauptmann* Alfred Horn and asked to meet the Duke of Hamilton.

Before long the British authorities realised that a far larger fish had been netted. The message issued from Downing Street at 11.20 p.m. on 12 May gave his true identity. 'Rudolf Hess, the Deputy *Führer* and Party Leader of the National Socialist Party, has landed in Scotland,' it announced.[1] Earlier, according to the *Daily Sketch*, German wireless had reported 'that Hess has gone mad, vanished in a plane, and was believed to have committed suicide'.[2]

'The thing's a mystery—was he in danger of his life?' a civilian diarist wondered. 'Why come to Scotland? Why didn't he fly to a neutral country?' The writer then expressed a general feeling. 'Wild hopes spring up that he is bringing terms for peace but of course no terms whatever would be acceptable, short of total surrender.'[3] An air of mystery has surrounded the event ever since, the fires of conspiracy theories fuelled by, for example, Costello's and Thomas's books, while Nesbit brings a balance of historical accuracy.[4] In terms of night air defence, which is the domain of this book, two points only are offered. First, Hess took off from Augsburg in Bf 110 VJ+OQ, not in machine NJ+CII. Second, Spitfires of No 2 Squadron were scrambled first to pursue Hess's aircraft, and it was only when the Controller believed that they would not catch him that Sergeant Pocock's Spitfire was dispatched.

The aims and circumstances of the Deputy *Führer*'s flight are still not fully known in Britain, or easily explicable, but obviously they were related to the Russian Campaign. Whether he was a messenger from the German Government offering Britain the opportunity of joining a Nazi crusade against Bolshevism, or whether his was a personal mission, is unknown. The effect was minimal. Britain remained the staunch enemy of Germany and six weeks later it was Russia who joined a crusade against Nazism.

Liddell Hart compares Hitler's attitude to Britain in 1940 with that of Napoleon 135 years earlier. 'Once again,' he asserts, 'a conqueror of the West was confounded by a people who "did not see that they were beaten".' While rejecting his peace offers, they were 'intent to keep their teeth in Hitler's skin at any cost'. His bafflement therefore led him, like Napoleon, to veer eastwards, to the conquest of Russia, before returning for a final showdown with Britain.

In Hitler' case, an innate hatred of Communism, expressed, for example, in his book *Mein Kampf*, was 'his most profound emotional conviction'.[5] Trevor Roper refers to 'his ultimate aim: the winning of living-space in the East'.[6] His agreement with Russia in the Soviet–German Pact of August 1939 was a wary acknowledgement by each side of the other's potential and more of a chess move than a statement of friendship. For the Russians, German victories in the West were ominous reminders of the power of the Nazi State. For the Germans, Stalin's seizure of the Baltic States in June 1940, followed by his demands on Romania, accelerated Hitler's fears of his eastern neighbour. Consequently, while the *Luftwaffe* were trying vainly to eradicate the RAF in the Battle of Britain, and then launching the Night Blitz, the German Army was preparing for a campaign against the USSR.

By November 1940 General von Paulus, Deputy Chief of the General Staff, had presented a plan which was then tested. On 18 December Hitler's Directive No 21 for Operation 'Barbarossa' set out the main principles of the forthcoming war. German armed forces would aim 'even before the conclusion of the war against England, to crush Soviet Russia in a rapid campaign'.

The final objective, he stated, 'is to erect a barrier against Asiatic Russia on the general line Volga–Archangel'.[7] With that achieved, and no possible ally remaining for Britain on the Continental mainland, he would return to the demolition of the United Kingdom.

According to Suchenwirth, Goering opposed the new war and told Hitler that 'the *Luftwaffe* is the only *Wehrmacht* branch which has not had a breathing space since the war began'.[8] Irving states that news of the proposed war came to Milch as a 'bombshell',[9] although he had already attended conferences where the matter had been discussed. Both men recognised that the demands on the *Luftwaffe* would be enormous, because its strength had to cover several theatres of war. On the Russian Front, in June 1941 the German Air Force had some 2,000 aircraft available. Remaining in France and the Low Countries were 660 machines, engaged particularly in offensive operations against Britain. In Germany itself were 190 fighters retained for home defence. Across the area of the Mediterranean and North Africa, the *Luftwaffe* had eight bomber and three fighter *Gruppen*, with five long-range reconnaissance squadrons. Other *Gruppen* and formations were retained in Norway. Consequently, by the opening of the Russian Campaign, and in spite of a number of savage attacks on British cities, the main *Luftwaffe* strength had been removed from the Blitz on the United Kingdom.

Although not apparent at the time to a nation which had, for a year, been the victim of German assaults and successes, the following six months were to bring unexpected and vital relief. Two allies joined Britain in the war. On 22 June the Germans began the invasion of Russia and, at a stroke, the centre of hostilities was turned to the Eastern Front. Then, in early December, when Japan commenced its unheralded attacks in the Far East, Hitler joined his Asiatic ally by declaring war on the United States. With these two moves the *Führer* signed his nation's death warrant. This, however, was not immediately obvious to the British people at the time. Once again, in each case, the new war brought initial rewards for the aggressors.

By the end of 1941 Britain was able to take stock. The two new allies were latent giants, as yet undeveloped in strength to strike back at the enemy. For the citizens of the United Kingdom, the Battle of Britain had uncovered the *Luftwaffe*'s weaknesses and frustrated Hitler's plans. The intensive Night Blitz had demonstrated the strength of civilians in standing up to the burdens of bombing. However, the Battle of the Atlantic, a campaign of attrition, was intensifying and posing equal threats to the nation's ability to stay in the war.

All over Britain enormous damage had been caused by explosive and fire-bombs, although mainly concentrated in urban areas. Yet the destruction, wherever it occurred, even in little villages, 'if small measured on the scale of the national war effort, had its local effects'.[10] Such disaster, nevertheless, could in the long run be repaired. Gradually, through patching up and reconstruction, the effects of devastation were smoothed away.

However, this was less easy with human beings, where the ledger columns of death and injury made grim reading. From the opening of the Night Blitz on 7 September 1940 to the end of that year, 22,069 civilians were killed in the British Isles, 13,390 of them in London. During 1941 a further 19,918 died and, of these, 13,431 met their deaths in villages, towns and cities outside the capital. The figures of those seriously injured were also daunting. In the first period, until 31 December 1940, 28,240 were admitted to hospital, 17,937 of whom were in London. For the year 1941 the nation's total was 21,165, of whom 13,524 were injured outside the capital. In addition, at least an equal number of civilians were slightly hurt. When these figures are set against the nation's totals for the whole war of 60,595 civilians killed and 86,182 seriously injured, the concentration of casualties into the eight months of the main Night Blitz becomes obvious.[11]

After reviewing civilian defence personnel on 14 July 1941, Churchill spoke of their bravery. It had impressed the world and especially opinion in the United States. All had been 'largely influenced by the conduct of Londoners and of the men and women in our provincial cities in standing up to the enemy's bombardments'.[12] Those who died and those injured were part of a British generation that neither sought nor gloried in war. Scots or Welsh, English or Northern Irish, they were self-reliant and peaceful people on whom the hardest burdens of war fell in the year following the collapse of France. In the cauldron of fire their independent spirit and determination ensured that Britain remained unconquered. Such sacrifice deserves everlasting acknowledgement and respect from later generations. Their example sets a benchmark for a nation in danger of losing one particular quality shown in abundance in 1940—the strength of national pride.

NOTES

1. Official communiqué, 12 May 1940.

2. *Daily Sketch*, 13 May 1941.

3. Beardmore, 113.

4. See R. Nesbit, *The Conspiracy Theories*; also see J. Costello, *Ten Days That Saved the West*, and H. Thomas, *The Murder of Rudolf Hess*.

5. Liddell Hart, *Second World War*, 142–3.

6. Trevor Roper, *Hitler's War Directives*, 48.

7. *Ibid.*, 49.

8. Suchenwirth, *Turning Points*, 75.

9. Irving, *Rise and Fall*, 116.

10. O'Brien, 428.

11. Figures taken from O'Brien, Appendix ii. For a comparison with casualties caused by later German attacks, note that during the whole of 1942 and 1943, 5,608 civilians were killed in the United Kingdom. In 1944–45, flying bombs and rockets led to 8,938 deaths.

12. C. Eade (ed.), *The War Speeches of the Rt. Hon. Winston S. Churchill*, vol. i (1951) 20–7.

APPENDICES

APPENDIX A
THE BLITZ NATIONWIDE

The effects of the Night Blitz were felt most heavily in the areas of large cities, where bombing was often concentrated. Nevertheless, many smaller towns, villages and hamlets also suffered, as was shown in figures published in German newspapers early in 1941. They referred to day and night raids made between 8 August and 31 December 1940, which constituted only about one-half of the final total. Even at that stage, the following places in Britain had been bombed: London—126 times; Liverpool—60; Birmingham—36; Southampton—26; Bristol, Dover—22; Coventry—21; Plymouth, Portsmouth, Thameshaven—13; Portland—12; Cardiff, Swansea—11; Chatham, Manchester, Yarmouth—9; Newcastle—8; Brighton, Pembroke—7; Rochester—6; Bournemouth, Filton, Norwich, Weymouth—5; Avonmouth, Dundee, Edinburgh, Eastchurch, Hastings, Hull, Middlesbrough, Manston, Tilbury, Weybridge—4; Aberdeen, Aldershot, Billingham, Birkenhead, Chester, Derby, Detling, Exeter, Faversham, Grantham, Hawkinge, Leith, Newport, Port Victoria, Poole, Reading, Sheerness, Sheffield—3; Banbury, Bexhill, Cambridge, Canterbury, Canvey Island, Devonport, Dungeness, Bridlington, Eastbourne, St Eval, Falmouth, Glasgow, Hartlepool, Hornchurch, Kenley, Kingston, Lowestoft, Lympne, Merryn, Newhaven, North Killingham, Penrose, St Athan, Wattisham, Yeovil, York—2. One raid each had been made on 81 other towns and important targets.

In that period, the German High Command claimed that the *Luftwaffe* had made more than 1,130 air attacks on Britain. Of these, 130 were termed 'mass raids', during each of which between 100,000kg and 700,000kg of bombs had been dropped. The totals were 43 million kilograms of high explosives and 1.6 million kilograms of incendiaries. During the same period, Bomber Command delivered only 4 per cent of these totals on Germany.

The German Press added that the *Luftwaffe*'s aim was to strike not only at military and economic targets, but also to hit 'British arrogance, the boundless conceit of Lords and Gentlemen'.

Figures taken from *The Aeroplane*, 21 February 1941.

APPENDIX B
MAJOR *LUFTWAFFE* NIGHT ATTACKS
7 SEPTEMBER 1940–16 MAY 1941

The numbers below are based on German figures for 'major' attacks, in each of which at least 100 tons of bombs were dropped on the target. They show particularly the extent of the burden carried by civilians in London.

Target	No of major attacks	Tonnage of HE dropped
London	71	18,291
Liverpool/Birkenhead	8	1,957
Birmingham	8	1,852
Plymouth/Devonport	8	1,228
Bristol/Avonmouth	6	919
Glasgow/Clydeside	5	1,329
Southampton	4	647
Portsmouth	3	687
Hull	3	593
Manchester	3	578
Coventry	2	818
Belfast	2	440
Sheffield	1	355
Newcastle/Tyneside	1	152
Nottingham	1	137
Cardiff	1	115

Source: AIR 41/17, Appendix IV

APPENDIX C
CIVILIANS IN DEFENCE SERVICES

The immense part played by civilians, full- and part-time, in the defence of Britain during the Night Blitz is shown by the accompanying figures (given in thousands; M= male, F= female)

	ARP		Fire		Casualty		Police (Reg/Aux)	
	M	F	M	F	M	F	M	F
June 1940	828.1	151.8	233.8	13.6	61.6	167.2	255.6	1.1
June 1941	869.3	163.2	256.2	15.4	61.7	158.2	258.8	1.4

ARP services: wardens, rescue and first-aid parties, report and control centres, messengers
Fire services: regular fire brigades, Auxiliary Fire Service, Works' Brigades
Casualty services: emergency ambulance service, first aid post service
Police services: Regulars, Police War Reserve, First Police Reserve, Special Constables, Women's Auxiliary Police Corps

Figures extrapolated from O'Brien

APPENDIX D
MINISTRIES AND THEIR RESPONSIBILITIES

Ministry of Health: Welfare of homeless; evacuation; re-housing; first-aid repairs to housing; disposal of the dead; repairs to sewers; casualty services; repairs to water undertakings.
Ministry of Home Security: Civil defence services; clearance of debris; salvage of furniture; military aid; disposal of UXBs; some road repairs; some communications.
Ministry of Transport: Some road repairs; rail and road transport; communications.
Ministry of Food: Emergency feeding; mobile canteens; food shops; food salvage.

Assistance Board and Ministry of Pensions: Relief of distress; claims for injuries.

Board of Trade: Emergency supplies; repairs to some factories; repairs to some shops; repairs to gas undertakings; salvage of goods.

Ministry of Works: Repairs to some shops; repairs to some factories; emergency repair services.

Home Office: Law and order.

Ministry of Information: Public information.

Source: O'Brien, Appendix VII.

APPENDIX E
FIGHTER COMMAND ORDERS OF BATTLE

The growth in importance of night fighters to Britain's defence is shown by Fighter Command's Order of Battle on three dates during the Night Blitz.

Group	Squadron	Sector	Aircraft type
14 November 1940			
10	87	Exeter	Hurricane
	604	Middle Wallop	Blenheim
11	23	Tangmere	Blenheim
	219	Kenley	Beaufighter
	141	Biggin Hill	Defiant
	85	Biggin Hill	Hurricane
	264	Hornchurch	Defiant
12	151	Digby	Hurricane
	29	Digby	Blenheim
16 February 1941			
9	96	Speke	Hurricane
	307	Speke	Defiant
10	87	Filton	Hurricane
	604	Middle Wallop	Beaufighter
11	219	Tangmere	Beaufighter

	264	Kenley	Defiant
	141	Biggin Hill	Defiant
	85	Debden	Hurricane/Defiant
12	25	Wittering	Blenheim/Beaufighter
	151	Wittering	Hurricane/Defiant
	29	Digby	Blenheim/Beaufighter
	255	Kirton–in–Lindsey	Defiant (one Section)
13	600	Catterick	Blenheim

11 May 1941

	96	Speke	Defiant/Hurricane
9	96	Speke	Defiant/Hurricane
	256	Speke	Defiant/Hurricane
	68	Turnhill	Blenheim/Beaufighter
10	600	Colerne	Beaufighter
	87	Charmy Down	Hurricane
	307	Exeter	Defiant
	604	Middle Wallop	Beaufighter
	93	Middle Wallop	Harrow (for aerial minelaying)
11	219	Tangmere	Beaufighter
	264	West Malling	Defiant
	29	West Malling	Beaufighter
	85	Debden	Havoc
12	25	Wittering	Beaufighter
	151	Wittering	Defiant
	255	Kirton–in–Lindsey	Defiant/Hurricane
13	141	Ayr	Defiant

Source: AIR 41/17, Appendix 18.

APPENDIX F
GERMAN BOMBER STRENGTH

Figures of German bomber strength in Western Europe for 1940–41 show the extent to which the *Luftwaffe* prepared for both the Balkan and Russian campaigns by moving aircraft to the East.

Date	Establishment	Strength	Serviceability
7 September 1940	1,504	1,241	787
16 November 1940	1,687	1,333	709
1 March 1941	1,867	1,443	781
21 June 1941	261	213	136

Source: AIR 41/17, Appendix 10

APPENDIX G
FINDING THE ENEMY

The difficulty of intercepting enemy aircraft in darkness before the use of GCI and AI radar is shown by these statistics of a typical Luftwaffe 'crocodile' of bombers on a night raid.

Average speed of aircraft	180mph
Influx strength	One aircraft crossed the coast every five minutes
Average linear distribution	One aircraft every twelve miles
Average superficial density	One aircraft per 180 square miles
Average volume distribution	Since the aircraft flew between 10,000 and 20,000 feet, there was an average of one aircraft per 345 cubic miles.

Source: AIR 41/12, 143.

APPENDIX H
GERMAN RADIO BEAM SYSTEMS

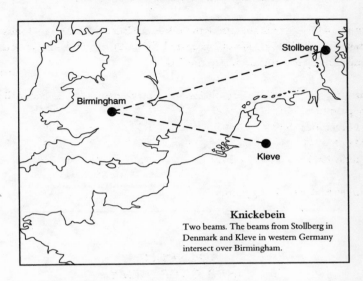

Knickebein
Two beams. The beams from Stollberg in Denmark and Kleve in western Germany intersect over Birmingham.

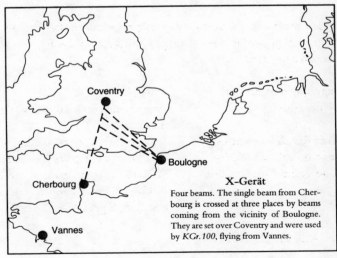

X-Gerät
Four beams. The single beam from Cherbourg is crossed at three places by beams coming from the vicinity of Boulogne. They are set over Coventry and were used by *KGr.100*, flying from Vannes.

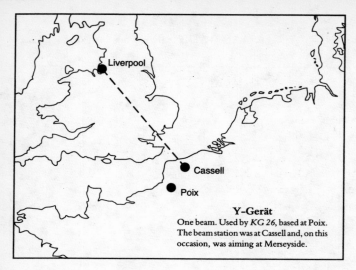

Y–Gerät
One beam. Used by *KG 26*, based at Poix.
The beam station was at Cassell and, on this
occasion, was aiming at Merseyside.

ABBREVIATIONS

AA	Anti-aircraft
AAAF	Advanced Auxiliary Air Force
ACAS	Assistant Chief of the Air Staff
ACM	Air Chief Marshal
ADGB	Air Defence of Great Britain
AFS	Auxiliary Fire Service
AFZ	Air Fighting Zone
AI	Airborne Interception
AM	Air Marshal
AOC	Air Officer Commanding
ARP	Air Raid Precautions
ARW	Air Raid Warden
AVM	Air Vice-Marshal
BBC	British Broadcasting Corporation
BDS	Bomb Disposal Squad
BOT	Board of Trade
CAS	Chief of the Air Staff
CD	Civil Defence
CH	Chain Home (radar)
CHL	Chain Home Low (radar)
CID	Comittee for Imperial Defence
CIGS	Chief of the Imperial General Staff
C-in-C	Commander-in-Chief
CO	Commanding Officer
COS	Chiefs of Staff
CSBS	Course-Setting Bomb Sight
DCAS	Deputy Chief of the Air Staff
FAP	First Aid Post
FAS	Fixed Azimuth System
GAF	German Air Force

GC	George Cross
GCI	Ground-Controlled Interception
GHQ	General Headquarters
GL	Gun Laying (radar)
GOC-in-C	General Officer Commanding-in-Chief
GM	George Medal
HE	High Explosive
IAF	Independent Air Force
IAZ	Inner Artillery Zone
JG	*Jagdgeschwader* (German fighter unit)
JPC	Joint Planning Committee
KG	*Kampfgeschwader* (German bomber unit)
LADA	London Air Defence Area
LCC	London County Council
LMF	Lack of Moral Fibre
MAP	Ministry of Aircraft Production
MO	Mass Observation
NADC	Night Air Defence Committee
NFS	National Fire Service
NIC	Night Interception Committee
OKL	*Oberkommando der Luftwaffe*
OKW	*Oberkommando der Wehrmacht*
PM	Prime Minister
PPI	Plan Position Indicator
RAF	Royal Air Force
RDF	Radio Direction-Finding
RFC	Royal Flying Corps
RN	Royal Navy
RNAS	Royal Naval Air Service
SC	*Sprengbombe-Cylindrisch*
SD	*Sprengbombe-Dickwandig*
TRE	Telecommunications Research Establishment
UP	Unrotating Projectile (rocket)
UXB	Unexploded Bomb
VCAS	Vice-Chief of the Air Staff
VCNS	Vice-Chief of the Naval Staff
WAP	Western Air Plans
WVS	Women's Voluntary Service

BIBLIOGRAPHY

UNPUBLISHED SOURCES

1. Government Records: Public Record Office

AIR 2: Correspondence
AIR 5: Air Ministry Registered files, 1921—World War Two
AIR 8: Chief of the Air Staff papers
AIR 14: Bomber Command
AIR 16: Fighter Command
AIR 19: Private Office papers
AIR 20: Unregistered papers
AIR 41: Air Historical Branch: Narratives and Monographs
AVIA 15: Ministry of Aircraft Production files
CAB 55: Committee of Imperial Defence, Joint Planning Committee, Minutes
CAB 65: War Cabinet, Minutes
CAB 66: War Cabinet, Memoranda (WP) Series
CAB 69: Defence Committee
CAB 81: Chiefs of Staff Committee and its sub-committees
CAB 120: Ministry of Defence, Secretariat
PREM 3: Prime Minister's Office: Operational papers
PREM 4: Confidential papers

2. Private and Unpublished Collections

Beaverbrook Papers: Papers of Lord Beaverbrook, House of Lords Record Office (HLRO), Historical Collection 184.
Beryl Cleveley's Diary: The Papers of Mrs B. Houson, Riverhead, Kent.
Conservative Party: The Minute Book of the Conservative Party 1922 Committee, 1938–1943, Bodleian Library, Oxford.
Dean Papers: Papers of Sir Maurice Dean, Liddell Hart Centre for Military Archives, King's College, London.
Douglas Papers: Papers of Marshal of the Royal Air Force Lord Douglas, Department of Documents, Imperial War Museum, London.
Dowding Papers: Papers of Air Chief Marshal Lord Dowding, Department of Aviation Records, Royal Air Force Museum, Hendon.

Ellender Notes: The Workings of Anti-Aircraft Defence, from the papers of Captain A. R. Ellender, Maidstone, Kent, formerly of AA Command.

Newall Papers: Papers of Marshal of the Royal Air Force Lord Newall, Department of Aviation Records, Royal Air Force Museum, Hendon.

Ogilvie Notes: Notes on Lord Dowding, from the papers of Squadron Leader D. B. Ogilvie, Tunbridge Wells, Kent.

Portal Papers: Papers of Marshal of the Royal Air Force Lord Portal, Christ Church, Oxford.

Salmond Papers: Papers of Marshal of the Royal Air Force Sir John Salmond, Department of Aviation Records, Royal Air Force Museum, Hendon.

Thurso Papers: Papers of Lord Thurso, formerly Sir Archibald Sinclair, Churchill College, Cambridge.

3. Air Historical Branch: Monographs, Narratives and Translations

Monographs

Skelley, R. E., Signals (3), vol. 4, 'Radar in Raid Reporting', CD 1063, AHB/II/116/21 (C) (1950); also as AIR 41/12.

Spaight, J. M., 'The Expansion of the RAF 1914–1939', AHB/II/116/17(1945), also as PRO AIR 41/8.

Stephenson, C., Signals (3), vol. 5, 'Fighter Control and Interception', CD 1116, AHB/II/116/21(D).

Translations

AHB Translation, vol. 2, VII/10, 'The Course of the Air War over Central and Western Europe', 21 November 1946.

AHB Translation, vol. 1, VII/11, 'The Douhet Theory in its Application to the Present War': also as AIR 20/7700.

AHB Translation, vol. 2, VII/26, 'The Course of the Air War against England', 7 July 1944.

AHB Translation, vol. 2, VII/30, 'Proposal for the Conduct of Air Warfare against Britain', 22 November 1939.

AHB Translation, vol. 9, VII/123, Survey of British Fighter Strength', 17 August 1940.

AHB Translation, K15410, *Hauptmann* O. Bechtle, Operations Officer of *KG 2*, 'German Air Force Operations against Great Britain: Tactics and Lessons Learnt, 1940–41'. Lecture given for German Air Force General Staff, 2 February 1944.

PUBLISHED SOURCES

1. Parliamentary Records
Parliamentary Debates (House of Commons). Official Report, 5th Series.

2. Memoirs, Autobiographies, Diaries

Anon. (P. Gribble), *Diary of a Staff Officer* (1941)

Beardmore, G., *Civilians At War* (1984)

Broad, R., and Fleming, S., *Nella Last's War: A Mother's Diary 1939–45* (1981)

Chandos, Lord, *The Memoirs of Lord Chandos* (1962)

Churchill, W. S., *The Second World War. Vol. I: The Gathering Storm* (1948)

———, *The Second World War. Vol. II: Their Finest Hour* (1949)

Colville, J., *The Fringes of Power: Downing Street Diaries 1939–1945* (1985)

Crozier, W., *Off the Record: Political Interviews 1933–1943* (1973)

Dalton, H., *The Fateful Years: Memoirs 1931–45* (1957)

Dean, Sir Maurice, *The Royal Air Force and Two World Wars* (1979)

Demarne, C., *The London Blitz* (1991)

Dilks, D., (ed.), *The Diaries of Sir Alexander Cadogan 1938–1945* (1971)

Douglas, Lord, *Years of Command* (1966)

Firebrace, Sir Aylmer, *Fire Service Memories* (1949)

Galland, A., *The First and the Last* (1955)

Henrey, Mrs R., *London Under Fire 1940–45* (1969)

Hermann, H., *Eagle's Wings* (1991)

Hudson. L., (trans.), *The Memoirs of Field Marshal Kesselring* (1953)

Hunt, H., *Bombs and Booby Traps* (1986)

Ickes, H., *Secret Diaries*, vol. iii (1967)

Ismay, Lord, *The Memoirs of General the Lord Ismay* (1960)

James, R. R., *Chips: The Diaries of Sir Henry Channon* (1967)

Johnstone, S., *Enemy in the Sky* (1976)

Jones, R. V., *Most Secret War* (1979)

Joubert, Sir Philip, *The Fated Sky* (1952)

Leutze, J., *The London Observer: Journal of General Raymond E. Lee 1940–41* (1972)

Lewis, C., *Sagittarius Rising* (1936)

Maisky, I., *Memoirs of a Soviet Ambassador* (1967)

Mayhew, P., (ed.), *One Family's War* (1985)

Middlebrook, M., and Everitt, C., *The Bomber Command War Diaries* (1985)

Moynihan, M., (ed.), *People At War 1939–1945* (1989)

Nicolson, N., (ed.), *Diaries and Letters 1930–64* (1980), of Harold Nicolson

Nissen, J., *Winning the Radar War* (1989)

Nixon, B., *Raiders Overhead* (1943)

Panter-Downes, M., *London War Notes 1939–1945* (1972)

Peel, Mrs C., *How We Lived Then* (1929)

Perry, C., *The Boy in the Blitz* (1972)

Pile, Sir Frederick, *Ack-Ack* (1949)

Pimlott, B., (ed.), *The Second World War Diary of Hugh Dalton 1940–1945* (1986)

Pritchett, V., *A Cab at the Door* (1968)

Rawnsley, C., *Night Fighter* (1957)

Reckitt, B., *Diary of Anti-Aircraft Defence 1938–1944* (1990)

Rowe, A., *One Story of Radar* (1948)

Sawyer, T., *Only Owls and Bloody Fools* (1982)

Scott, Sir Harold, *Your Obedient Servant* (1959)

Shirer, W., *Berlin Diary* (1941)

Slessor, Sir John, *The Central Blue* (1956)

Stahl, P., *The Diving Eagle: A Ju. 88 Pilot's Diary* (1984)

Strachey, J., *Post D* (1941)

Thomas, H., *With an Independent Air* (1977)

Thompson, W., *I Was Churchill's Shadow* (1951)

Townsend, P., *Duel in the Dark* (1986)

Ustinov, P., *Dear Me* (1977)

Vassiltchikov, G., (ed.), *The Berlin Diaries, 1940–1945, of Marie 'Missie' Vassiltchikov* (1987)

Warlimont, W., *Inside Hitler's Headquarters* (1964)

Watson–Watt, R., *Three Steps To Victory* (1957)

Wickes, B., *Waiting for the All-Clear* (1990)

Winant, J. G., *Letter From Grosvenor Square* (1947)

Winterbotham, F., *The Ultra Secret* (1974)

Zuckermann, S., *From Apes to Warlords* (1978)

3. Contemporary Publications: Books

Ashmore, E., *Air Defence* (1929)

Austin, A., *Fighter Command* (1941)

Brittain, V., *England's Hour* (1941)

Charlton, L., *War From the Air* (1935)

Douhet, G., *The Command of the Air* (1943)

Fuller, J., *The Reform of War* (1923)

———, *Towards Armageddon: The Defence Problem* (1937)

Grey, C., *A History of the Air Ministry* (1940)

Groves, P., *Behind the Smoke Screen* (1934)

Haldane, J., *Air Raid Precautions* (1938)

Harris, Sir Arthur, *Bomber Offensive* (1947)

Harrison, T., (ed.), *War Begins At Home: Mass Observation* (1940)

Idle, D., *War Over West Ham* (1943)

Jones, H. A., *The War in the Air* (1934)

London County Council, *Fire Over London* (1941)

Liddell Hart, B., *The Defence of Britain* (1939)

Mass Observation, *War Begins At Home* (1940)

Matthews, W., *St Paul's Cathedral in Wartime* (1946)

Mitchell, W., *Winged Warfare* (1930)

Monks, N., *Squadrons Up!* (1940)

Morris, J., *The German Air Raids on Great Britain 1914–1918* (1927)

Murrow, E., *This is London* (1941)

Reynolds, Q., *Only the Stars are Neutral* (1942)
Sanson, W., *Westminster in War* (1947)
Spaight, J., *The Sky's the Limit* (1940)
Sykes, F., *From Many Angles* (1940)
Wassley, M., *Ordeal By Fire* (1941)
Women's Group on Public Welfare, *Our Towns: A Close Up* (1943)

4. Official Publications: HMSO
Admiralty, The, *The Battle of the Atlantic* (1946)
Butler, J., *Grand Strategy. Vol. II: September 1939–June 1941* (1957)
Collier, B., *The Defence of the United Kingdom* (1957)
Flight Lieutenant, *We Speak From the Air* (1942)
Hammond, R. J., *Food* (1951), 2 vols.
Hinsley, F., *British Intelligence in the Second World War*, vol. i (1979)
HMSO, *Fire Over London: The Story of the London Fire Service 1940–41* (1942)
———, *The Protection of Your Home Against Air Raids* (1938)
———, *Protection Against Gas and Air Raids* (1939)
———, *Passive Air Defence* (1939)
Kohan, C. M., *Works and Buildings* (1952)
Medlicott, W. N., *The Economic Blockade. Vol. I: 1939–1941* (1952)
Ministry of Information, *Front Line* (1942)
———, *Roof Over Britain* (1943)
Ministry of War Transport, *Transport Goes To War* (1943)
O'Brien, T. H., *Civil Defence* (1955)
Penrose, H., *British Aviation: Widening Horizons, 1930–`1934* (1979)
———, *British Aviation: Ominous Skies, 1935–1939* (1980)
Postan, M. M., *British War Production* (1952)
Probert, H., *High Commanders of the Royal Air Force* (1991)
Richards, D., and Saunders, H., *Royal Air Force 1939–1945*, vol. i (1961)
Savage, C. I., *Inland Transport* (1957)
Titmuss, R. M., *Problems of Social Policy* (1950)
Webster, Sir Charles, and Frankland, N., *The Strategic Air Offensive Against Germany 1939–1945*, vol. i (1961)

5. Biographies
Andrews, A., *The Air Marshals* (1970)
Birkenhead, Earl of, *Cherwell* (1961)
———, *Halifax* (1965)
Boyle, A., *Trenchard* (1962)
Bradford, S., *George VI* (1989)
Bullock, A., *Hitler: A Study in Tyranny* (1962)
———, *Life and Times of Ernest Bevin* (1967)
Clark, R., *Tizard* (1965)

Collier, B., *Leader of the Few* (1957)

Colville, J., *Churchillians* (1981)

Cooper, A., *Born Leader* (1993)

Cosgrave, P., *Churchill at War. Vol. I: Alone* (1974)

Gilbert, M., *Winston S. Churchill. Vol. V: Prophet of Truth,* (1976)

————, *Winston S.Churchill. Vol. VI: Finest Hour,* (1983)

Irving, D., *The Rise and Fall of the Luftwaffe: The Life of Luftwaffe Marshal Erhard Milch* (1974)

————, *Goering* (1989)

Lacey, R., *Majesty* (1977)

Laffin, J., *Swifter Than Eagles* (1964)

Lee, A., *Goering: Air Leader* (1972)

Orange, V., *Sir Keith Park* (1984)

Overy, R., *Goering: The Iron Man* (1984)

Richards, D., *Portal of Hungerford* (1977)

Roberts, A., *'The Holy Fox': A Biography of Lord Halifax* (1991)

Saward, D., *'Bomber' Harris* (1984)

Soames, M., *Clementine Churchill* (1979)

Taylor, A. J. P., *Beaverbrook* (1972)

————, *The War Lords* (1976)

Taylor, F., (ed.), *The Goebbels Diaries 1939–1941* (1982)

Wheeler-Bennett, Sir John, *King George VI: His Life and Reign* (1958)

Wright, R., *Dowding and the Battle of Britain* (1969)

Young, K., *Churchill and Beaverbrook* (1966)

6. Books: Blitzes on provincial cities

Abrahams, J., *Sheffield Blitz* (1942)

Arthur, N., *Swansea At War* (1988)

Blanchard, V., (ed.), *City of Portsmouth: Records of the Corporation 1936–1945* (1970)

Brode, T., *The Southampton Blitz* (1977)

Boyle, G., *The Clydebank Blitz* (1980)

City of Coventry, *Information Officers' Guide* (1943)

Dallat, C., and Gibson, F., *Rooms of Time: Memories of Ulster People* (1988)

Dike, J., *Bristol Blitz Diary* (1982)

Douglas, A., *Birmingham at War* (1982)

Geraghty, T., *North-East Coastal Town: Ordeal and Triumph [1951]* (1989)

Hardy, C., *Hull at War* (1993)

Hardy, C., and Harris, P., *Tyneside at War: A Pictorial Account* (1988)

Harris, P., *Glasgow and the Clyde at War* (1986)

Hodgkinson, G., *Sent To Coventry* (1970)

Jeffrey, A., *This Present Emergency* (1992) (Eastern Scotland)

Jenkins, P., *Battle over Portsmouth* (1986)

Knowles, B., *Southampton: The English Gateway* (1951)

Longmate, N., *Air Raid* (1976) (Coventry)

MacInnes, C., *Bristol At War* (1962)

McPhail, I., *The Clydebank Blitz* (1974)

Morris, W., *Rescue Services and Other Services of the Hull City Engineer and Surveyor's Department* (1942)

Newbold, E., *Portrait of Coventry* (1975)

Peake, N., *City At War* (1986) (Portsmouth)

Perrett, B., *Liverpool: City At War* (1990)

Portsmouth Evening News, *Smitten City* (1942)

Rance, A., *Southampton Blitz: The Unofficial Story* (1991)

Scrivener, K., *Plymouth At War* (1989)

Stedman, J., *Portsmouth Reborn: Destruction and Reconstruction 1939–1974* (1995)

Twyford, H., *It Came To Our Door* (1945)

———, *Plymouth Blitz* (1947)

Underdown, T., *Bristol Under Blitz* (1942)

Wasley, G., *Blitz* (1991) (Plymouth)

Williams, H., *Annual Report on the Health of the County Borough and the Port of Southampton for the Year 1945* (1945)

Winstone, R., *Bristol in the 1940s* (1970)

———, *Bristol Blitzed* (1976)

7. Books: General

Air Ministry, *The Rise and Fall of the German Air Force*, Pamphlet No 248 (1948)

Ansel, W., *Hitler Confronts England* (1964)

Armitage, Sir Michael, *The Royal Air Force* (1993)

Bartz, K., *Swastika in the Air* (1956)

Bates, I., *The Thames on Fire* (1985)

Batt, R., *The Radar War* (1991)

Baumbach, W., *Broken Swastika* (1960)

Bialer, U., *The Shadow of the Bomber* (1980)

Bisset, I., *The George Cross* (1961)

Bekker, C., *The Luftwaffe War Diaries* (1969)

Bowyer, C., *Fighter Command* (1980)

Briggs, A., *The History of Broadcasting in the United Kingdom*, vol. iii (1970)

Calder, A., *The People's War* (1969)

Calder, A., and Sheridan, D., (eds), *Speak For Yourself: A Mass-Observation Anthology 1937–49* (1984)

Calvocoressi, P., *Top Secret Ultra* (1980)

Cooper, B., *The Story of the Bomber 1914–1945* (1978)

Clark, R., *The Rise of the Boffins* (1962)

Cross, R., *Bombers* (1987)

Dierich, W., *Kampfgeschwader 'Edelweiss': The History of a German Bomber Unit 1939–1945* (1975)

Eade, C., (ed.), *The War Speeches of the Rt Hon. Winston S. Churchill*, vol. i (1951)
————, (ed.), *Secret Session Speeches of Winston Churchill* (1946)
Faber, H., (ed.), *Luftwaffe* (1979)
Fitzgibbon, C., *The Blitz* (1957)
————, *London's Burning* (1970)
Foreman, J., *Battle of Britain: The Forgotten Months, November and December 1940* (1988)
Frankland, N., *The Bombing Offensive against Germany* (1965)
Gelb, N., (ed.), *Scramble* (1986)
Glover, M., *Invasion Scare 1940* (1990)
Gombrich, E., *Myth and Reality in German War-Time Broadcasts* (1970)
Graves, C., *Women in Green* (1948) (The WVS)
Gunston, W., *Fighters 1914–1945* (1951)
————, *Night Fighters* (1976)
Harrison, T., *Living Through the Blitz: Mass Observation* (1976)
Liddell Hart, B., *History of the Second World War* (1970)
Hibbert, C., *The Court at Windsor: A Domestic History* (1964)
Hinsley, F., *Hitler's Strategy* (1951)
Historical Radar Archive, *Radar Bulletin, 60 Group* (1991)
Horne, A., *To Lose A Battle* (1969)
Hough, R., and Richards, D., *The Battle of Britain* (1989)
Irving, D., *Churchill's War* (1987)
Ishoven, A. van, *The Luftwaffe in the Battle of Britain* (1980)
Jacobsen, H., and Rohwer J., (eds), *Decisive Battles of World War Two* (1965)
Johnson, D., *The City Ablaze* (1980)
Lawrence, W., *No 5 Bomber Group RAF* (1951)
Lee, A., *Blitz On Britain* (1960)
Lewin, R., *Ultra Goes To War* (1978)
Longmate, N., *The Home Front* (1981)
Lynn, V., *We'll Meet Again* (1989)
Marwick, A., *Britain in a Century of Total War* (1968)
————, *The Home Front* (1976)
McClaine, I., *Ministry of Morale* (1963)
Middleton, D., *The Sky Suspended* (1960)
Mowat, C., *Britain Between the Wars 1918–1940* (1955)
Murray, W., *The Luftwaffe* (1985)
Overy, R., *The Air War 1939–1945* (1980)
Parry, S., *Intruders Over Britain* (1987)
Peake N., (ed.), *The People's War 1939–1940* (1989)
Penley, W., and Batt, R., *Dorset's Radar Days* (1994)
Porten, E. von der, *The German Navy in World War Two* (1972)
Powers, B., *Strategy Without Slide-Rule* (1976)
Price, A., *Instruments of Darkness* (1967)

————, *Luftwaffe Handbook 1939–1945* (1977)

————, *Blitz on Britain 1939–1945* (1977)

————, *The Hardest Day* (1979)

Probert, H. and Cox, S., *The Battle Re-Thought* (1991)

Ramsey, W., (ed.), *The Battle of Britain: Then and Now* (1980)

————, *The Blitz: Then and Now*, vol. i (1987)

————, *The Blitz: Then and Now*, vol. ii (1988)

Richardson, W., and Freidin, S., (eds), *The Fatal Decisions* (1956)

Ray, J., *The Battle of Britain: New Perspectives* (1994)

Roger, G., *The Blitz* (1990)

Schliephake, H., *The Birth of the Luftwaffe* (1971)

Scutts, J., *Luftwaffe Fighter Units: Europe 1939–41* (1977)

————, *Luftwaffe Bomber Units 1939–41* (1978)

Smith, G., *How It Was in the War* (1979)

Smith, M., *British Air Strategy between the Wars* (1984)

Smith, P., *Stuka Squadron* (1990)

Suchenwirth, R., *Historical Turning Points in the German Air Force War Effort* (1968)

————, *Command and Leadership in the German Air Force* (1970)

Taylor, A. J. P., *English History 1914–1945* (1965)

Taylor, T., *The Breaking Wave* (1957)

Terraine, J., *The Right of the Line* (1985)

Trevor Roper, H., (ed.), *Hitler's War Directives* (1964)

Waller, J., and Vaughan Rees, M., *Blitz: The Civilian War 1940–1945* (1990)

Webb, E., and Duncan, J., *Blitz Over Britain* (1990)

Wellington, N., *Firemen At War* (1981)

Wheeler-Bennett, J., (ed.), *Action This Day: Working with Churchill* (1968)

Williamson, M., *The Luftwaffe 1939–1945* (1986)

Wood, D., and Dempster, D., *The Narrow Margin* (1961)

Wykeham, P., *Fighter Command* (1960)

Wynn, K., *Men of the Battle of Britain* (1989)

8. Articles

Banus, J., and Murray, H., *North London Collegiate Magazine*, December 1939

Bialer, U., 'Humanization of Air Warfare in British Foreign Policy on the Eve of the Second World War', *Journal of Contemporary History (JCH)* 13, 1 (1978)

Cox, S., 'A Comparative Analysis of RAF and Luftwaffe Intelligence in the Battle of Britain, 1940', *Intelligence and National Security (INS)*, 5, 2 (1990)

Haslam, E. B., 'How Lord Dowding Came to Leave Fighter Command', *Journal of Strategic Studies (JSS)*, 4, 2 (1991)

Hillgruber, A., 'England's Place in Hitler's Plans for World Dominion', *JCH*, 9, 1 (1974)

Hyde, H. Montgomery, 'Lord Trenchard: Architect of Victory in 1940', *The Times*, 15 September 1973

Kingston-McCloughry, E. J., 'The Strategic Air Offensive', *Journal of the Royal United Services Institute (JRUSI)*, 107, 1 (1962)

Koch, K. W., 'The Strategic Air Offensive Against Germany: The Early Phase, May–September 1940', *Historical Journal (HJ)*, 34, 1 (1991)

Overy, R. J., 'Hitler and Air Strategy', *JCH*, 15, 3 (1980)

———, 'German Air Strength 1933 to 1939: A Note', *HJ*, 27, 2 (1984)

Palmer, A., 'Operation Punishment', *Purnell's History of the Second World War*, 2, 1 (1967)

———, 'The Balkan Campaign', *Purnell's History of the Second World War)*, 4, 64 (1969)

Searth, R., The Sound Mirrors at Hythe', *Sanctuary*, 23 (1994)

Smith, M., 'Sir Edgar Ludlow-Hewitt and the Expansion of Bomber Command', *JRUSI*, 126, 1 (1981)

Wark, W., 'British Intelligence on the German Air Force and Aircraft Industry 1933–1939', *HJ*, 25, 3 (1982)

INDEX